CHEYENNE SUMMER

CHEYENNE SUMMER

THE BATTLE OF BEECHER ISLAND:
A HISTORY

TERRY MORT

PEGASUS BOOKS

NEW YORK LONDON

CHEYENNE SUMMER

Pegasus Books, Ltd.
148 West 37th Street, 13th Floor
New York, NY 10018

Copyright © 2021 by Terry Mort

First Pegasus Books cloth edition July 2021

Interior design by Maria Torres

Map on page ix © 2design art co.

All photographs unless otherwise stated are courtesy of
The Fort Wallace Museum, Wallace, Kansas. Used with permission.

ISBN: 978-1-64313-710-0

10 9 8 7 6 5 4 3 2 1

Printed in the United States of America
Distributed by Simon & Schuster
www.pegasusbooks.com

For Izabella, Brooks, Penelope and Zoe

CONTENTS

—ᴟ—

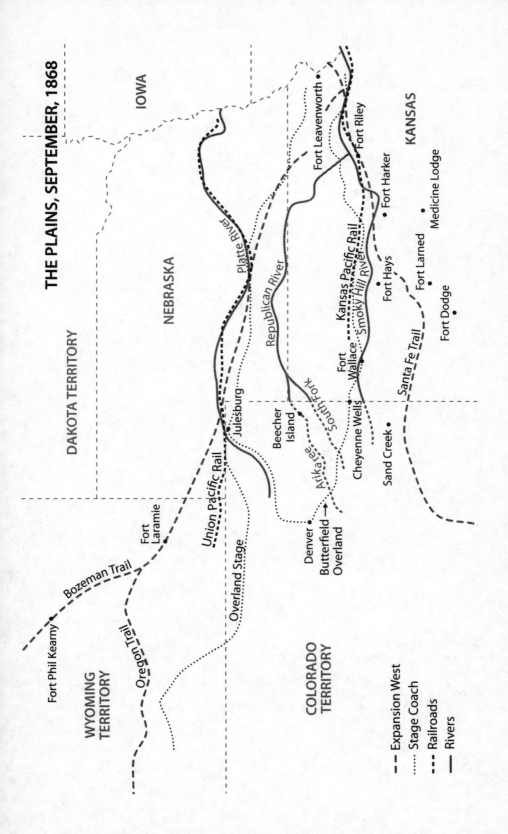

THE PLAINS, SEPTEMBER, 1868

INTRODUCTION

In the summer of 1868 General Phillip Sheridan was commander of the US Army's Department of the Missouri. He was responsible for the vast Plains that were the homelands of some of the most warlike and troublesome of the Native tribes. His territory comprised Missouri, Kansas, Colorado, and New Mexico. And he had a problem. Those tribes—notably, the Sioux, Cheyenne, and Arapaho—were raising havoc in the settlements, along the construction route of the Union Pacific Railroad and the emigrant wagon trail routes. Major George A. Forsyth, Sheridan's inspector general of the department, wrote:

> Upon the reoccupation of the southern and western frontier by government troops at the close of the [Civil War], the Indians, who had grown confident in their own strength, were greatly exasperated, and the construction of the Union Pacific Railroad across the continent to the Pacific coast, directly through their hunting grounds, drove them almost to frenzy. The spring of 1868 found them arrogant, defiant, and confident, and late in the summer of that year, they boldly threw off all concealment, abrogated their treaties, and entered upon the warpath. I have lying before me, as I write, tabulated statement of the outrages committed by the Indians within the Military Department of the Missouri from June until December of that year, and it shows one hundred and fifty-four murders of white settlers and freighters, and the capture of numerous women and children, the burning and sacking of farmhouses, ranches, and stage-coaches, and gives details of horror and outrage visited upon the women that are better imagined than described.

Sheridan didn't have enough troops or enough experienced officers to deal with the highly mobile Indian warriors who traveled the Great Plains as they wished, attacked where they chose, and disappeared into the seemingly endless prairie. Officers and men who knew anything about that business were very rare in the regular army. Jim Bridger, the old scout, summed up Sheridan's dilemma when he said, "Your boys who fought down South [i.e., in the Civil War] are crazy. They don't know anything about fighting Indians."

In fairness to the army, it could hardly have been otherwise. Most of the officers learned their trade in the Civil War. They fought in appalling battles that involved thousands of men marching shoulder to shoulder to attack enemy positions defended by thousands more, while both sides exchanged devastating artillery barrages that covered the field with the fog of gun smoke, confusion, noise, and sheer terror. Those tactics were absurdly inappropriate and useless against an elusive enemy like the Plains tribes. (Some thought the tactics were absurd, period.) Those few Indian leaders who heard about such battles were amazed that anyone could fight so foolishly and wastefully. The officers who survived and even prospered in the Civil War bloodletting might be competent soldiers in conventional, set-piece battles, but most of them didn't know what they were doing when it came to the warlike tribes. What's more, newly minted graduates of West Point—those who were sent to western outposts—were completely unprepared. The subject of Indian fighting was not, and had never been, a part of the Academy's curriculum.

As one possible response to his problem, Sheridan decided to raise a company of frontier civilians who were experienced Indian fighters. Sheridan figured that a relatively small, well-armed group of frontier scouts might be worth many times that number of regular—and often green—army troops. And although these civilian scouts would necessarily be under the command of regular army officers, a few wise old heads among the frontiersmen might balance their officers' tactical naiveté. What's more, these men would not be used *instead* of the army patrols but *in addition to* the initiatives that were already underway, such as they were.

There was another reason why Sheridan's idea seemed to make sense. The Indians were almost impossible to find—unless they wanted to be found. And when they wanted to be found, it was because they had selected a time and place where they had a marked tactical advantage. An army patrol led by officers new to the business might wander fruitlessly for days across the Plains and never see an enemy. Then they would return with horses played out and nothing to show for the effort. Or they might never be heard from again, if they stumbled on a hidden and waiting enemy. But frontiersmen, who understood tracking and understood the ways of the tribes, might at the very least locate some significant pockets of hostiles. The officer commanding the scouts would then have the choice of attacking then and there, or, if the enemy force was too large, sending for the regulars.

So in Sheridan's mind, it made a lot of sense to create an independent unit of experienced frontiersmen to scout against the tribes—and to engage them, if the opportunity presented itself. And there were other good reasons—the army could use the extra manpower. After years of the Civil War and the burgeoning national debt, Congress was not keen on spending for troops whose enlistment meant financial commitments of several years. The army was therefore stretched thin across the Western frontier, and the troops it did have were a mixed bag, at best. A team of temporary scouts therefore made some financial sense and was really the only alternative to budget-strapped departments like Sheridan's. There was also a precedent for this kind of unit. The estimable scout Frank North and his brother Luther had organized and now commanded the Pawnee Battalion—two hundred or so Pawnee warriors who were assigned to patrol and protect the Union Pacific Railroad as it moved slowly west. The Pawnee were the eternal and inveterate enemies of the Sioux and Cheyenne and were happy to take the white man's dollar to do what they had always done, anyway—fight their tribal enemies.

So Sheridan decided to go ahead with the idea. He offered the job of recruiting and commanding the new unit of scouts to one of his favorite staff officers, George "Sandy" Forsyth, his inspector general. Forsyth jumped at the chance for a field command. He was a veteran of the Civil War and a competent soldier and had been breveted colonel for his conduct in the war. Like most professional officers of this time, he had no experience of Indian fighting. What little he knew about them was almost entirely secondhand. As he wrote in his memoirs:

My experience of military life having been gained solely in our civil war, the only fairly accurate knowledge I had of Indians had been picked up during a year's service in the Department of the Missouri, as I travelled through its limits on duty as an inspector, and not-withstanding I had assimilated, or tried to, all that I had seen or heard regarding them, my knowledge was most meagre. It might have been summed up under three heads. First, that they were shrewd, crafty, treacherous, and brave. Secondly, that they were able warriors in that they took no unnecessary risks, attacked generally from ambush, and never in the open field unless in overwhelming numbers. Thirdly, that they were savages in all that the word implies, gave no quarter, and defeat at their hands meant annihilation, either in the field, or by torture at the stake.

Forsyth's opinions were understandable in view of the army's recent history of action against the tribes. Only a year and a half before, in December of 1866, in northern Wyoming, eighty-one troops under Captain William Fetterman were ambushed, over-whelmed, and quite literally annihilated by a huge force of Sioux and Cheyenne under the leadership of Red Cloud. Not a soldier survived. Until Colonel George Custer's defeat in 1876, the Fetterman battle was the army's greatest disaster in its campaigns against the Native tribes. And the tactics used by the Indians were precisely those that Forsyth described—they decoyed the troops into an ambush and overwhelmed them with vastly superior numbers. Fetterman's overconfidence, inexperience, and disobedience to orders certainly contributed to his defeat, but that did not mitigate the army's anger or shock. Nor did it change anyone's opinions about the nature of their adversary. Quite the contrary. The aftermath of the Fetterman battle was, in the army's mind, nothing less than barbaric savagery, for the Sioux and Cheyenne followed up their victory by turning the battlefield into a charnel house of stripped and grotesquely mutilated bodies. Scalping was the least of it. And while apologists might later explain this as an understandable expression of Indian rage, the army did not see it that way. So, Forsyth's three judgments about the enemy he was sent to look for reflected the virtually unanimous opinion of the professional officer corps.

It's worth noting that Forsyth's remarks display none of the overconfidence and contempt for the Indians that doomed Fetterman—and would doom some others in the future. It's also fair to mention, however, that Forsyth wrote his memoirs twenty-five years after the events, so it's possible his opinions in 1868 were not quite so temperate. Wounded Knee had happened by the time of his writing, and understanding of the tribes' attitudes and tragedies was more widespread, even among veterans who had fought against them. Besides, by then the tribes had been defeated, and the victors could afford to be less rancorous. On the other hand, Forsyth was not unique among army officers in apparently having little, if any, bitter hatred of the Indians as a people. The hostile tribes were the enemy, and if you were a soldier, you understood that your enemy was in the legitimate business of trying to kill you, any way he could. A professional soldier like Forsyth accepted that, and while he would deprecate scalping and savage mutilation, he would be able to appreciate their qualities as warriors.

Virulent hatred of the Indians was vastly more widespread among the civilian populations of the territories; they were, after all, the main targets of Indian attacks. In fact, a division of opinion about the "Indian question" was one aspect of Sheridan's strategic and political problem, for the Western settlers were loud in their demands that the army do something about the attacks. Western editorialists frequently advocated "extermination." The financiers who were building the railroads, operating stage lines, building new towns, and opening mines pressured their cronies in Congress to act. More than a few politicians had been bought and paid for, and their sponsors wanted some vigorous action in return for their investment. On the other hand, there were other politicians and editorialists, mostly in the east and far from the scenes of strife, who complained about the expense of maintaining an army to protect settlers and emigrant trains. This attitude was in direct line with a strong anti-army tradition, dating back before the Civil War and expressed by Horace Greeley: "Of all solecisms, a Standing Army in a Republic of the XIXth Century is the most indefensible. We have no more need of a Standing Army than of an order of nobility." Greeley might suggest that a young man "go west" to seek his fortune, but that same young man should not expect the federal government to protect him on the way or when he got there. State and territorial volunteer troops, militias, and rangers should handle things in their areas, and the people directly affected by Indian depredations should bear the cost of their own defense. There were also philanthropists and religious leaders who urged understanding, moderation, and negotiation with the tribes, although they didn't explain how that might work. Pacifists, like the Quakers, had trouble understanding that the tribes were decidedly not pacifists— quite the contrary. Their culture glorified and rewarded the warrior. So the arguments raged, and throughout the settlement of the West, the army felt ill-used and in the middle of an unwinnable argument between competing civilian interests and political opinions.

Sandy Forsyth didn't know much about fighting Indians, but at least he realized it. And he was quite sure that his adversaries were not to be underestimated or disdained. Contempt and pride had killed Fetterman and his men. Forsyth understood that. He also knew that superior firepower and discipline could overcome numerical disadvantages. He could reasonably assume that fifty well-armed men—men who could shoot well—could defeat, or at least discourage, many times that number of attackers, especially if the men were placed in a reasonably good defensive position. Army doctrine at the time postulated that in order to have a chance of success, an attacking force needed three times the number of well-entrenched defenders. Maybe that also would apply against the mounted tribesmen. There was no reason not to believe that. The key, though, was not getting caught in the open. And on the endless, often featureless Plains, that might be easier said than done. A soldier didn't need experience to figure that out; it was common sense.

Forsyth's second-in-command was Lieutenant Frederick H. Beecher, of the Third Infantry. A Civil War veteran who had been severely wounded at Fredericksburg and Gettysburg, Beecher was now assigned to Fort Wallace, the westernmost post in Kansas and the site of the Union Pacific Railroad's farthest construction point to date.

As Lieutenant Beecher had directed a secret mission that consisted of a group of four select scouts who kept surveillance over the Indians during the summer of 1868 and reported their strengths, locations and activities directly to General PH Sheridan, it is understandable that General Sheridan appointed Lieutenant Beecher as Major Forsyth's second in command. Lieutenant Beecher was a dedicated soldier [and] a skilled scout . . .

Major Forsyth was glad to have Beecher with him. He described the young lieutenant as "[e]nergetic, active, reliable, brave and modest, with a love of hunting and a natural taste for plainscraft, he was a splendid specimen of a thoroughbred American and a most valuable man in any position requiring coolness, courage and tact."

Forsyth also hired Dr. John H. Mooers, another Civil War veteran, who was now a civilian practicing in Hays, Kansas. According to one of the scouts, Mooers volunteered "more for fun than anything and because he always wanted to see a real, live wild Indian."

Forsyth and Beecher recruited and hired the scouts at two forts in Kansas—Harker and Hays. They had no trouble raising the required number. Forsyth said he could choose from hundreds of men, many of them veterans of the Civil War who had flocked to the Western settlements after the end of the war—some of them glad for a job, however potentially hazardous. One in particular had fallen on hard times. He was William H. H. McCall, who had been a colonel of a Pennsylvania regiment of volunteers, had been brevetted brigadier general, and "like many another good man in either army, had drifted West since the close of the war, been unsuccessful, became a bit dissipated, and just at this period was ready and willing to take the chances in anything that offered an opportunity for advancement or distinction." Forsyth appointed the former general, now sadly reduced, apparently, to be his first sergeant. The scouts would remain civilian employees, but Forsyth organized his company along the lines of a cavalry troop. Many of the other men had served in either the US or Confederate forces and had, like former General McCall, drifted west. Martin Burke, an Irishman who had served in the English army in India and then in a New York regiment during the Civil War, was a veteran who had only been recently discharged from the Third US Cavalry. On the other hand there was Sig Schlesinger, a Hungarian immigrant who had tried more odd jobs than most men at his time of life and was more or less desperate for any kind of job. Although only twenty, he looked even younger. One of the scouts described Sig as "a little New York tenderfoot Jewish lad, Sigman was about sixteen years old, wanted to enlist but Beecher told him, 'You are too young and inexperienced. You wouldn't know how to take care of yourself.' But little Schlesinger went to Forsyth and begged so hard to go with us that the major turned to Beecher and said, 'Oh, hell, Beecher, sign him up.'" Schlesinger hardly fit the ideal of an experienced frontiersman, but something about him must have appealed to Forsyth, if only his eagerness.

Other volunteers were local ranchers or farmers who had their own reasons for fighting Indians. Some were experienced scouts, like Forsyth's chief guide, Abner "Sharp" Grover: "a plainsman of somewhere between forty and fifty who had passed his life hunting and trapping along the northwestern border." Forsyth surmised that Grover was descended from French voyageurs and probably had some Indian blood, for he spoke Sioux language and was well versed in the crafts of a plainsman. "A keen eye, a good shot and a cool head made him a valuable man." Grover would end his days in a barroom shoot-out in Pond Creek, Kansas—a wretched stage stop on the western Kansas border.

The scouts would be paid a dollar a day. They would provide their own horses and receive an additional thirty-five cents per day for their upkeep. The army would provide each man with a Spencer repeating rifle and a Colt pistol, 140 rounds of rifle and 30 rounds of pistol ammunition. They would also be issued "a blanket, a haversack, butcher-knife, tin plate and tin cup."

Having recruited his fifty men, Forsyth was ready to head west by the end of August 1868. Forsyth's outfit included "a pack-train of four mules, carrying camp-kettles and picks and shovels, in case it became necessary to dig for water, together with 4000 extra rounds of ammunition, some medical supplies, and extra rations of salt and coffee. Each man, officers included, carried seven days' cooked rations in his haversack."

It's significant that the men carried only seven days' worth of rations. There may have been extra food with the pack mules, but there were only four of them, and they were also burdened with heavy ammunition and tools. So there could not have been too much extra food. The men probably assumed they could supplement their food by hunting, but experienced frontiersmen would know that game animals did not always show up when they were most needed. The men could not rely on living off the country. After all, Indians who did live off the country were nomads who searched for their quarry across great expanses of the Plains—and often went hungry.

Even more important was food for the horses. Unlike Indian ponies, the white man's horses could not live for long on grass alone. They were larger, bulkier, and had not been forced through generations to adapt to life on the Plains. To remain healthy, army and civilian horses needed to supplement grazing with an equal amount of grain. The army regulations stated that their horses required fourteen pounds of oats or corn per day—in addition to grazing—in order to maintain fitness. To state the obvious, grain was the army's fuel, just as vital as the gasoline that powered armored columns in twentieth-century wars. But this necessity meant that the army's major campaigns against the tribes required long wagon trains filled with grain for the horses, and that, by its very nature, restricted the army's movement and dictated where they could go and not go, how far they could go, and how long they could stay before having to turn back. For example, the army in the Southwest was continually frustrated chasing after the hostile Apache, who were a mountain-dwelling people and who traveled fast through country that was impossible for wagons to traverse. It was only when General George Crook abandoned wagons and switched to pack-mule trains that the army began to have any success and could mount campaigns instead of sending out short-lived, small-unit patrols. (It also helped that Crook hired Apache scouts.) The point here is that even Forsyth's small column was limited in the time it had for its patrol. Horses would begin to break down quickly once their normal fodder was exhausted. And since the scouts were supplying their own horses at the rate of thirty-five cents a day, and since there were only four mules in their train, we can assume that each scout carried his own horse's fodder. It also meant extra weight for the horse to carry. That, added to the rider's weight and the weight of his equipment, meant that the horse's strength would be depleted even sooner than usual, especially if Forsyth anticipated making a normal cavalry march, which was usually twenty to twenty-five miles per day. Some of the men probably thought that their horses could exist on grass alone for a short patrol and decided to pocket the thirty-five cents instead of spending it on grain. On the other hand, it was late summer, and the prairie grass had long ago turned brown under the intense summer sun. It was an interesting logistical problem for even a small-unit patrol. The men might be able to shoot a buffalo or antelope, but that would mean nothing to their horses.

And the prospect of having their horses break down and being afoot in the midst of the vast and hostile Plains was not something anyone wanted to think about, much less risk.

So if the men only carried seven days' worth of rations, it was no doubt because they didn't expect to stay out much longer than that.

When Forsyth's little command left Fort Hays, Kansas, he was a happy man:

I sprang into the saddle with a light heart, and no little elation, at the thought of having a field command and a roving commission—a state of affairs that any true cavalry man can thoroughly appreciate. In less than ten hours' time we were practically beyond civilization and well into Indian country. Looking back [. . .] I find it almost impossible not to rhapsodize somewhat over the freedom of the life we led: the fresh air of the plains, the clearness of the atmosphere, the herds of buffalo, which scarcely raised their heads from their feeding-grounds as we passed, the bands of antelope that circled around us [. . .] and, above all, the feeling that civilization was behind us, and the fascination that the danger of campaigning in an enemy's country ever holds for a soldier was before us.

Quite a feeling. Ironically, these were the same feelings that often animated the tribesmen that Forsyth and his men were looking for. And it seems fair to think that Forsyth would have realized that, too, had he thought about it. Quite possibly, he did.

It was August 29, 1868—the part of summer that the Cheyenne called "the time when the cherries are ripe." The scouts would be looking primarily for those same Cheyenne—warriors Captain Frederick Benteen of the Seventh Cavalry once described as "good shots, good riders and the best fighters the sun ever shone on."

I

THE ANTAGONISTS

—~—

We are to consider the subject of mankind,
not as we wish them, but as we find them.

—SAMUEL JOHNSON

1

THE CHEYENNE

THE PEOPLE

The tribe popularly known as Cheyenne called themselves Tsist-sistas. The word means, roughly, "people." They were not the only tribe that referred to themselves that way. The Apache and Navajo tribes called themselves Dine, which also means "the people." The Sioux called themselves Lakota, which meant "the men." Most likely the Cheyenne meant the word to signify "our people," as opposed to other tribes who might be enemies or allies, depending on fluctuating intertribal politics. The word *Cheyenne* is sometimes assumed to come from French voyageurs who called them *chien*, the French word for "dog." Since one of the fiercest and most famous of the Cheyenne warrior societies was called the Dog Soldiers, people assumed the connection. It's more likely, however, that the word comes from the Sioux word *shahiena*, which means, roughly, "foreign speakers." The wandering voyageurs probably learned it from the Sioux and adopted it, perhaps misunderstanding the meaning. Perhaps not. But as with many questions about preliterate cultures and their slow migrations through territories of other tribes speaking other languages, it is impossible to be certain about how the word *Cheyenne* evolved.

The Cheyenne language is part of the great collection of tongues called Algonquian, one of the largest and most widespread of the major Native language families. Speakers of Algonquian dialects lived in the Canadian provinces, from the Maritimes to the Rockies, down the east coast of the mid-Atlantic United States, and out through Ohio and both sides of the Great Lakes. The Iroquoian group in New York and Ontario formed a mostly eastern island in the midst of this, as did the Siouxan group in the central regions and on the western edges. But obviously these geographical distinctions are pretty arbitrary, for the Native peoples were not bound by language and they intermingled both for peaceful trade and war. Other Algonquian speakers were the Arapaho, who became the fast friends and allies of the Cheyenne, when the latter arrived on the Plains. The Blackfeet, however, spoke a similar tongue but were troublesome and fought with the migrating Cheyenne. Similarities of language conveyed no particular allegiances among the tribes. Nor did they convey any particular cultural advantages. Alvin Josephy notes that the Uto-Aztecan language was spoken by the highly sophisticated Aztecs and the impoverished and destitute Gosiute. It was also the language group of the Ute, Comanche, and Kiowa—all tribes the Cheyenne would encounter and fight with, now and then, and trade with occasionally. In short, there were dozens of different languages and dialects at work among the Native tribes of North America, and those languages are just one of the many differences among them. And while it is sometimes necessary to use a collective term, neither *Native Americans* nor *Indians* conveys the incredible diversity of people and cultures and, in fact, tends to group them all into one vast monolith, which further tends to foster sweeping and often inaccurate generalizations about them. The pueblo-dwelling Zuni of the Southwest spoke, and speak, a language that is unique—sui generis—and they are as different culturally from the Plains nomads as Basques and Cossacks.

The great diversity of languages resulted in the evolution of a sophisticated sign language, especially on the Plains, in order to facilitate trade among the tribes, the Mexicans, and later the whites. Forsyth's "guide," Sharp Grover, spoke the Sioux language, and Forsyth may have thought that would be useful. But Forsyth's little command would instead run into the Cheyenne, and if he wanted to communicate, Grover would have to resort to sign language, which he undoubtedly understood, too. In the event, though, there was not much of an opportunity for talking.

The popular image of the Cheyenne is of a mounted warrior either chasing buffalo or attacking a wagon train or cavalry troop. And there is some truth to that image, of course. They were among the most warlike of all the Plains tribes. But they had come to the Plains only recently, as migrations go. In generations past, they were driven from their homelands in the northern Great Lakes regions by intertribal warfare. One story has it that their primary enemies at the time were the Ojibwa, whose early contact with the French traders gave them access to firearms. Guns allowed the Ojibwa to terrorize enemy tribes and drive them west. (The Lakota were also sufferers at the hands of the Ojibwa, whose name for them was *naddowessioux* meaning "enemy." The French Canadian voyageurs merely shortened the name to Sioux.

A different Cheyenne story has it that the Siouan-speaking Assiniboins were the first to use firearms against them. But whatever the truth of the matter, there's not much doubt that the Cheyenne migrated to the banks of the Upper Missouri River sometime in the eighteenth century because of pressure from enemy tribes to the east and north. And again contrary to popular images, the Cheyenne at the time were semi-agriculturalists. They planted corn, squash, beans, and tobacco. That in turn meant that their villages were more or less permanent. Like the other tribes of the Upper Missouri—the Mandan, Arikara, and Hidatsa—the Cheyenne lived in circular earth and timber lodges. The nomads who lived in buffalo-skin tepees would not become a reality until the next century, although the early Cheyenne of the Upper Missouri did venture on to the edges of the Plains to hunt game—buffalo, antelope, and small game—to supplement their crops. But they traveled on foot. Dogs dragged travois that held camp essentials. Typically, the Cheyenne would plant their crops in the spring, leave for an extended hunt during the summer, and return to the harvest in the autumn. In this they were no different from most of the tribes of North America who existed on a combination of agriculture and hunting. (The fierce Chiricahua Apache of southern Arizona and northern Mexico were an exception. They planted nothing and existed by hunting and plundering less warlike tribes and Mexican ranches and farms. They also relied to some extent on trade with other tribes and traders, both Mexican and Anglo.) By all accounts the Cheyenne got along reasonably well with their immediate neighbors on the Upper Missouri. The Arikara at the time were a large and powerful tribe and were the deadly enemies of the Sioux, who were also gradually being pushed west from the Upper Great Lakes. But after some early tension and fighting with the Arikara, the Cheyenne settled down and lived as fairly friendly neighbors. The tribes of the Upper Missouri were ravaged by smallpox in the early nineteenth century. The Mandan were virtually extinguished, and the Arikara lost roughly half their numbers. Their permanent villages on the banks of the Missouri—a primary trade route—exposed them to the contagion. By that time, though, the Cheyenne had migrated on to the Plains and therefore avoided most of the devastation. There would be other epidemics in their future, however.

Though perhaps it is obvious, the migration of these peoples happened very slowly and in small bands. Whole tribes did not pack up and leave; rather, small villages would move—either from pressure from enemies or from some depletion of food resources—and they would wander off to find a better location. Like most immigrants, they heard from some who had gone before about an attractive place to move. The same is true of other tribes who are now thought of as synonymous with the Great Plains horse culture—Kiowa, Comanche, Crow, and Arapaho, in addition to the Sioux, who came probably a little later. Eighteenth-century Mexican traders who wandered north encountered all these tribes in the area of the Black Hills (of south-western South Dakota). Not surprisingly these hills were often the scene of intertribal strife, warfare, and shifting alliances. The Black Hills were rich in game animals, clear streams, timber for lodge poles, and they were a huge island in the midst of the Plains and a refuge from the searing summer sun. They were therefore a greatly coveted territory and much fought over. But they were also centers of trade. Not only Mexicans but also the French voyageurs arrived in the area well before Lewis and Clark's expedition, and were probably the source of the first firearms for the Cheyenne and others. And having a firearm naturally led to a continuing need for ammunition—powder and ball. That in turn led to an increased need for trade and for contacts with the Europeans or with other tribes who acted as middlemen. And so semi-regular trading patterns evolved.

But there was one key to all this movement onto the Great Plains— the horse.

THE SACRED DOG

It would be virtually impossible to overstate the importance of the horse to the Cheyenne and indeed to all the Plains tribes. The horse was the means of transportation that allowed the Cheyenne to venture farther out onto the Plains in search of game. Whereas before they were afoot and accompanied by dogs that carried their goods and dragged their travois, now they had a powerful animal that would allow them to carry more, go faster and farther. Even in the days when they were making the transition away from semi-agricultural life, a few mounted Cheyenne hunters could stay away from their fields longer, and remain in distant hunting grounds longer, because they could return quicker. When villages acquired more horses and became fully mobile, they were able to abandon their farms for good and follow the migrations of the buffalo herd. They could go wherever opportunities presented themselves. They could meet with other tribes, other villages for trade. They could more easily find and attack their enemies. They could meet wandering European traders and acquire supplies. No longer part-time farmers, they became full-time nomads.

Most of these changes occurred in the eighteenth century:

> The Spanish brought horses to the Rio Grande. Some escaped, and Indian raiders seized others. By the opening of the eighteenth century the grasslands of the Great Plains nourished multiplying herds of wild horses. Trade and raids hastened their spread north and east. By late in the century virtually all the Indians of the Trans-Mississippi West had horses.

Surely the horse was known to the tribes, when they were living along the rivers and lakes toward the east and north. European settlers, traders, and explorers had them, but not in great numbers. And at the time, the Native tribes like the Cheyenne were largely woodland, riverine, and hunter/farmer people. The horse was not an essential animal and therefore not particularly coveted—not the way it would become. Travel was by canoe on rivers and lakes and by forest path. Hunted quarry were predominantly woodland creatures, many of them small game, who were best stalked on foot. Fish and waterfowl were important supplements, but no one needed a horse to catch them. What's more, the geography of the north and eastern lakes and woodlands would not support huge herds of grazing animals—neither horses, buffalo, nor even domestic cattle of the kind that flourished later on western ranches. (There were bison east of the Mississippi, but they were less numerous and traveled in much smaller herds, unlike their cousins in the West.) It was the geography of the western Plains that elevated the horse to a place of preeminent value to the tribes, as they migrated west and south. It was the grass of the Plains that supported the buffalo and then later the wild horse, and it was the mounted hunter who was able to search for and efficiently kill the buffalo. A hunter afoot would have only a few chances to kill one or two buffalo before probably frightening the rest of them into a stampede, assuming he could even find a herd. And a hunter afoot is vulnerable to a buffalo that takes exception to being shot at or speared. But a hunter on horseback can ride with them, shooting arrows into the panicked beasts and killing numbers of them. And he can avoid their counterattacks much easier than a man on foot. The buffalo, horse, and hunter became inextricably bound together. But it was man who benefited. Remove either of the other two, and the Native man could not survive independently on the Plains. (That was so glaringly obvious that it became both a matter of strategy and tactics. Killing off the buffalo became one strategic solution to the Indian problem. And running off or destroying the hostile horse herds was a common tactic. Colonel Ranald Mackenzie's successful campaign in Texas was capped by the destruction of the vast herds of Comanche horses.)

But on the Plains, the horse was much more than transportation and a hunting partner. Because it was so essential, the horse also became a unit of exchange. It was the Plains Indians' primary currency and therefore the most important indication of wealth. Unlike the European, who thought of wealth mostly in terms of money and land, the wealthy Cheyenne's portfolio consisted mostly of horses. One popular image of the Indian is that of a man who disdained material goods and was immune to the attractions of wealth. But that is not true. The Cheyenne liked wealth as much as the whites; they just thought of it in different terms. Land was never part of the equation, because no one "owned" land. The concept of deeded real estate didn't exist. Tribes fought over prime hunting grounds and thought of them as their territory, once they had evicted their enemies. But no one claimed to own that land. Tribes often had friendly—or wary—relationships with other tribes and might honor vague territorial hunting "rights." But those informal agreements would last only as long as game in their own territory was abundant. When game became depleted, there would be war over territory, and the law of conquest was applied ruthlessly. When the tribes talked about "our land," they were talking about hunting territory they had conquered and from which they had driven out previous tribes. A Sioux chief expressed the prevailing attitude of all the warlike tribes: "'These lands [the Black Hills] once belonged to the Kiowas and Crows, but we whipped these nations out of them, and in this we did what the white men do when they want the lands of the Indians.'"

That said, the concept of individual ownership of pieces of the earth was foreign to them. This idea is often romanticized as a kind of religious/ philosophical principle utterly foreign to the acquisitive white culture— "no one owns Mother Earth." And there is certainly something to that. But when your means of subsistence is a creature that wanders for miles in all directions, the idea of surveyed and fenced real estate is a practical absurdity. It seems likely that when the Cheyenne were farming plots along the Missouri River, they had a somewhat different idea about ownership and property. That said, horses—those useful and vital creatures—were another story. Individual people of the tribe coveted them, owned them, and accumulated them. And they were so valuable a tool that they also became a unit of exchange, a currency. Unlike money, which is only a *representative* of value, the horse had *intrinsic* value. Even gold, which is pretty widely recognized as a store of value, really has none, intrinsically. You can't do much with it, except make jewelry and cap teeth. (Indians never could understand the white man's mania for gold.) But a horse! You could obviously use it to improve your hunting and therefore your way of life, but it was also a commodity that other people valued equally. It was a fungible medium of exchange. You could trade it for other goods you desired—and in dire circumstances, you could even eat it. And the value of the horse as a currency was pretty well agreed upon by your trading partners. Everyone understood how to evaluate a horse. Of course, there were other recognized items of value that were bartered—buffalo robes and fur-bearing animal skins, tools and weapons, whiskey. But the horse was a unit of value conceptually like the dollar in the foreign-currency markets—the principle unit against which others could be measured. (Even Hollywood, which has perpetrated decades of ridiculous images of the tribes and the West, accurately portrays the horse as a currency, usually used to acquire a wife.) Even better, a horse was a unit of wealth that could reproduce itself without any human agency. An annual foal was nature's compound interest. What's more, a horse was—and is—a reliable, social, herd animal. Put two horses in a five-hundred-acre pasture, and they will be standing next to each other, most of the time. That meant the tribes could accumulate large herds of the animals and not worry about them running off and scattering in all directions at the first opportunity. They did not take much management or effort to control. A few preteen boys could easily watch over the village herd. Even better, most Indian horses were descendants of the wild mustangs—or even captured wild mustangs, themselves. They could live off the grass of the Plains without any supplement, and the only concession the tribes had to make to managing their herds was to move along when the horses had eaten all the grass around the camp. (People who study the Battle of the Little Big Horn wonder what Custer would have found if he'd arrived a few days later, for the unusually large Indian camp would have had to split up and move to get grazing for the huge horse herd.) Thus the animal that allowed the tribes to be greater nomads, also required it, as did the wandering buffalo, of course. And that in turn brought the tribes into greater contact with other similar tribes who coveted the same hunting grounds. Hence the horse encouraged intertribal strife, which is not to suggest that there was none before, but just to say that it became more widespread. And easier. Tribes were more likely to bump into other tribes. That could lead to fighting, but it could also lead to alliances and peaceful trade.

What's more, the horse was a unit of wealth that was pretty easily acquired, either by capturing wild mustangs or, even better, by stealing them from other tribes, other villages. An enterprising Cheyenne warrior might make himself wealthy in just one raid against a Crow or Pawnee village. With wealth came prestige within the tribe, and that prestige was enhanced in the manner of achieving the wealth, for it took daring and courage to raid an enemy camp and run off some of their horses. This was especially true because the tribesmen had a practice of keeping their best horses tied just outside their lodges, rather than with the night-grazing herd. Stealthily coming into a sleeping enemy camp, cutting loose the best horses, and leading them quietly away, took particular courage and skill and therefore conveyed great prestige, in addition to wealth. And, as one of the horse's many virtues, it would probably not even resist being stolen and would come away obligingly, either singly or with the others in the herd. The successful horse stealer might then add to his prestige by giving away some of his prizes to less able or more needy people in his village. His motives were both charitable and self-interested, and not all that different in spirit from a banker endowing a college building. The banker sees his name in stone, the warrior hears his name in story. Both do good works; both enjoy a sense of pride.

In addition to being a way of gaining wealth and prestige, raiding for horses was a great game. It was exhilarating. A successful raid was an artistic triumph—to drive off an enemy's wealth and leave him no way to pursue? It was the ideal adventure. And speaking of story, it was a perfect story with a beginning, middle, and end—the planning, the execution, the escape, and return. It would sound good with the retelling around the campfire later. It was also an expression of the individual freedom that the Cheyenne and like-minded tribes cherished above all other human values. The expression of wild freedom in both raiding and hunting was the Cheyenne's greatest satisfaction.

The Cheyenne were a warlike tribe, but combat was not the only expression of the warrior's virtues. Raids to steal horses were an equivalent, or perhaps even greater joy, and brought the greatest financial rewards. In terms of satisfying risk and reward, raiding and hunting were coequals.

The horse meant wealth and freedom. Little wonder then, that while the Cheyenne valued their individual horses, they also ascribed a mystical meaning to the *idea* of a horse. The Sioux called it "the sacred dog"—albeit in a different language, but a very similar sentiment.

The horse made the Cheyenne nomadic way of life possible, and it also made it irresistible and nourishing, in more ways than one. Not that life on the Plains was always easy. It might now and then involve periods of hunger, or months of desperate weather. Winter on the Plains can be harsh—and worse. In fact, late winter was the best time for horse hunters to capture wild mustangs, because the horses were thin and weak from months of barely getting by. They were easier to capture, as they might flounder in late snow drifts or early mud. The army gradually learned that these same winter months were a useful time to attack the villages. The Indians traditionally did not fight or move during these months precisely because their horse herds were worn down from lack of forage. It was only when the grass turned green that the Cheyenne and other Plains tribes began to think about raiding or going on the warpath.

NOMADISM VERSUS SETTLEMENT: AN IRRECONCILABLE DIFFERENCE

Even though living on the Plains was not easy, the life of a nomad was irresistibly attractive to the Cheyenne and the other Plains tribes. The growing number of Western settlers—miners, ranchers, farmers, villagers—regarded nomads with incomprehension and alarm. The two modes of life were fundamentally incompatible.

Settled people, particularly people of settled habits seeking to impose them over a nomadic zone, simply cannot comprehend the fulfilment that the roaming existence brings to the migrant pastoralist and the hunter. The settler is a creature seeking the certainties of boundaries, fixed habitation, mine and thine. The nomad, by contrast, relishes uncertainty, movement, adventure, random reward, chance wealth, and values no possession that does not serve his restless, rootless, irresponsible habits. [. . .] [T]he nomad regards himself as a superior being, because he enjoys the greatest of all human endowments, personal freedom and detachment from material burdens. Nomadism, anthropologists have concluded, is the happiest of all human ways of life, and *because of the happiness it brings, those who enjoy it react with violence against outsiders who seek to limit or redirect it.*

And that is exactly what happened. The tribes "reacted with violence" to the growing incursion of the white *settlements*. But anyone who thought about it knew with absolute certainty that the nomadic way of life could not possibly coexist with the expanding white civilization. It could not continue. Over time the environment—the very space—that supported the nomad's way of life would be swallowed up by settlement, and the game animals would be replaced by domestic cattle. Settlement was coming inevitably; there was no stopping it; there was no stopping the hordes of miners heading for the goldfields, or the railroads moving inexorably west, or the Mormons heading for Zion, or any of the other thousands of people heading for somewhere that promised to be better than the place they left. And no one but the Plains nomads *wanted* to stop the settlement. Quite the contrary.

People are fond of calling this attitude an expression of manifest destiny. Some use it with something of a sneer, implying that the term represented discredited nineteenth-century assumptions about the superiority of Anglo-Saxon civilization and the inevitable correctness of its expansion at the expense of lesser cultures. Some did think of it that way at the time, perhaps. But in fact the country's destiny *was* manifest—not in the sense that it was somehow the will of divine providence but in the sense that the country's westward destiny was glaringly *obvious. Manifest.* Anyone who could look at a map could see that. The Louisiana Purchase and then the Mexican War settled that question once and for all. It was inconceivable that the nation would leave vast swathes of land empty in the middle of the country to be used solely by a relatively small number of wandering tribes of hunters—tribes that fought with each other for the right to go wherever they pleased and shoot whatever they wanted. Even if such an absurdity were granted, the two sides of the settled country would have to communicate with each other. California was already a state; Colorado was clamoring to become one. The two halves of the country had to be connected in order to *be* a country. And that meant installing the telegraph and building the railroads across the land that the United States *owned* by right of conquest, treaty, or purchase. And as soon as the railroads came, so, too, would come towns and farms and ranches and all the elements of white civilization that would cluster along the tracks, elements that indeed were part of the basic planning for the railroads and essential to them. The Plains qua Plains could not and would not continue to exist as a vast ocean of grass occupied only by wild grazing animals and their occasional predators. And as the Plains were settled and filled, the *feasibility* of nomadism would slowly but surely fade. Even the most tenderhearted philanthropist and friend of the Indian understood that. And there were many such white people, mostly in the east and far from the scenes of conflict. This is not to imply that their philanthropy was insincere or largely self-congratulatory, but merely to say it's easier to be a philanthropist when no one is running off your cattle or burning down your homestead—*and* when the risk of that is nonexistent. Furthermore, no honest philanthropist would disagree with that. In any event, even the strongest advocates for the Indians understood that the Plains nomads would sooner or later have to surrender their way of life. There was no alternative. People only differed about the best way to arrive at that inevitable end. Because it *was* inevitable. And so the settlers knew that the sooner the Indians stopped "wriggling against their doom," as General William Tecumseh Sherman put it, the sooner the barriers to civilization in all its forms would fall. (Sherman also referred to the Indians as "[a] singular race of brave men fighting against destiny." And if the Indians refused to comply, sterner measures were called for.

In the years just after the Civil War, the Plains tribes may have suspected what was coming. But none of them could quite imagine the extent of it. They would sit on their ponies and look around all points of the compass and see nothing but rolling grassland all the way to the horizon. It was hard to imagine that this could ever change. And so they continued to assert their nomadic imperatives. Kiowa chief and fierce antagonist of the whites, Satanta, said: "I have heard you intend to settle us on a reservation near the mountains. I don't want to settle there. I love to roam over the wide prairie, and when I do, I feel free and happy, but when we settle down we grow pale and die." It could hardly be more clear—the nomadic life *was* life. To be forced to abandon it—to become settled—was death. But very few white people, whether in the government or civilian life, really cared whether Satanta and his comrades felt free and happy, or not. Those few who did care also understood that in the long run it really didn't matter.

As mentioned, it was the Western settlers who were loudest in their calls for the government and the army to do something about the nomadic tribes. And they were the ones who could not understand or countenance the nomadic way of life. And, in fairness, they were the ones whose farms and ranches made them easy targets for Indian raiders. It was their cattle that were run off, their barns and houses that were burned, their families who were murdered. The rage of the settlers was understandable. Those who lost property or had family members killed or kidnapped wanted revenge immediately. In its attitudes toward the tribes, the *regular* army tended to be far less violent than civilian settlers, although the army was tasked with carrying out vacillating government policies and was therefore often frustrated and placed in situations that resulted in mistakes and even atrocities. Sherman understood the Indians' dilemma and admired their bravery, but his determination to do his job was "uncomplicated by sentiment." That job was to eliminate the possibility of a nomadic culture. If the tribes agreed to stay in one place, the violence could end. If they refused to do that, the violence would continue. And there was no doubt about the eventual outcome. Sherman knew as others must have that nomadism would inevitably fade away—become impossible—as the nation grew. But Sherman also knew he could not afford to wait for time to do the job, while the tribes and the whites were literally at each other's throats. The cost in blood and treasure was unacceptable. And the political pressures to accelerate the process were irresistible.

But the Cheyenne and their native allies would not go quietly.

THE MARK OF THE WARRIOR

The Cheyenne culture was a warrior culture. As difficult as it may be for the more settled or pacific person to understand, the mark of the warrior is that he actually enjoys fighting. For the nomadic horse warrior "violence [was] a way of life, an expression of joy and belief, unlinked to any strategic or tactical necessity." The Latin for it is *gaudium certaminis*—the joy of battle. It's not that the warrior is never afraid but rather that fear is a controllable emotion and can be over-ridden by the fierce exhilaration of the fight. This ethic was instilled in Cheyenne boys from the first moments they were able to understand:

> The fighting spirit was encouraged. In no way could a young man gain so much credit as by the exhibition of courage. Boys and youths were trained to feel that the most important thing in life was to be brave; that death was not a thing to be avoided; that, in fact, it was better for a man to be killed while in his full vigor rather than to wait until his time was past, his powers were failing, and he could no longer achieve those feats which to all seemed so desirable.

Furthermore:

The Indian lived in public. He was constantly under the eyes of his tribe, and most of his doings were known to them. As he was eager for the approval of his fellows, and greedy for their praise, so public opinion promised the reward he hoped for and threatened the punishment he feared.

The path to acclaim was clear from a boy's earliest years—success in hunting, success in raiding, success in war. The boy learned these lessons directly, through instruction from his elders, and indirectly, through observation of the village's warrior/heroes. To succeed in these arenas was to be a great man in the village and in the tribe as a whole. To fail brought shame and ignominy.

Of abstract principles of right and wrong, as we understand them, the Indian knew nothing. He had never been told of them. The instructor of the Indian child did not attempt to entice him to do right by presenting the hope of heaven, nor to frighten him from evil by the fear of hell; instead, he pointed out that the respect and approbation of one's fellow men were to be desired, while their condemnation and contempt were to be dreaded.

The clearest route to acclaim was raiding and war. And in a raid, it wasn't even necessary to kill anyone—not that the Cheyenne were averse to killing. Far from it. But an equally and perhaps superior expression of their ethic was counting coup—touching an enemy, preferably when he was still alive. Being the first to do so was the greatest honor. Even counting coup on a dead enemy meant something.

The chief applause was won by the man who could first touch the fallen enemy. In Indian estimation, the bravest act that could be performed was to count coup on—to touch or strike—a living, unhurt man and to leave him alive, and this was frequently done. [. . .] It was regarded as evidence of bravery for a man to go into battle carrying no weapon that would do harm at a distance.

The key phrase there is *at a distance*. If you were going to kill an enemy, it was far better to do it with a knife or club at close range than with a rifle at three hundred yards. But if circumstances dictated that you had to shoot him, it was still an honorable act to ride up and touch the dead or wounded man. You might then scalp him or leave it for someone else to do it:

[T]o scalp an enemy was not a notable feat and in no sense especially creditable. If scalped, the skin of the head was taken merely as a trophy, something to show, something to dance over—a good thing, but of no great importance; but to touch the enemy with something held in the hand, with the bare hand, or with any part of the body, was a proof of bravery—a feat which entitled the man or the boy who did it to the greatest credit.

The warrior's desire for acclaim affected the way the Cheyenne fought.

Much has been written about the great chiefs, Sitting Bull, Red Cloud, Spotted Tail, Crazy Horse and, American Horse of the Sioux and Tall Bull, Dull Knife, and Roman Nose of the Cheyenne. They have been described as great leaders and in a fashion that is true. Besides being themselves brave, these men were orators, able to stir the emotions and were looked up to with great respect. Some of them were great warriors, but in battle not one of them could have given an order that would have been obeyed, for among the Indians there was no such thing as discipline. If some great warrior wished to charge the enemy, he would say "Now I am going," and if a group of young men felt disposed to do so they would follow him. But if Red Cloud or Sitting Bull had picked out two or three hundred men and ordered them to charge the enemy in a body, no attention would have been paid to the order. *The individual Indian fought just in his own way and took orders from no one.*

Red Cloud and many of the others mentioned here were the same chiefs who authored the destruction of Fetterman and his men. But the tactics involved were simple and agreed upon by all—wait in ambush, send a few mounted warriors to decoy and lure the feckless soldiers into the ambush, and then overwhelm them. The decoy tactic was common and well understood by all warriors. So was ambush. It required little discipline, because it was the way things were usually done. And although there's no way of knowing for sure, it's likely that when the Indians attacked, it was a spontaneous eruption, rather than an organized charge—"Now I am going."

If the acclaim of the village was the primary goal and if that was achieved through war and raiding, it's clear why well-meaning and earnest Christian missionaries had slow going when they approached the Cheyenne and suggested things like meek pacifism and turning the other cheek. And while that may seem to be a facile observation, it becomes relevant to remember when it's time to discuss the government's peace initiatives, which were driven in large part by well-meaning missionary efforts from both Catholic and Protestant denominations. The missionary's Christianity was the principal barrier to understanding the Indian, in the same way the Indian's worldview was a barrier to comprehending the missionary. It was not that the warrior misunderstood what the Christian was saying; it was that he fundamentally disagreed with it, just as he disagreed with the reformers who told him the life of a settled farmer would be an improvement over the life of a wandering hunter.

Probably the only thing the Cheyenne could agree with in Christianity was the notion of charity. That was a communal value they embraced long before the missionaries arrived. But this was not the result of some sort of naturally inherent communitarian feelings that were absent in much of the white society. Nor was it an expression of the sentimental fiction known as the Noble Savage. The Cheyenne lived in small villages. Everything and everyone was there to see and hear. It was impossible to ignore the fact that someone was starving or had needs that could easily be satisfied by the transfer of some sort of wealth. Some of those in need might even be relatives. The feeling that something should be done was inescapable and would be abroad in the village. So that although a buffalo killed belonged to the hunter who killed it, and to his immediate family, it was impossible to ignore the fact that an ancient wizened woman with no means of support should be given something of the successful hunter's game. And it was natural that this sort of feeling and action should be applauded and become part of the ethic of the village. Charity—especially a warrior's distributing the spoils of a raid—was not only useful in keeping the village supplied but also another way to achieve acclaim. It seems unlikely that the Cheyenne people were intrinsically more charitable than other people, and more likely that they adapted and responded to the village environment with natural human instincts. Anything less would have been unusual cruelty, and the Cheyenne were not cruel—not to their own. Quite the opposite. To their enemies, however, it was another story. And it's also natural and reasonable that the successful hunter or raider should receive praise for giving away what he had won through an exercise of his skills. So charity leads to gratitude and praise, which encourages more of the same. Nor was charitable giving insincere or politically cynical; it was a natural thing to do, and it was an equally natural thing to receive praise for doing it. (Having said this, it is also undeniable that any generalization about human nature will have exceptions.)

That same sort of reasoning applies as well to the fame a warrior sought and cherished. The way of the warrior was more than simple self-assertion and vanity, more than "seeking the bubble reputation, even in the cannon's mouth." It was necessary for the survival of the family and the village. As mentioned, the villages were necessarily small, because they relied on hunting to survive. (Once again, the huge village Custer encountered was an anomaly and a very temporary one, at that.) The villages were also at risk to raiders from enemy tribes who came not only to steal horses, but to enhance their own reputation as fighters and to express their hatred of an enemy tribe—hatred that was possibly driven by desire for revenge—an extremely powerful motive for all the Plains tribes. Or attacks may have simply been economically driven—a raid for horses. And so with a small village population to draw from, and few if any ways to replace casualties, the men of the village had to become warriors and *effective* warriors at that. It is not enough to have courage and a dauntless spirit. Without the requisite skills, a warrior is nothing more than a courageous casualty. And so the tribe and its various villages had no choice but to nourish the warrior's skills and mentality, and part of that process involved reward. Rewards meant not only wealth but also, more important, the acclaim and gratitude of the village—from comrades and the old people and the women and the children, who were even then imbibing the ethic, by observation and instruction. The vast and numerous white culture could afford psychological and professional specialization—could accommodate cavaliers and pacifists, settlers and soldiers, businessmen and pastors—but the Cheyenne could not. Even at the height of their power the Cheyenne tribe probably numbered somewhere around 3,500 people. And those were further divided into villages that, because of the villagers' wanderings on the vast Plains, were necessarily often isolated and left to their own devices in both hunting and defense. They were warlike because they had to be, and because they had to be, the culture of acclaim developed and continued the cycle from generation to generation. Of course, not every man was a fearless warrior or tribal hero, but every man had to be able to fight, just as he had to be able to hunt. They were a people who adapted to their environment in ways that seem, on reflection, perfectly reasonable.

Had they not so adapted, they would most likely not have survived; certainly not in their recognized form. And so a warrior, who reveled in the arts of hunting, raiding, and war, was an expression of a fundamental tribal imperative. If he was proud and vainglorious, well, that went with the territory. And it was a well-earned privilege. But he had to be the way he was. The more one looks at the context and conditions the Cheyenne and the other tribes faced, the more it seems that the adaptations of their culture could hardly have been otherwise. British general and military theorist J. F. C. Fuller wrote:

> Rude tribes [. . .] have had continually to carry on an external self-defense and internal co-operation—external antagonism and internal friendship. Hence the members have acquired two different sets of sentiments and ideas, adjusted to these two kinds of activity. A life of constant external enmity generates a code in which aggression, conquest, and revenge are inculcated, while peaceful occupations are reprobated. Conversely a life of settled internal amity generates a code inculcating the virtues conducing to a harmonious co-operation—justice, honesty, veracity, regard for each other's claims.

It seems logical that the greater the external threat, the sharper and more intense this Manichean worldview would be. And if Fuller is correct that "peaceful occupations would be reprobated," it goes some way to explaining why the threatened tribes resisted adopting the "peaceful occupations" of white civilization. Or rather, it is an additional insight into their reluctance, for that reluctance, even refusal, had a variety of sources, not least the nomad's love of being a nomad.

The Plains Indians' way of life was profoundly different from the whites, of course, but when faced with the same environmental conditions and historical context, would a collection of whites have reacted much differently? That is not a rhetorical question; it's one that seems interesting to think about. On the other hand, maybe the answer is obvious.

VILLAGE POLITICS

Discipline and the desire for individual acclaim—glory—are, if not incompatible, then at the very least uncomfortable bedfellows. The Cheyenne culture encouraged an individual warrior's desire for glory, because it depended on it for survival. And that was understood and accepted—even unquestioned—by the leaders who would be chiefs and tribal influences. And for that reason, the chiefs had only moral power to sway opinion and advocate policy. There was little, if any, hierarchical command and control structure to the tribes. The chief could not order his people to do something. He could only suggest and explain his thinking about why one course of action seemed to be the better way. On other hand, the chiefs were selected by the people, and the people naturally gravitated toward men they respected. Chiefs were chosen on the basis of their record as warriors, their wisdom, their skills in oratory and persuasion. But their authority still resided in the "will of the people." Chiefs were keenly aware of the general consensus on any weighty matter, such as peace or war, tribal alliances, and treaties with the ever increasing, ever encroaching whites. Even decisions such as moving the camp, because of scarcity of food resources, were generally taken after the chief understood public opinion. After all, he lived among his people, in close proximity, so it was not hard to assess the way people felt about anything. Half-caste Cheyenne warrior George Bent said:

[F]ew white people understand the position of an Indian chief. There is no such thing as a "war chief"; those so called war chiefs being simply the leaders of the warrior societies and not chiefs at all. [. . .] A chief was a peace official. Many chiefs were famous fighters in their younger days, yet others who gained fame as wise leaders were never noted as warriors. [. . .] A chief was the headman of the village, directed its movements, selected camping places, and appointed the soldier societies to maintain order in the camp; he settled disputes and was just to all, else he fell into disfavor.

If he fell "into disfavor," he could be deposed.

Sometime in the 1830s the Cheyenne tribe decided to divide into two groups. One would stay in the north in the area of the Black Hills and environs; the other would go south to what is now Oklahoma and had not yet been officially designated as Indian Territory. There was no schism involved in this division. The two groups continued to intermingle socially, and sometimes whole families would live in one location for a while and then move to the other.

There were chiefs selected in all the Cheyenne bands, and periodically these would meet in grand council of the tribe. Of these, there were four elected principal chiefs. Councils were conducted in grave dignity and decorum. One speaker at a time spoke his mind, while the others listened and said nothing. They would have been shocked to observe, for example, the unruly behavior of members of Parliament during the Prime Minister's Questions. The chiefs had significant moral power and significant responsibility as a result, but they could not order anyone to do anything, nor would they consider it right or proper, or even wise to do so. But they all felt the weight of responsibility, and some warriors who had made famous names for themselves refused the honor of becoming a chief because of that responsibility. Roman Nose, one of the most famous of the Cheyenne warriors, was elected several times but always refused the office. William Tecumseh Sherman would have understood the decision, although Sherman's refusals had more to do with contempt for politics and politicians as a species, while Roman Nose seemed to feel himself unequal to the responsibilities of leadership in anything but war. Quite a difference.

Or, since it's possible that the Cheyenne were at base not much different from other human creatures, maybe Roman Nose was having too much fun raiding and didn't want to be bothered with the cares of the Cheyenne senate. This same Roman Nose, by the way, would soon be meeting Forsyth and his band of frontiersmen.

The inability of the white government officials to understand the way the Cheyenne (and the other Plains Indians) governed themselves played havoc with their relations with the tribes. The whites simply could not understand that the chief's mark on a treaty meant nothing necessarily to his village, let alone to the whole tribe. And it certainly meant nothing at all to the young warriors who went off on a raid. The raid was an expression of the eternal ethic of the warrior's culture, not a violation of it. It was a proclamation of identity and authenticity. The older chiefs might lament that they "could not control their young men." And that was true, but not for reasons that the frustrated white politicians believed. It was not because the chiefs were weak or duplicitous; it was because such discipline and authority were utterly foreign and obnoxious to all "the people." In an 1867 council with the tribes, General Winfield Scott Hancock, hero of Gettysburg and commander on the southern Plains, said, "Every tribe ought to have a great chief, one that will command them. For any depredations committed by any one of his tribe, I shall hold the chief and his tribe responsible."

Hancock was an effective general when it came to commanding an army corps, but he knew no more about the Plains Indians and how and why they acted as they did than the greenest new recruit just off the boat from Ireland. Now and then the white politicians would try to appoint a compliant individual as a chief and get him to agree to something. That ploy fooled no one and only led to more white frustration, when the rest of the tribe ignored the ersatz chief, his policies and his agreements.

In fairness, the white officials had of course all been raised in a hierarchical structures—starting in the family and passing through school and college and perhaps the armed services and then into business or government. They knew no other model and could not imagine any other kind of organization. In fact, "organization" and "hierarchy" were virtually synonymous. Everyone had a boss who must be listened to, like it or not. It's no wonder that they could not understand how the Indians thought. Besides, the whites really had no one to explain things to them. The language barrier in itself was almost insuperable, and it was only one barrier to understanding. And even if someone tried to explain Indian thinking, some officials wouldn't have believed what they were told. Or cared. Others would have realized that the Indians' ideas about society simply could not work in any group other than a small village of nomads operating in an empty country that offered abundant game. And so the discussion ultimately was academic, because sooner or later the empty country would be a thing of the past. So would the abundant game. And, therefore, so would the small villages of nomads. It was not a question of whether; it was a question of when and how.

"WE FEW, WE HAPPY FEW."

The Cheyenne had a reputation for being bold and aggressive warriors. But of course they were people, and not every individual man was as courageous as he might wish himself to be. But here again, the culture supported his resolve, not only because of its rewards for daring deeds but also because of the public nature of his life. The warriors all knew each other. And even in the odd situations when several villages happened to be camped together, and when the warriors from each went out in their hundreds, as in the case of the Fetterman battle, the warriors from a same village would naturally associate as usual, almost like an army's squad system. So even in the rare actions when hundreds were involved, the warriors still thought in terms of small units. "[F]our brave men who do not know each other will not dare to attack a lion; four less brave, but knowing each other well, sure of their reliability and consequently of mutual aid, will attack resolutely."

People who write about soldiers in combat routinely and correctly point out that soldiers fight primarily for each other, rather than for any cause or idea, however valid or noble. To help a comrade and not to be seen shirking were two sides of a powerful motive. The more desperate the situation, the more that is true. The nomadic village was by necessity a small group, and its warriors were the very definition of a small-combat unit. And the small-combat unit supported and reinforced the individual's courage and martial ardor, or at least his steadfastness. Even the less aggressive could join in to attack "the lion," because he trusted his mates. He also knew that any failure or shirking would bring certain disgrace back in the village. And the Cheyenne were keenly aware that when they were fighting against invaders, they were not fighting to protect some abstract idea of home and country but the real thing. A Cheyenne warrior's family and the families of his comrades were threatened. The celebrated idea of a "band of brothers" was often literally true of the Cheyenne. When you combine these three factors—small-unit support, the acclaim or shame of the village, and the defense of loved ones and property—it's not at all surprising that the Cheyenne warrior was a fierce and formidable opponent—especially when his adversary was an army private who was there primarily for his thirteen dollars a month and not much else. And the fact that the private was probably a recent immigrant and possibly not even fluent in English meant that he might be isolated even from the others in his company and have little or no feelings of comradeship.

To say that the Cheyenne fighters enjoyed a high degree of comradery does not mean that every village was a harmonious gathering that was free of personal jealousies and rivalries. The famous Lakota warrior Crazy Horse was shot in the face by a jealous husband. Jealous husbands and wandering wives are not the sole province of the Europeans, although the Cheyenne women were famously virtuous. But the

Cheyenne village was vulnerable to the same kind of minor pathologies that surfaced in any small town. When the Cheyenne called themselves "the people," they were perhaps saying more about themselves than they intended. It's just that the Cheyenne way of life fostered and perpetuated the unanimous warlike mentality—and the warriors—it needed to survive.

Unit comradery was enhanced by membership in one of the famous Cheyenne warrior societies. There were six of these—the Kit Foxes, the Elk Horn Scrapers (or Crooked Lance), the Red Shields, the Bow Strings, the Crazy Dogs, and the Dog Soldiers. A teenage boy might choose to join any of these societies, each of which had its own ceremonial dance, talismans, taboos, and rituals, and each enforced a discipline of a kind on its members. The discipline was compatible with the Cheyenne's fierce individualism, because it operated within the strictures of prescribed rituals on the one hand and in the practical sphere of camp management on the other. And it was voluntary. A society might be assigned as the police force for the movement of the camp. The chiefs in the camp might get together and decide it was time to move, and the announcement would be made by the assigned society, who would then go ahead to the selected new site and establish themselves for the rest to follow. A society might also be chosen to manage a group hunt, which would involve more complicated tactics than simply chasing after buffalo on horseback. Often hunts involved surrounding a herd of buffalo or antelope and driving them into an enclosure or defile, where they could be killed en masse by specially placed hunters. It could be a relatively complex operation and had to be organized. Also, individuals were discouraged from hunting because they might stampede a herd and thereby deprive the village of the chance to harvest numbers of animals. The warrior societies were appointed to police the errant individuals who threatened to ruin things for the village.

In other words, the Cheyenne were individualists, but they were not anarchists, and they understood the value of cooperation for the management of the village supply and movement. Part of the role of these warrior societies was to help in that management.

But in one sense the societies were also a little like the traditional European regiment, especially the famous British regiments, like the Royal Horse Guards or Black Watch. Each society spawned comradery and pride in the group and provided prestige. And although not all young men chose to join (individualism at work), many, if not most, chose to do so. On the other hand, the societies were definitely not like the British regiments, with their layer upon layer of ranks and rigid hierarchy. The societies may have a war leader, but individuals followed him only when and if they wanted to. And they went off on their own whenever they chose to.

Probably the most famous of the Cheyenne societies was the Dog Soldiers. Unlike the other societies, the Dog Soldiers camped separately. Upon joining, a young man agreed to move with his family to the separate camp. And since there were many half-Sioux, half-Cheyenne warriors in the society (the tribes having established friendly relations), and since they camped separately, the Dog Soldiers became almost another tribe. At the height of their power, they numbered anywhere from seventy-five to one hundred lodges. They were also the most warlike of the societies, especially in their attitude toward the whites. ("Most warlike" is a relative term, though; the Elk Horn Scrapers also became known as the Blue Soldiers, because they wore the jackets of troops they killed, stripped, and mutilated in the Fetterman fight.) But the Dog Soldiers were more likely to ignore the counsel of others in the tribe and to go off on raids of their own, both to steal horses from their enemies and to attack white settlements. And they were not so exclusive as to reject other young men who wanted to join the attack, even though they were not members. To go along with the Dog Soldiers on a war party or raid was almost a guarantee of enough action to garner a reputation, or at least the beginnings of one. The aforementioned Roman Nose was officially a member of the Crooked

Lance society, but he enjoyed the company and aggressiveness of the Dog Soldiers and often camped with them.

All the societies had their own ceremonial dances and rituals and taboos. As an example, if a mounted Dog Soldier dropped something, he was not permitted to stop and get off his horse to retrieve the object, whatever it was. Someone else might come along and pick it up and return it, or another warrior might come along and lead his comrade's horse back to the object, whereupon the rider might get off and pick up the object. None of the other Cheyenne societies or the warriors as a whole were troubled by this taboo. And it is unclear what it meant or what sort of reaction it brought, if violated. A more understandable custom was the dog rope, which was carried and worn by a particularly brave warrior. The leather rope was about ten feet long. At one end was a picket pin. The other end was either wrapped over the warrior's head and shoulder or tied to his belt. In battle, the warrior might dismount and pound the pin into the ground, thereby swearing not to retreat. He would die on that spot rather than run. Aside from displaying his courage, the prime object was to encourage the men around him who might appear to be giving way before the enemy. He would either be killed or rally his retreating comrades. If things got worse, one of his comrades might pull out the pin for him and allow him to retreat. But he could not do it for himself. (Other tribes, notably the Kiowa, had a similar practice.) Carrying the dog rope was an honor unique to the Dog Soldiers among the Cheyenne societies, but it carried with it an unusual responsibility. If the wearer's wife ran off with someone else, the rope holder could not object and was obliged to accept the usual forms of payment as compensation for her wandering ways. Whether this obligation figured into a warrior's decision about accepting the rope is not clear. Perhaps he did not worry much, because the Cheyenne women were well-known for their chastity: "[I]t was most unusual for a girl to be seduced, and she who had yielded was disgraced forever. The matter at once became known, and she was taunted with it wherever she went." The Arapahoe, who were close friends of the Cheyenne, would have been a better place to look for loose women; they looked at sexual matters quite differently from the modest Cheyenne. As an aside, it has long been a story among the Cheyenne and the whites that George Custer had a romance with a young Cheyenne woman, and even had a child by her—a son. It's not hard to believe, because Custer certainly had an eye for the ladies. But it would be inconsistent with the young Cheyenne girls' traditional mores. On the other hand, maybe the story has persisted because it was so uncharacteristic of the Cheyenne. Her name was Mo-nah-see-tah.

Once a rope carrier felt he had carried it long enough, he would then sell it to the highest bidder from among some brave men selected by the society's chiefs. The usual currency made up the offer—horses and, most likely, weapons and ammunition. There was no disgrace in relinquishing possession of the rope. The only disgrace was in pulling the pin and running away.

THE EDUCATION OF A WARRIOR

The warrior needed more than martial ardor to succeed. He needed skills.

Both boys and girls learned to ride as soon as they could walk. Children had to be able to ride soon after they left their mothers' bundling boards, not just because the Cheyenne were nomads but because when the village was attacked by an enemy, the men would fight a rearguard action while the women and children escaped. And of course a boy who grows up on horseback takes the first step toward being a competent hunter, raider, and warrior.

Children started out on gentle old village horses and gradually progressed to more ambitious mounts, until they became adults, when each man had one particular horse, his warhorse, that was strongest and fastest and most trustworthy in the noise and chaos of battle or the hunt. These were the horses that warriors tied to their lodges and the horses that were the prime objectives of enemy raiders. And the boys grew into men who were the finest light cavalry in the hemi-sphere—the combination of the years of being on horseback plus the universal ethic of the warrior created what Captain Benteen of the Seventh Cavalry called "the best fighters the sun even shone on."

It's worth mentioning that these environmental conditions affected other Plains tribes in a similar way and that they, too, adapted in a similar fashion with a similar ethic. Some of those tribes, like the Arapaho, allied themselves with the Cheyenne. Others, like the Pawnee, were inveterate enemies. But if the Cheyenne were, as Benteen suggests, the finest warriors, it may well be that they simply adapted better than the other tribes. And if that is the case, there is no obvious explanation for it. But after all, some schools are better than others in all cultures. Perhaps the Cheyenne just did a better job of training their young people.

Their training methods with horses were illustrative of their approach to educating the young. After catching a wild mustang, the warriors did not break him rodeo-style. Instead, they tied him to the tail of an old gentle mare and let him follow her around for several days, until he got used to the new herd and new community, used to the scent of people, dogs, smoke from the fires, and used to the sight and sounds of the camp. Now and then a rider might sit on his back for a moment or two so that the horse grew to understand that nothing evil was in store for him. After a while he became agreeable to the notion of a human on his back, and that was that. In other words, the Cheyenne liked to teach lessons by example and indirection, rather than by didac-tics. (On the other hand, a particularly incorrigible animal might be tied down to a snubbing post, until he calmed down.)

The skills involved in hunting are obviously transferrable to war, and hunting did not always mean riding after buffalo. Little boys learned the value of stealth and quietness by hunting small animals on the prairie and along the banks of the rivers where the villages camped—tactics that he would later use to steal horses and to attack his enemies. The boys hunted small birds, and the successful hunter who brought back a sparrow to his mother was praised as other little boys in other cultures were praised for bouquets of dandelions. And in order not to diminish the small hunter's achievement, the sparrow would be plucked and put in the pot. The lesson was—hunting success brought praise from the ones who matter most and would later bring praise from the entire village. And praise and acclaim of the village were the greatest rewards.

Many writers have noted that the Cheyenne and many of the other Plains tribes did not discipline their children with punishment. Whites who spent time in the villages routinely reported that the children were treated kindly and with affection. As both boys and girls grew, their games involved mirroring the roles they would have as adults until they became proficient at the arts of managing the home, for the girls, and hunting and war games, for the boys.

"[A]s his strength grew and skill increased [the boy] began to make excursions on the prairie for rabbits, grouse, and even turkeys. Little boys eight or ten years of age killed numbers of small birds with the arrows, and sometimes even killed them on the wing." Any hunter who has shot game birds will understand the difficulty of wing shooting with a bow and arrow. But constant practice shooting at targets and at real game honed the boy's skill to a razor's edge.

The bow was the Cheyenne's principal weapon even after they acquired firearms. Ammunition for firearms was sometimes difficult to acquire—and expensive, even if available. (This was especially true before treaties with the whites gave them access to firearms and ammunition—much to the disgust and fury of the army.) But a Cheyenne could make his own bow and arrows.

Bows were made either from wood or the horns of elk, buffalo, or bighorn sheep. The process of making a bow from horn involved gluing together "pieces of flat bone and then wrapping them with sinew." The result was a compound bow that was extremely powerful. A hunter could shoot an arrow through a buffalo from close range, and one story has it that a Cheyenne hunter killed two buffalo with one arrow by shooting through the first and killing the second, which was running alongside.

"At its most effective range—say from forty to seventy yards—an Indian could handle a bow and arrow more rapidly and more effectively than the average man could use a revolving pistol of that time." It's safe to say that no soldier and very few Old West gunfighters could expect to hit anything with a pistol at seventy yards, or forty yards for that matter. Wild Bill Hickok might've managed such a shot, but he would've known in his heart that it was mostly luck. The maximum range of Cheyenne bows was approximately four hundred yards— just about the effective range of the carbines Forsyth's men were carrying.

The Cheyenne were famous for the quality of their arrows. There were arrow makers who sold their products to others in the village. The shafts were made of shoots of the cherry bush or red willow. Great care and technique went into straightening and feathering these shafts so that they flew straight. Initially, the points were made of stone, but after the Cheyenne got access to metal they made steel points. Interestingly, the stone points were thought to be more deadly than the metal. Unlike the Sioux, the Cheyenne arrowheads were not barbed.

Captain Benteen's remark that the Cheyenne were "good shots" probably referred to their skill with a firearm, although many, if not most, of the tribes in the West struggled to get enough ammunition, and as a result had limited opportunities for target practice. As the US government became more and more generous with their "gifts," which were tantamount to bribes for good behavior, they provided more and more guns and ammunition—much to the loud complaints of the army officers who were often on the receiving end. So it's possible Benteen was talking about the Cheyenne skill with guns. But it's also possible that he referred to their skill with the bow and arrow, and there was no doubt about their training and practice from the earliest age. Little boys who could shoot game birds on the wing grew up to be deadly marksmen.

BARDS

Much of a boy's training and education was supervised by the older men of the village—typically the "grandfathers"—men who knew the codes and the history of the tribe. And the lessons were taught both by direct instruction and indirectly by stories. And stories were both real events of tribal history, as well as myths and legends or parables.

It is commonly understood that many preliterate cultures had bards who were charged with remembering and reciting the stories of the culture. Homer is the most obvious example. It has been said that the *Odyssey* and the *Iliad* were not really composed by Homer but by someone else with the same name. Witticism aside, the point is a preliterate culture's important myths, legends, and history are passed along orally by many, mostly anonymous bards. The Cheyenne were no different. Great store was placed on maintaining the accuracy of each story, and so memory was honed through repetition. And because of the importance of accuracy and memory, there are those who believe the Cheyenne versions of battles with other tribes, and with the whites, are as accurate, if not more accurate, than the accounts of white soldiers who were there. On the other hand, there are so many different Indian versions of what happened at the Little Bighorn battle, that the theory of Indian accuracy becomes questionable. Still, it is undeniable that a bardic culture values accuracy in its storytelling about not only its myths but its actual history.

As the estimable Jacques Barzun said: "Reading history remakes the mind by feeding primitive pleasure in story." The Cheyenne were no different from any other people in their love of story. And many of their stories had to do with their tribal myths—"Mythology is what never was, but always is." So said philosopher Stephen of Byzantium in the sixth century. When it comes to that aspect of mythology, not much is different among all people.

One of the first stories the grandfathers would have told was about the chief god of the Cheyenne, the Creator, whose name was Heammawihio, the Wise One Above. The name is interesting because it is a combination of the word for "above"—*heamma*—and *wihio*, which refers to both wisdom and perhaps, strangely, the spider. To the white man's sensibility, the spider conjures up few, if any, positive images. Nor does it suggest intelligence. But on reflection, the spider becomes an interesting association with the creative force, and the web is an astute image of the Cheyenne cosmology. The spider creates something out of nothing, spins an intricate web of interconnected strands, each delicate in its own right, but strong in context. Strands are nothing alone but become beautiful in their interlocking design, a design that is able to catch both the sunlight and the moisture after a rain and seems immune to the strongest wind. But it is also a snare to trap the inattentive or unobservant, those who are blind to its existence. It is both a work of natural art and a trap for those who do not see clearly. It is intricately designed and dangerous, aesthetically divine and sinister. Viewed that way, the spider as a representative of the Creator seems to make sense, especially as a Creator of the Cheyenne world, where life hung on a delicate thread. It was a world where the powers of nature— and mystery—always threatened to catch the unwary or the unskilled, or especially, those who paid no attention to the ways that life should be lived and its rituals, those who ignored their responsibilities both to the tribe and to the supernatural powers, who were everywhere. Aesop told of the grasshopper and the ant, and the Cheyenne would have understood and appreciated the lesson in its story form, especially since the feckless grasshopper would be far more likely to become ensnared than the careful ant. In the Cheyenne world, all creatures were part of a carefully interlocking design. You ignored that truth at your peril. Interestingly, *wihio* also came to be used to describe the white man—smart with his technology, but also potentially sinister, an intelligent creature that laid snares. In that, he was related concep-tually to a mythical creature, also called *wihio*, who is a trickster and shape-shifter. That *wihio* often took the form of a coyote—a clever creature that was sometimes dangerous, sometimes amiable, sometimes a jokester, and sometimes a fool. But rarely trustworthy.

Wherever the Cheyenne looked there was complexity, and so, too, it would seem, in their imagery and mythology. And because of that complexity and perhaps elusiveness, the lessons were best communicated in stories and parables. The Cheyenne had no texts or dogma, but their beliefs were best expressed in story form anyway, and stories could be and were transmitted orally by tribal authorities.

The Cheyenne did believe in an afterlife. It was above with Heammawihio, but it was not much different from life here on earth. The warriors hunted and raided, the people of the village carried on pretty much as they had done in life. And everybody went there; there was no reward and no punishment. Why would the lowest scoundrel or thief go to the same place as the virtuous warrior or the beloved grandmother? Why wouldn't heavenly reward mean some increase in happiness, some transformation of daily life? That may suggest a failure of the Cheyenne theological imagination. But another way of looking at it is that life here on earth seemed just about right to the Cheyenne. Their life here was as good as it gets, and the afterlife was therefore more of the same. Seen that way, the ultimate destruction of the Plains Indians' culture seems all the more sad. And to them, catastrophic. (The celebrated Ghost Dances promoted by the occasional mystic revivalist invariably promised a return of the buffalo and the disappearance of the white man—in short, a return to how it used to be.)

Principle among the myths of the Cheyenne were their culture heroes. The grandfathers would have explained that the Cheyenne of the nineteenth-century Plains were composed of two tribes—the Suhtai and the Tsistsistas—the latter having absorbed the former in fairly recent times. But the two have two culture heroes—mythic figures who brought the people lessons in how to live and gave them sacred objects to remind them of the message and to guarantee success in the vital areas of life: "The medicine arrows and the buffalo hat are the two cherished talismans handed down to protect the Cheyenne . . . to give them health, long life, and plenty, and strength and courage to conquer their enemies."

The Suhtai hero was Stands on the Ground, who delivered the sacred buffalo hat with the instructions: "You must tell whoever you pass it over to that he must take great care of it and never injure it in any way. If in any manner the cap is abused or hurt, the buffalo will disappear, because the cap is the head chief of the buffalo." The other was Sweet Medicine, who delivered the four sacred arrows. He received these from supernatural beings somewhere near Bear Butte, which is close to the Black Hills. In periods of strife they would have to be "renewed," which involved prescribed, complicated ceremonies.

The ceremony was thought to insure the health of the people and an abundance of buffalo, cherries, berries, roots, grass, and all animals for the coming year.

The arrows were therefore extremely powerful talismans, and their desecration or loss would be a calamity. Disastrously, the arrows, which were carried into battle to guarantee success against the Pawnee, were carried incorrectly by the wrong warrior. Consequently, the arrows were captured by the Pawnee, who then practically annihilated the Cheyenne war party. The arrows were eventually recovered, but their loss was viewed as a tragedy for the tribe. And the loss was dramatic proof that violation of a ritual or sacred precept could bring catastrophe. Or to put it differently, it was further proof of the direct connection between ritual and result, ceremony and outcome. This was not theoretical but intensely practical. Note that both of these sacred objects—the buffalo hat and the medicine arrows—were real, physical objects that stayed with, traveled with the Cheyenne, and were venerated by both branches of the tribe. Certain men were charged with their care. It was a sacred responsibility and honor.

MEDICINE

Not surprisingly, the Cheyenne cosmology led to the development of elaborate rituals that had to be followed to make sure the individual acknowledged and appreciated the various spirits that were subordinate to the Creator but that interacted with humans, both for good and ill. Many have tried to explain this idea of the spirit world, but these explanations never seem to do full justice to the concept. It is perhaps impossible to express the meanings the Cheyenne attached to these ideas without understanding the Cheyenne language. Rich and varied as English is, it does not seem to have the vocabulary to express what the Cheyenne felt about the spirit world that surrounded them—or more properly, that they were immersed in. That may say something about the relationship of language to evolving cultures. But suffice it to say that no one has been able to express in English what the Cheyenne understood about the mysterious world around them. *Spirit* and *medicine* don't quite do the job.

Perhaps one way to approximate the Cheyenne's thinking is, strangely enough, the platonic notion of the ideal—the belief that while there are individual manifestations of creatures, there is also an ideal form somewhere apart. The *idea* of a buffalo, the *idea* of a horse. To the Cheyenne, these ideal beings interact with man and need to be propitiated with rituals in order to ensure their continued benevolence. Grinnell puts it slightly differently trying to explain the mostly inexplicable: "[T]he Cheyennes personified the elements; to certain birds, animals, and natural objects they attributed mysterious powers, and believed in the transference of such powers from the birds and animals to man. Prayers were offered to these natural objects; yet [. . .] not to the actual animals, but rather to the qualities, or forces, which these animals typified or which took their shape." The Cheyenne were the direct opposite of philosophical materialists who believe that only matter exists, that there is nothing more than what can be perceived. The Cheyenne believed there was a lot more going on than could meet the eye.

Visions and instruction on any subject could come to anyone. Sometimes, they were sought through fasting or self-torture (such as the celebrated Sun Dance—a Sioux term, but a ceremony performed by the Cheyenne and other Plains tribes). Sometimes they arrived in dreams. Somewhere along the line of adolescence the young warrior would probably receive a vision from one of the supernaturals. Often the vision would come in the form of a horse or a snake or a burst of thunder, and that voice would speak to him and instruct him and from then on would be the boy's personal guide and protector. His medicine. Thereafter he would offer prayers to his spirit, asking for help in a number of different contexts. In operation, the concept is not all that different from a Catholic's patron saint, although the warrior's "patron saint" could come in many forms other than human and was probably more active in the warrior's life—more consistently called upon, more consistently present.

Not surprisingly, in the Cheyenne worldview, there were minor deities associated with natural phenomena and geographical locations. They wanted their obeisance, too. The Cheyenne were immersed in a miasma of supernaturals, each of whom expected respect in the form of prayers and ritual. The observant Cheyenne was busy. In fact, the distinction between the natural and supernatural world really didn't apply. It was all one existence—sometimes magical, sometimes frightening, sometimes mysteriously beautiful, sometimes reasonable, sometimes inexplicable, but always multidimensional. Here again, although the comparison may seem outlandish, the Cheyenne were not all that different from the ancient Greeks, who were also surrounded by deities and spirits who interacted with humans for good or ill and often were in conflict with one another. They, too, needed to be propitiated, regularly and according to precise rituals and ceremonies. Of course, not all the ancient Greeks believed everything they were told by their priests and seers. And it's hard to believe that all the Cheyenne were uniformly pious. But even the skeptics would agree there was no sense taking any chances. They would have understood Pascal's wager. (Essentially, what have you got to lose by believing?) Rituals and ceremonies should therefore be ceremoniously observed, and they were.

There were men in the tribe—and now and then women—who were more in touch with this spirit world than others. They are commonly called "medicine men," although, here again, the English language struggles to do justice to the idea. At the risk of seeming overly sensitive, the term seems to emit a whiff of condescension and charlatanism, like stuff peddled in Old West medicine shows. The word *priests* may be better, but it has obvious associations with organized religion, and *shaman* is a bit obscure. And so *medicine man* has come down to us, and although it seems inadequate, it will have to suffice.

Since disease is believed to arise from supernatural as well as natural causes, the work of healing is a mingling of natural and supernatural remedies.

Medicine men who became healers got their information in two ways—one from a supernatural visitation, often in a dream. That vision outlined procedures for ritual remedies and may have also indicated which plants would be useful in treating different ailments. But even when specific herbs were used, the medicine man would always accompany the treatment with songs and shaking a rattle. The rattle was designed to chase away the "bad spirit" that had caused the sickness, and the song was an invocation to the benign powers and a request for a cure.

One cause of disease was thought to be malevolent spirits who dwelled around springs or watercourses. Offended somehow, they shot invisible arrows that had to be extracted through prescribed ritual. (Interestingly, the cholera epidemic of 1849 that devastated the Cheyenne tribe originated in contaminated river water—invisible arrows that were immune to ritual.)

These procedures would be followed even in the case of a gunshot or arrow wound, and while a warrior's friends might hold the wounded man down as someone cut out an arrow head or bullet, the medicine man would accompany the procedure with rattle and song. If the warrior recovered, credit would be shared. There is, of course, no way to know the survival rates among wounded Cheyenne. Loss of blood and infections most likely did severe work among them. As a comparison, it's worth considering soldiers wounded at the Battle of Gettysburg: "The wounds themselves were made all the more horrible by the weaponry that inflicted them, for while the rifle musket might fall considerably short of its reputation for accuracy, the weights of the unjacketed lead rounds (between .45 and .69 caliber) were heavy enough that when they did strike a human target, the damage would almost always be life threatening." The regular army troops who were sent west after the Civil War were armed with these same rifled muskets, and although most of them, especially the new recruits, were not very good shots, when they did hit someone, the wounds they inflicted were beyond the scope of prayer and ritual. (Forsyth's men were carrying seven-shot Spencer repeaters that fired a .56 caliber round and Colt revolvers that fired .45 caliber rounds.)

A young man or woman who wished to become a doctor might not wait for a vision and go to an established man in the tribe to request instruction. In this way, the folk wisdom that had over the years accumulated about effective herb remedies would be passed along. As in all formal requests for a favor, the supplicant would present the medicine man with a pipe. If he agreed to become a tutor, he would signify by accepting the pipe and smoking it. Presenting a pipe in this fashion was considered a mandatory preliminary in any important or formal negotiation.

Importantly, medicine men did not only receive information (in dreams, visions, or formal instruction) about how to treat sickness and wounds. They also received instructions in how to prepare charms and amulets that could prevent disease and, perhaps more important, injuries and wounds in battle.

ROMAN NOSE

Roman Nose was the most famous of the Cheyenne warriors and often led war parties against the whites, although not so many as the army claimed. In that way he was like Jesse James or other folk rebels who were blamed for more adventures than even they claimed. Roman Nose was a member of the Elk Horn Scrapers society, who were also called the Crooked Lances because of the object carried by the society leader. (They were the same who were also known as the Blue Bellies.) As mentioned, he was not a member of the Dog Soldiers, but he often lived with them in their separate camps, because their warlike spirit suited his temperament. In battles against the whites, he would often charge single-handedly on his horse after saying, "Now I am going to empty their guns," and in this way draw the fire of the soldiers. He obviously understood that most of the troops after the Civil War were using single-shot muskets, and so after their first volley, they would be vulnerable to attack from Roman Nose's waiting followers. But it was not merely—or even primarily—a military tactic or an act of leadership. It was a display of the kind that garnered the warrior fame and respect. And if he was killed? Well, that was better than to live in obscurity and wither away in impotent old age.

This sort of display garnered Roman Nose great acclaim and fame. But he had a secret weapon, of sorts. He believed he was invulnerable. In battle he wore a war bonnet that was made for him by his friend and medicine man, Ice Bear. The bonnet made him bulletproof.

As a boy Roman Nose had fasted for four days on a lake island in Montana, and during his fast he dreamed of a snake with one horn on its head. Ice Bear adopted this important image into the war bonnet he made for Roman Nose:

> Instead of having two buffalo horns attached to the headband, one on each side, it had but one rising over the center of the forehead; it had a very long tail that nearly touched the ground even when Roman Nose was mounted. The tail was made of a strip of young buffalo bull's hide and had eagle feathers set all along its length.

Ice Bear then informed Roman Nose about the strict rituals and taboos that accompanied the bonnet. We assume these instructions came to Ice Bear in the process of making the bonnet. These included wearing "sacred medicine paint" for his face in carefully prescribed manner: "for the forehead, Indian yellow, red across the nose, and black across the mouth and chin." And because many Cheyenne disliked using metal implements when they were eating (because it was felt food touched by metal might attract bullets), Roman Nose was warned to avoid any food that had been cooked or served using the white man's metal utensils. If he violated these or any of the other taboos or improperly performed any of the preliminary ceremonies, he would destroy the bonnet's protective power.

To the Cheyenne this was not a fanciful idea. Many believed in mysterious talismans or rituals that would make them invulnerable, whether to bullets or arrows or any other weapon.

"Owing to the protective power of the bird, a man wearing a war bonnet of gray eagle feathers believed that he would not be hit by either bullets or arrows. These bonnets were worn therefore not merely because they made a man look fine, but for protection as well. Some men, however, would not wear war bonnets, because they made one conspicuous; and the enemy was more likely to shoot at a man wearing a war bonnet than at one without decoration. [. . .] It was [also] generally believed that, if in a fight, a man imitated the call of a sand hill crane, he would not be hit by a bullet." The call is a short, softened blend of a squawk and a police whistle. Attacking warriors also blew whistles made from the bone of eagle wings.

One warrior, who became known as Bullet Proof, devised a pre-battle ritual that, if followed precisely, would render the soldiers' guns useless. The bullets would simply drop out of their guns and fall to the ground. In order to prove his power, Bullet Proof and a half dozen or so warriors planned to attack an army wagon train. The warriors would ride against the train one at a time. They located a supply train and attacked as planned. The first two charged, and both had their horses shot out from under them, but the warriors walked away, unharmed. The next two charged, one after the other, and both were shot and killed. Bullet Proof (who did not participate but only observed) afterward said that they had not followed instructions, and the people of the village accepted that. In other words, neither the idea of invulnerability through talisman and ritual, nor the firm belief in the necessity of precisely following the ritual instructions, was challenged or invalidated. And the father of one of those killed said to Bullet Proof, "Friend, it is well. It is better for a man to be killed in battle than to die a natural death. We must all die. Do not let the killing of these young men make you feel badly."

Roman Nose's war bonnet served him well from the time he first wore it in 1860. Whenever he charged white soldiers "to empty their guns," he was never hit. Cheyenne warrior George Bent described one fight with the soldiers:

> We crossed over, and now Roman Nose rode up on his fine white pony, wearing his famous war bonnet that nearly touched the ground when he was mounted, and with his face painted in a peculiar way, to protect him from bullets. As soon as he came up he called out to the warriors to form a line and get ready for a charge, as he was going to empty the soldiers' guns. The Indians formed a long line from the river nearly to the bluffs and sat on their ponies facing the troops. Roman Nose then put his pony into a run and rode straight out toward one end of the line of troops. When he was quite close he turned and rode at top speed straight along the front, from the river clear to the bluffs, the troops firing at him at close range all the way. Reaching the bluffs, he turned and rode back along the line again. In this way he made three, perhaps four, rushes from one end of the line to the other, and then his pony was shot and fell under him. On seeing this the warriors set up a yell and charged.

Although he certainly attributed his almost miraculous escape in these charges to his medicine, Roman Nose also knew that it was much harder to hit a fast-running rider who was crossing in front of the enemy instead of coming straight at them. The relative motion required the trooper to swing his long, heavy, one-shot musket and lead his galloping target—even at fairly close range. In the frightening noise and smoke of battle it's not an easy shot to make, as Roman Nose surely understood. And it's obviously easier to hit the rider's horse than to shoot him out of the saddle, even if he is sitting tall—something the Cheyenne were smart enough and expert horsemen enough not to do. Still, that does not diminish Roman Nose's bravery nor his ability to inspire his comrades, nor, undoubtedly, his belief in the power of his medicine hat.

Although presumably shaken up by his fall, Roman Nose was not hurt in that fight—or in the many others that followed. He would be wearing his war bonnet and paint again eight years later, when he led a similar charge against Major Forsyth's frontiersmen.

BEAU SABREURS AND CAVALIERS

The horse and the buffalo created the nomad and allowed him to exist. And the joy in that way of living, the freedom that it involved, was also understood and appreciated by many of the white soldiers who were tasked with chasing down hostile tribes. They fought the native warriors, because it was their job, not because they didn't understand their adversaries or felt them so very different from themselves. Recall Forsyth's comments on leaving for his scout with his fifty frontiersmen: "I sprang into the saddle with a light heart and no little elation at the thought of having a field command and a roving commission—a state of affairs that any true cavalry man can appreciate."

George Custer famously said, "If I were an Indian I often think I would greatly prefer to cast my lot among those of my people adhered to the free and open Plains, rather than submit to the confined limits of a reservation, there to be the recipient of the blessed benefits of civilization with its vices thrown in without stint or measure." This is not to say that the attitude was universal among the cavalry officers. There was very little unanimous opinion about the tribes among the professional army—or the civilians, for that matter. But it is to say that some of the officers understood the warrior's point of view, because it was not all that different from their own. It's perhaps a little ironic that Custer's pen name when he wrote articles for magazines was "Nomad." Or perhaps, it's not ironic at all. Custer was and is, of course, the most famous and controversial Indian fighter. He proved himself to be a very competent soldier and leader of cavalry during the Civil War, but he came west knowing no more about Indian fighting than most of the other regular officers. But he was to learn that he had something in common with the Cheyenne warriors he would face. It was a self-image of the mounted warrior, the beau sabreur.

History and literature are littered with characters who were handsome, vainglorious, aristocratic, often dim-witted but appealing, and, above all, glamorous. The cavalryman was the dashing ideal of centuries of European wars. He was in the Charge of the Light Brigade. (Tennyson didn't write about the attack of the foot soldiers.) And of course throughout European history the mounted man—the knight—was different from the common herd. His horse signified his exalted status. (Even the knight on a chess board is a horse). In battle, he was literally above the plodding peasants carrying pikes. He may be a dim-witted aristocrat like Lord Cardigan, but he *was* an aristocrat—if not in fact, at least in his role and in comparison to the infantry and artillery. The word *cavalier* descends from *chevalier*, which derives from the French for "horse"—*cheval*. And while the Cheyenne warrior like Roman Nose did bedeck himself in war paint and feathered bonnets, his outfit was not much more gaudy or outlandish than a hussar's gold lace and tasseled shako and cavalry mustache. Custer himself sported a red scarf and buckskins, flowing hair, and a wide-brimmed hat—all that was missing was a feather. The word *panache* not only means great style and self-assertion, it also means "feather." Many cavalrymen felt a certain kinship with the Indian warrior, because on some level they recognized that the warrior's self-image and psychology were not very different from their own. A staff officer in the Civil War said of Custer: "As far as I could see, his ambition seemed to be more to startle and surprise friend and foe with the brilliancy of his deeds than anything else." That in a nutshell also describes the ambition of the Cheyenne warrior.

(Along the same lines, a French general of hussars, the Comte de Lasalle said: "Any Hussar who is not dead by thirty is a blackguard." Lasalle was killed at age thirty-four.)

In their villages, the Roman Nose and his comrades were as glamorous and celebrated as any strutting European hussar, and they basked in their glory and reveled in the knowledge that the people admired them and would tell stories about them. The warrior on horseback enjoyed prestige, freedom, and adventure—wealth in all its forms, material and psychological.

Perhaps it's fair to say, then, that when the Cheyenne and other similar tribes called themselves a variation on the word "people," they were unconsciously affirming an ironic truth. Their warriors weren't all that different psychologically from General Custer, the soldier historian Robert Utley called the "Cavalier in Buckskin." Whether Custer and his comrades perceived that kinship or not—and Custer's writings suggest strongly that he did—he and many of his comrades understood it on a deeper level. The horse was a common denominator between the Cheyenne warrior and the professional cavalryman—both perceived themselves as nature's aristocrats. They had *style*. Some like Custer were not shy about displaying it, but even the more modest officers felt it as keenly. (It's also worth noticing that the modern myth of the cowboy is a variation of this theme—the free man on horseback. What is a cattle drive, after all, except another form of wandering with purpose?)

IN SUM

Before they were the warriors of the Plains the Cheyenne were a semi-agricultural people living in the area around the northern Great Lakes. Pushed out of their territory by hostile tribes, primarily the

Ojibwa, they migrated to the regions of the Upper Missouri River, where they farmed and lived in semipermanent earth-and-wooden houses along the river. They wandered seasonally onto the fringes of the Great Plains to hunt. But when they acquired the horse, they gradually began to follow the buffalo and soon became entirely nomadic, and they abandoned earthen houses for the buffalo-skin tepee used by other Plains tribes who were following a similar pattern of life. Their way of village life, their reliance on hunting, and the enmity of other tribes fostered a culture that celebrated the warrior both as a provider of material wealth and as a protector of the village. Fiercely individualistic, these warriors were, as Captain Frederick Benteen said, "the best fighters the sun ever shone on." And these were the people Sandy Forsyth and his fifty scouts were looking for.

2

‒‒‒‒

THE ARMY

General Ulysses Grant had a talent for saying things clearly and succinctly: "The art of war is simple enough. Find out where your enemy is. Get at him as soon as you can. Strike him as hard as you can and as often as you can and keep moving on." Now faced with problems on the frontier, Grant, Sherman, and Sheridan—and their colleagues—might wonder whether this theory really applied and, if it did, whether the instrument they were being given was adequate, or even appropriate, to do the job. More fundamental, was the nation really at war with the hostile tribes—at war in the way Grant and everyone else understood it? Or were the troubles on the Plains more properly understood as a regional police action? If so, what did that mean for the composition and deployment of the nation's army? Were whole tribes involved, or were the depredations the work of a few hundred malcontents or opportunists? And who was in charge, if anyone? Satisfactory answers seemed to be as elusive as the mounted raiders themselves. The situation was fraught with frustration, primarily because of political squabbling over the nation's resources and over the fundamental policies toward the Indians. The generals might well have had moments of nostalgia for the Civil War. At least then Grant's straightforward understanding of the art of war was not hampered by disagreements about whether there was even a war going on or who the enemy was.

When the Civil War erupted, the regular army numbered only 18,000 officers and men. By the end of the war it's estimated that 900,000 men fought for the Confederacy and 2,100,000 for the Union, and a modern estimate is that 750,000 men in both armies had been killed, either in action, or by disease. The single-day battle at Antietam created more casualties than the prewar regular army had ever mustered.

The huge numbers of the Civil War armies were therefore not filled by regulars but by volunteer units from each of the states. Often these were organized by state and local politicians who were then given command assignments, not especially because they knew anything about soldiering but because they were politically useful or powerful or both. And at the beginning of the war, almost all were genuinely dedicated to their cause, whichever it might be, and not a few of them also liked the idea of serving in an officer's uniform. There was nothing incompatible in those motivations. Vanity and patriotism can coexist in a single package. The volunteer enlisted men were less concerned with wearing gold braid but equally concerned with the issues at stake. But some of them signed on for as little as ninety days. Many, if not most of them, thought it would all be over in that amount of time.

These volunteer units were in many cases leavened with regular army officers who were used to train and introduce the amateur troops into the arts of soldiering and to help lead them in action. The regulars were the professionals. Many were veterans of the Mexican War and had no illusions about the nature of war. These officers were mainly graduates of West Point or perhaps some of the state military colleges like Virginia Military Institute. Some few had come up through the ranks. Not many, but some. Many of the regular enlisted men were career soldiers—lifers. These regulars, both officers and noncommissioned officers (NCOs), were invaluable in shaping the huge rabble of civilian soldiers into something like a fighting force. For all his well-documented faults as a field general, West Point graduate George McClellan was a superb organizer and trainer. And it's fair to wonder whether his noted reluctance to use his troops in combat was due at least in part to his hatred of seeing the splendid army he had created destroyed or even badly torn up. (A trait for which his men understandably loved him.) As some of the volunteer officers would learn, there is a great deal more to the arts of war and managing troops than leading a charge against the enemy. Something as mundane as setting up and managing a reasonably healthful camp was part of the job—not glamorous, but vital. In the Mexican War, which featured a similar division between the regulars and the volunteers, only about one in eight US deaths came from combat, the others came from disease. The volunteers suffered disproportionately from the regulars, because of their ignorance of basic military camp management and even elementary hygiene. The old army joke has it that the coffee always tastes better when the latrines are dug downstream from the camp. The record was better in the Civil War, but even so, twice as many soldiers died from disease as from combat injuries. The POW camps on both sides were disgraceful cesspools of disease and death, but even the ordinary soldiers' camps were breeding grounds of fatal illnesses that always come around whenever large groups of people gather without much thought for hygiene, sanitation, or water purity. What's more, the food was poor—bacon, beans, coffee, and hardtack were the staples. That was hardly a menu that discouraged disease. It was hardly a menu that encouraged vigorous health, and that in turn made soldiers who were wounded less able to fight off the effects of blood loss and infection. Fifteen percent of all wounded men would die, and the wounds tabulated included anything from a mere scratch to an almost always fatal wound in the abdomen.

The regular army officers knew a little more about such matters: castrametation (the art or science of setting up a camp) was a course studied at the Point. They also knew something about European-style warfare—the kind that Civil War armies would fight. In fact, it was essentially the only form of war they knew about. Regular officers were therefore promoted to senior rank in the volunteers, even though their regular rank might be a relatively junior. After distinguishing himself commanding the volunteer Brigade of Michigan "Wolverines" at Gettysburg and then in subsequent battles, George Custer moved up the ranks until he became a major general and division commander at the age of twenty-five. His regular rank was captain. Brevets, or honorary promotions, were also awarded to officers who distinguished themselves. Thus a lowly lieutenant like Custer's brother Tom might be awarded several brevet promotions and end up a lieutenant colonel for his conspicuous bravery in action. (He also won two Congressional Medals of Honor.) Brevets were honorary titles, but they were cherished by officers who had no other way to advance their careers in a regular army that promoted on the basis of seniority. That process continued after the war and into the era of troubles with the Indians. (Major Joel Elliott led a charge against the Cheyenne at the Washita in 1868, famously shouting, "Here's for a brevet or a coffin!" Along with the nineteen men he led, he—what was left of him—got the coffin.)

When the war was over, things returned to prewar procedures. The volunteer troops went home to their farms and families. The politically appointed volunteer generals and colonels on both sides went home to run for office again, or for the first time, while retaining their rank as an honorary title. Hence the well-known "Kentucky colonels." The professional officers, those who had been awarded exalted brevet ranks and/or placed in command of volunteer units, were returned to their regular army rank and given regular army assignments. Former major general George Custer was briefly a captain again before being promoted to lieutenant colonel and second-in-command of the Seventh Cavalry. Sandy Forsyth, who like Custer had been brevetted a general, was back to being a major. These were not demotions but merely reversions to their actual status in the regular army, which was in the process of returning to almost prewar manpower levels. Both men were also able to retain their brevet titles as honorifics, but they were paid according to the actual rank, and their places on the seniority list—the basis for promotion—were fixed accordingly. At the Little Bighorn, Custer died a lieutenant colonel, not a major general, despite what the newspaper headlines read. Some of the civilian volunteer officers who distinguished themselves in the war and developed a taste for army life, decided to stay in and transfer to the regulars. They were given regular army commissions. Benjamin Grierson, who commanded perhaps the most famous Union cavalry raid of the war, stayed on to become Colonel of the Tenth Cavalry. He had been a music teacher in civilian life and, although he disliked horses, he liked the army life better than conducting the town band. He was also one of the few officers who was happy, or at least willing, to take command of the newly created Tenth Cavalry—one of two cavalry regiments of mostly former slaves who came to be known as the Buffalo Soldiers.

By the end of 1865 the nation was understandably sick of war. And it was unhappy with the national debt that the war had run up. Reconstruction was underway with varying degrees of success, and units of the army were employed throughout the South as a police force to counteract criminal resistance from groups like the Ku Klux Klan. (Army units in South Carolina alone arrested some three thousand Klansmen.) Regular army regiments were broken into companies and scattered throughout the country so that they could cover wider regions, not only in the South for Reconstruction, but also in the West. As a result regiments rarely came together as a unit, and training and management of the men devolved to the company level, with little or no supervision from senior regimental officers. That was true throughout the army. What's more, the army began to take on the role of a constabulary, especially in the South, but increasingly on the frontier. Breaking up meetings of the Klan and arresting members

did not require much in the way of military skills or training. It was
police business that the army had to assume, because there was little
civilian appetite for enforcing the new laws of Reconstruction. Not
surprisingly, Texas was a particularly thorny problem—not only
did Texans dislike Reconstruction, but the Comanche and the
Kiowa and some Kiowa Apache were continuing their own form
of resistance and depredation. It was a situation that bedeviled army
command. On one of his visits General Sheridan once said if he owned
both hell and Texas, he'd live in hell and rent out Texas. And he wasn't
talking just about the weather. (The story sounds apocryphal, but it
also sounds like something he would say.)

Hell for General Sherman, aside from having to live in Washington
and deal with the politicians and newspapers, was that he didn't have
the resources to do what the army was being asked to do—not only
from the federal government but from the settlers on the frontier
who were clamoring for help against the hostile tribes. He didn't have
enough troops, and he didn't have enough of the right kind of troops.

CONGRESS AND THE POSTWAR ARMY

The army was divided into the line and the staff. Staff officers worked
in major centers, most notably Washington, of course. They were
responsible for the business of the army—supply and manpower
planning.

The line was divided into the engineers, the artillery, the cavalry, and
the infantry. The engineers were responsible for domestic projects—
building dams and bridges, surveying the vast territories of the West,
laying out proposed lines for railroads, and surveying boundaries and
mapping territories. In wartime they fought alongside the other arms
and were vital in areas such as fortification and siege warfare. In fact the
engineers were the most prestigious arm of the line, and the graduates
of West Point who did the best asked for and were assigned to the

engineers. Robert E. Lee for example finished second in his class at West Point and was assigned to the engineers. He did heroic service in the Mexican War scouting enemy positions and mapping out trails and roads around enemy positions.

West Point was originally established as an engineering school. The idea was to create a core of competent professionals who could build the young nation's infrastructure, and its graduates did live up to the task. West Point was called the "Best School in the World." While the French and British might take exception to that, West Point certainly did the job it was formed to do. And along the way the cadet would learn something about soldiering, but engineering, math, and natural sciences were the backbone of the curriculum. And since there was very little turnover among the instructors—there were decades of continuity—West Point's curriculum remained solidly devoted to the engineering subjects.

In addition the cadets would learn something about tactics and of course these mirrored the Napoleonic theories of war. Therefore artillery was considered to be second in prestige assignments. Sherman chose the artillery even though he had done well academically and might have gone to the engineers. But he thought the chances of combat were greater in the artillery, and at the time he graduated, there was trouble with the British and the idea of war was in the air.

Third in prestige was the infantry. The infantry was the place for fighting soldiers—the service that many if not most soldiers considered the only real service. They're the ones who did the work. "Ninety percent of all wounds in the Civil War were caused by gunshot and the remainder by shell fragments and other large projectiles." Notice that wounds from cavalry sabers did not figure in the accounting, although in fairness, troopers also used their carbines and pistols at close range, so their contribution was not nothing. Still "boots on the ground" did most of the work. That was an article of faith in the regular army. A Civil War infantryman spoke for many, if not most of his comrades when he said: "Our cavalry are too often satisfied with a few discharges of their pistols and carbines, and then 'retire' to give the infantry a chance."

At West Point, the last in line of *academic* prestige was the cavalry. The beau sabreur was a distant fourth to the methodical engineer.

With its emphasis on engineering and scientific studies combined with European tactics and the general subjects of man management, drill, and the details of organization—the curriculum was full. There was nothing said about the problem of fighting Indians, even though strife with the tribes had been going on for decades. The subject was thought to be unworthy of the curriculum. Or rather it was thought that any officer who graduated from West Point would be able to grasp the relatively small problems of Indian fighting once he got to the frontier, wherever that might be. Now and then a line officer with experience against the tribes would have a temporary assignment as an instructor of some academically suitable subject, like cavalry tactics, but his experience could only be tapped informally. The curriculum was watched over by professors of long standing who were sure they knew the best way to build a professional officer. And so the curriculum hardly changed.

Despite its lack of academic prestige, the cavalry was the army's glamorous arm to its officers and to the general public. Artists and writers appreciated them, too. But to the Congressmen who paid the bills, the cavalry was something of an expensive luxury. When it came to value for money, the cavalry didn't seem to make a very good case for itself.

[A] persuasive reason for minimizing cavalry in the US army was its sheer cost. Mounted troops were enormously expensive to maintain, requiring at least six months to train just in riding drill. Beyond that, admitted another veteran officer, another "three years had been regarded as necessary to transform a recruit into a good cavalryman"—all of which cost money with no sign of immediate return on investment. Cavalry horses were even more costly. A cavalry brigade in the Crimea consumed 20,000 pounds of fodder a day (in addition, each horse required five gallons of water) and that did not even begin to reckon with the cost of the horses themselves or their attrition (in a six month period in 1854–55 British cavalry in the Crimea lost 932 of its 2,216 horses to sickness).

It's worth mentioning that many US Army regular officers, such as George McClellan, went to the Crimea to observe the Europeans and the Turks fighting. Other officers—both staff and line—and politicians read their reports. Lots of water, lots of grain, lots of money to buy and maintain—horses did not appeal very much to the parsimonious Congress—nor did the idea of a trooper who could not become truly productive for years. (It's also worth mentioning that five gallons of water per horse could be a problem on the Plains, where branches of the rivers often went dry and there were no wells to draw from.) Therefore any congressman or staff officer thinking about the Indian problem on the Plains might wonder how useful the cavalry horse really was—especially a congressman who was looking for a politically acceptable or defensible reason to cut back on army appropriations. Certainly the horse had limitations that were not always apparent at first glance. Further, if that same Congressman was paying attention, he would understand that by breaking the army, including the cavalry, into companies and spreading them around the country, they were relying on company officers to supervise the training of new men. Some company officers and noncoms were good at the job, and conscientious, but others were not. And with no senior regimental officer to look over their shoulders, it was easy for a captain of a troop to neglect the training. Besides, they were often just doing police work, so what was the point of riding drills or saber and pistol practice? That meant that the lengthy training required to produce a productive cavalryman—someone useful against the superb Cheyenne horsemen— would take even longer than normal. That's assuming he received any cavalry training at all.

Added to congressional doubts about the cavalry's return on investment, there was a school of thought in both the United States and European militaries that regarded the cavalry with some skepticism. The cavalry may be glamorous—the men and horses may look very fine in a parade; the officers may look dashing in uniform when waltzing at the balls—but in a battle were they really all that useful? They were good for scouting—yes. Intelligence gathering and screening main body movement—yes. Raiding supply lines—yes. Harassing rear echelons or retreating columns—fine. But in a set-piece battle? That was a different matter. And although the Light Brigade did make a brave and famous charge against the Russian artillery in the Crimea, what did they achieve after all, except "to do and die?" Nothing. The charge was, after all, a mistake to begin with. And one-third of them were casualties for no discernable gain, except some lines of verse.

That question affected the way the European generals constructed their armies, and since the Americans took their lessons from the Europeans, they followed suit. For all of his well-known affection for the flamboyant J. E. B. Stuart, Robert E. Lee's ratio of infantry to cavalry was ten to one at Gettysburg (possibly in part because Stuart was missing for the first two days). The Duke of Wellington's ratio at Waterloo was four to one; First Baron Raglan at the Crimea had thirty infantry divisions versus ten of cavalry, and although Tennyson would go on to write about the glamorous cavalry charge, the bulk of the real work would fall to the foot soldiers and artillery. The infantry was "the queen of battle": the bayonet, the *beau ideal*. "[O]ld line General Edwin Sumner urged his officers . . . '[G]ive 'em the bayonet, give 'em the bayonet, they can't stand that.'"

So it was not just congressional parsimony that limited cavalry appropriations; it was professional military received wisdom and entrenched tradition. These ideas worked in the Mexican War, and they worked in the Civil War—if you could overlook the appalling casualties suffered by the infantry.

And there was also a fundamental question that both the army and the politicians asked themselves—where was the risk to the nation likely to come from? And what kind of future war would we be required to fight? What kind of army would be needed to counteract it? Certainly the nation was not at risk from a few bands of primitive brigands in feathers, carrying bows and arrows. If there was any risk at all it would come from another nation state with hostile intentions. (It should be remembered that the French were meddling in Mexico and had installed a puppet emperor in 1864, when the United States was otherwise engaged. European empire building and expansion was not something to be casually dismissed. The French army was still in Mexico in 1866, and there was, after all, the Monroe Doctrine to think about.)

Having just emerged from the huge bloodbath of the Civil War, having studied the history of war at West Point, having read history, period, the generals and politicians could not conceive of a legitimate threat other than from a hostile nation state that coveted our land or resources, or our influence in trade—or any other of the other classic motives for hostility. And yes, the antics of a few tribes of illiterate Indians was irksome, and their victims and the Western politicians and editorialists were noisy, and yes, of course, their complaints were legitimate and Indian atrocities were unfortunate. All that was true. But after all, even though there were a couple of hundred settlers killed in Kansas and thereabouts, no one sent them there. They were there of their own free will. The nation had just suffered over 700,000 dead and many more thousands impoverished. By contrast, the troubles on the Plains were rather small. And most important, the nation was in no danger from the tribes. Their way of life was unsustainable and on the way out, anyway. It might take a few years, but there was no existential threat to the United States, and there was no doubt about the outcome. Besides, there was the national debt to consider—as well as civilian projects, including Reconstruction of the ruined South, and those projects demanded attention and money. True, the transcontinental construction crews must be protected, but surely infantry could handle that. The crews moved along only a mile or so each day. In the light of all that, it was hard to make a good case for an extensive and therefore expensive commitment to the cavalry. Or, to put it differently, it was easy to reject the case for cavalry.

There was also the feeling that these troubles with the Indians were quite obviously a regional problem. It might therefore be best solved by regional or local action. The Civil War had mustered troops from the states. Now the states and territories could and should use similar mechanisms for dealing with their local problem. Ranger companies had fought the Comanche in Texas even as other Texans were off fighting for the Confederacy. The Arizona Territory also had Rangers to address the Apache problem. True, the action of the locals orga-nized into a temporary regiment had resulted in the unconscionable, egregious, and politically contentious massacre of the Cheyenne camp at Sand Creek, in 1864. There was no denying that that was an act of local barbarians and the sweepings of the Denver saloons, and there was no denying that the hideous displays of Cheyenne body parts by the drunken rabble known as the Third Colorado was a black mark on the territory that wanted to become a state. It didn't help that local opinion applauded their grisly massacre and that the *Rocky Mountain News* exulted that "[t]he Colorado soldiers have again cov-ered themselves in glory." But that whole sad incident was the result of fanatical leadership by that maniac John Chivington and did not by itself invalidate the concept of local action to solve a local problem. Did it? An honest politician in Washington might well ask himself that question as he pondered how to balance competing requests for limited federal resources.

Then there were the staff officers working hand in glove with the politicians in Washington. They were army officers, but they were attuned to budgetary constraints and political currents, and their separation from the line officers in the field made it relatively easy for them to go along with legitimate concerns about expense. Hence the preference for infantry among large sectors of official Washington—even though the dullest student of war knew that a hundred thousand marching infantrymen would not—and could not—bother, or even inconvenience, a half dozen mounted Cheyenne. Furthermore, if anyone was going to use a bayonet at close quarters, it was more likely to be a Cheyenne warrior counting coup with a weapon he took from a private.

Despite the arguments in favor of the infantry as a cost-effective branch of the service and despite the tradition of the "queen of battle," the fact remained that infantry were only marginally useful on the frontier. They were fine for garrison duty or for guarding a plodding supply train, but they were designed for attacking or defending fixed lines or fortifications, and the Plains Indians never had fixed fortifications, and they never fought in Civil War–style fixed positions. The Cheyenne and Sioux and their allies did not fight set-piece battles, and if they thought about it at all, they realized that the very idea was absurd. They were also hard to find, much less bring to battle, unless it was by their choice, and so the infantry was tactically useless against a mounted, nomadic enemy. Across the West the Plains Indians scorned the infantry as "walk a heeps." The only possible way for the infantry to be effective in an offensive campaign against the Plains tribes was during winter, when the tribes were in their permanent camps. They could then be surprised and attacked. But that strategy was better suited for the cavalry, because getting to those camps was far more feasible on horseback than by marching on foot through the winter weather of the Plains and risking the loss of the command. (As an aside, General Nelson Miles did employ this idea late in the Indian Wars and more or less succeeded, but his infantry suffered terribly from the weather, and Miles could easily have suffered Napoleon's fate in Russia.)

But infantrymen were cheaper, and if they received any training, it was rudimentary and therefore over quickly, so that the new recruit could be sent to the field relatively soon after putting on his uniform.

He knew how to march, and he knew the difference between a sergeant and a lieutenant. But unless he was already familiar with firearms, he probably didn't learn much about his rifle. Training budgets were slim and restricted practice firing to a "handful of cartridges a year." As Captain Albert Barnitz of the Seventh Cavalry wrote: "Our men are in the main a set of uninstructed recruits, who can't hit a barn door at three hundred yards . . . much less an Indian." Barnitz was describing his cavalry troop, but it was much the same with the infantry. It's interesting to wonder how much of this Roman Nose knew or suspected when he went to "empty the soldiers' guns." As mentioned, it's not easy to hit a man on a fast horse crossing in front of you, especially when you're handling a long, heavy, single-shot musket. It's even harder when you don't really know how to shoot.

It should come as no surprise, however, that the infantry had its advocates. Their argument was counterintuitive, but persuasive, especially to anyone who wanted to be persuaded. Simply put, it was that the infantry may not be better against the Indians but they were no worse than the cavalry. The reasons centered around the intrinsic liabilities of the cavalry horses on campaign: "After the fourth day's march of a mixed command, the horse does not march much faster than the foot soldier, and after the seventh day, the foot soldier begins to outmarch the horse, and from that time on the foot soldier has to end his march earlier and earlier in the day to enable the cavalry to reach the camp the same day at all." During a campaign, as opposed to a routine patrol, cavalry horses broke down too easily, too quickly. This was the view of General William B. Hazen, an advocate of the infantry's virtues (and a bitter enemy of George Custer) as well as being notably dyspeptic and irascible. His opinions therefore are hardly objective. But he was not alone. He and those who shared his opinion also pointed out that the cavalry troopers were so poorly trained as horsemen that they typically dismounted to fight on foot, because they knew no other way. What's more, their lighter cavalry carbines were less effective than the infantryman's heavier caliber, longer-range musket. And there was some truth to that. What's more, every fourth trooper had to be assigned as a horse holder, so a cavalry troop by definition went into action with only three-fourths of its men on the line. And that was also true. (It should be mentioned that Hazen made his remarks to a congressional committee in 1878 during another of those contentious debates about funding the army. But the points were equally valid just after the war. The fundamentals of the debate had not changed.)

Looked at objectively, Hazen's argument essentially boils down to this—if neither the cavalry nor the infantry can campaign efficiently against the mounted tribes, what's the point in spending money on horses, especially since on the march a cavalry troop requires three times the number of accompanying supply wagons as an infantry company? And so a congressman who was being asked to support an army appropriations bill and who either knew nothing about the West or cared nothing about it, could feel he had done his duty by his constituents by saving them tax dollars and favoring the infantry over the cavalry. There were solid arguments in favor of the infantry, anyway, and they provided political "cover" as well as a salve for any tender political consciences that needed it. It might also quiet the clamoring of the settlers in the West by sending a few blue coats to the forts near the new towns. Congress could be seen to be doing something. Whether that something was an effective response to the problems was another question, but that was at least legitimately debatable. The politicians could tell themselves they were addressing the problem in a reasonably honest and disinterested fashion. Not all of them were, of course, but unquestionably *something* was being done. And so the army appropriations bill of 1866 allowed for an army that was heavily weighted toward the infantry. The cavalry would be allowed ten regiments; the infantry, forty-five; and the artillery, five.

No one thought that artillery was very useful against the hostile tribes. Cannons required horses to haul them and their heavy limbers, and in action they were by definition stationary weapons. They obviously could be moved here and there, but in order to be fired, they had to be immobile. Beloved of Napoleon and his students, they were extraordinarily effective in set-piece battles and in classic military situations—bombarding enemy lines in preparation a for a charge by infantry, counterbattery fire, defensive fire against an attacking lines of enemy, battering down enemy fortifications, bombarding his installations, and protecting your own fortifications against assault. But none of that mattered in fights against Indians. Almost the only piece of artillery that was useful against the tribes was the mountain howitzer, because it could be disassembled and carried on mule back. The Indians did not like this gun "that shoots twice" (meaning it fired an exploding shell), and in at least two notable engagements against hostile tribes, the mountain howitzer averted disaster (in Apache Pass, Arizona, against the Apaches in 1862, and against the Comanche and Kiowa at Adobe Walls, Texas, in 1864). But the mountain howitzer was a weapon that could be employed by infantry or dismounted cavalry. The only other possibly useful piece of artillery was the Gatling gun, but it was ponderous, and the barrels had a tendency to foul after a few rounds. It will be remembered that Custer didn't bother to take his along when he left for the Little Big Horn. It was probably just as well. They wouldn't have helped.

According to the 1866 appropriations bill, each army regiment would have ten companies (or "troops" in the case of the cavalry) and the War Department was given the latitude to decide on the size of the companies—anywhere from fifty to one hundred men per company were allowed. In 1866 the War Department "fixed company strength at 64 privates, so that the total paper strength of the army, both staff and line, thus became 54,302 officers and enlisted men." Of these, roughly one-third were sent to the South for Reconstruction duty. And in a burst of common sense, the bill also allowed for the hiring of one thousand Indian scouts.

In coming years the number of men authorized per company would fluctuate according to War Department policies. More important, the actual numbers available for duty would fall short of even the authorized numbers. The companies were chronically short-handed because of attrition due to normal turnover, to disease and combat, and, most important, to desertion. So the key phrase in assessing the army's strength in the immediate postwar period is "on paper." The army on the frontier almost never had its authorized number of men.

THE RANK AND FILE

The volunteers who fought in the bloodbaths of the Civil War were like most soldiers in combat—when the firing was heaviest and the dangers most intense, they fought pretty much for each other, for their messmates, for the men on either side of them. But the vast majority of them were there, in uniform, because they believed in their cause. They joined because of idealism or patriotism. In combat, unit cohesion and loyalty kept them in the fight, kept them from running away, most of them. But they had volunteered because they believed in their country's cause—whether their country was the United States or, like Robert E. Lee's, Virginia. (Later in the war, conscription and enlistment bounties provided far less motivated men.) But most of those idealistic soldiers went home after the war—along with almost all of the draftees. The patriotic beliefs of the volunteers on both sides may have been unchanged, even though their bodies and psyches might have been sadly altered. But very few of the citizen soldiers stayed on in the regular army. And so the composition of the postwar army became a very different story, and the motivations of the soldiers to join and then to serve were very different from those of the Civil War volunteers. There were, of course, the old veterans, the lifers, the regulars. They were the backbone of the army. And a handful of soldiers of fortune remained, along with some others who liked the army or couldn't think of something else to do. But the new recruits? The ones who filled the rolls of those ten cavalry regiments and forty-five infantry regiments? Their motivations were nothing like the patriotism of the volunteers. More than half weren't native-born Americans.

Who would want to be a soldier after the dreadful war that just ended? One answer came from an editorial in the *New York Sun*: "The Regular Army is composed of bummers, loafers, and foreign paupers." The poor and the derelict of the cities were candidates, because they had no skills, no prospects, and because they were close to the recruiting offices. The phenomenon was not unique to the United States. The Duke of Wellington famously said that the soldiers who prevailed at Waterloo had joined to escape all manner of previous sins, legal troubles, and bad habits and that they were "the very scum of the earth." (He went on to say, however, that life in the army had transformed them somehow into "fine fellows." Even so, while Wellington's officers might have been aristocrats from "the playing fields of Eton," the rank and file were anything but.)

More than half the rolls of enlisted men were made up of recent immigrants, two-thirds from Ireland and many of the rest from Germany. Few of the immigrants to this country were coming from the top of the social, professional, or educational heap in their home country. Emigration is more often than not the act of someone who has no prospects at home and who has heard of opportunities overseas. In the postwar era of nation building in the United States, much of this good news was spread by advertisements and agents who went to Europe, primarily to Germany and Scandinavian countries to recruit farmers to come to the United States and flesh out the new townships that were growing up along the railroads, as they crept west. There was not as much recruiting among the Irish, who were regarded pretty much as useless when compared to the sturdy German and Swedish farmers who knew something about hard work and efficient agriculture. But the Irish heard about the land of opportunity, too, and so they came. There were already Irish communities in the cities on the eastern coast. The famous New York Irish Brigade fought gallantly in the Civil War, and there was an established pipeline between Boston and New

York, especially, and the Auld Sod. And there were established German communities as well, notably in and around St Louis. There were German regiments in the Civil War commanded by German-speaking officers. Roughly 25 percent of the Union soldiers were foreign-born. But that does not mean they were recent immigrants. Many had established themselves here and joined for many of the same reasons as their native-born comrades.

But while the specially recruited European farmers continued west to claim their new homesteads, many newly arrived immigrants ran aground in the cities. Lacking money and having no prospects for a job, they drifted into the army-recruiting depots and made their marks on enlistment papers. They signed for three years in the infantry or for five years in cavalry. The pay was thirteen dollars a month. To a malnourished and unemployed foreigner, that sounded pretty good. Some spoke very little English. Even the Irish, many of them, came from the wretchedly poor west counties where the people spoke the Irish language (often called Gaelic) and knew almost no English. Those who did speak English spoke with such heavy accents as to be nearly incomprehensible. Most immigrants who could do anything useful went on to do it in their new land; everyone else was a candidate for the army—another generalization, of course, but not far off the mark. Some foreign recruits came with prior military experience and soon proved to be efficient soldiers; many were promoted to noncoms and performed well, especially the Irish and the Germans. But experienced men were in the minority.

There was another class of recruits—men who heard about the rich prospects of the gold and silver fields in Montana, Colorado, and the Southwest, to say nothing about the still-glittering opportunities in California. Civilian miners—native-born and immigrant—who could pay their passage to the West were streaming to the goldfields. In fact, their travels across the immigrant trails of the Plains were a major source of irritation to the tribes—as well as a major source of opportunity to raiders. But men without much more than a few coins in their pockets needed another way to get there. Joining the army temporarily was one answer. Soldiers were needed in the West, and the West was where the gold was. All it took was a signature and a few weeks of basic training to get a ride west. And it mattered little if you signed up for three years, five years, or five decades, if you intended to desert as soon as you got within running distance of the goldfields. Many did. One army captain was sent eighty-six new recruits to San Francisco, and within a few weeks two-thirds of them had deserted. Desertion created a vicious cycle—the postwar army was no longer seen as a patriotic duty, the quality of the men was declining and so, too, the reputation of the force. Since many of those who did join quickly deserted, that created a continuing need to fill the rolls, which in turn caused a decline in the standards of selection. Virtually anyone would do. And many of those who did arrive at their frontier post were such poor examples of manhood that the officers and sergeants despaired of turning them into anything like useful soldiers. Some simply gave up trying. This is perhaps an exaggeration but not by much. As an example: a complement of 325 new recruits arrived in New Mexico, and an inspection of their muskets revealed that 140 of the men had loaded the bullet first and then poured the charge of powder on top of it. There is also the fact that the frontier officers and noncoms had their normal responsibilities of patrolling, managing supply, maintaining the post and its animals, as well as all the usual problems of man management and discipline. Even the most conscientious of junior officers and noncoms had their hands full with their regular duties. The more conscientious they were, the busier they were. Training inevitably suffered, especially given the budget constraints that even limited the amount of ammunition available for target practice. An officer at a remote post that was by definition at the end of a very long supply chain—and a very slow one, at that—would be careful about his supply of ammunition and reluctant to use even the allocation for training. He might need it for the real thing. But if his men couldn't shoot, it wouldn't matter much if he had sufficient ammunition on hand. Alternatively, if his men were trained to shoot well, he might be short of ammunition when he most needed it. The third way was often to compromise and end up with the worst of both worlds—mediocre marksmen and very limited ammunition. As George Custer wrote in *My Life on the Plains*: "Some of the troopers were quite inexperienced as horsemen and still more inexpert in the use of their weapons, as their inaccuracy of fire when attempting to bring down an Indian within easy range proved." Small wonder that Roman Nose felt he was invulnerable to bullets.

The army's problem with recruiting was severe and chronic—each year the turnover was anywhere from 25 to 40 percent. Some was caused by death from disease, others by expiration of the enlistment, some by injuries and death suffered in combat—although that was the least of it. And to state the obvious, when an experienced man left after his three- or five-year enlistment expired, he was replaced by a poorly trained rookie, and so the army's core of professional soldiers who knew what they were doing was constantly being whittled away. But the primary cause of turnover was desertion. In 1871, at the height of the troubles with the Indians, the army lost as many as 30 percent of its men from desertion. And it was not just because men had gold fever.

BUFFALO SOLDIERS

The army could draw from another class of people—the freed slaves, some of whom were veterans of the Civil War.

At the close of the Civil War 33,380 black Union soldiers were dead from either combat or disease. That was from a total of almost 180,000 in uniform. Precise casualty figures for the war are very difficult to come by, because of the poor record keeping and reporting. The number of total war deaths among combatants has traditionally been put at 620,000 but has since been raised by subsequent studies to as high as 750,000. Given the inaccuracy of all figures, it's difficult to assume the figures for black casualties are absolutely correct. Nor do the figures differentiate between deaths from combat and deaths from disease, although it's certain that disease killed far more. In nineteenth-century war, disease was always much more lethal than combat. Most estimates place the ratio at three to one—three deaths from disease for every one from combat, for black troops. This compares to two to one for white troops. There are various theories about the reasons for this disparity, ranging from the fact that black troops were more likely to be serving in rear-echelon positions (and therefore more exposed to disease than enemy fire) to less-than-adequate medical care for the sick.

As an aside, Civil War casualty rates will probably never be known with any precision—a wounded man might be listed as a casualty in one fight, returned to action, and wounded again in the next battle. The after-action reports by his unit would list him as a casualty both times. (As an example, Fred Beecher, who was Sandy Forsyth's second-in-command, was wounded at Fredericksburg, recovered, and was wounded again at Gettysburg.) Having said that, it's interesting to remember that the *casualty* rate of troops under General Grant was 16 percent, while Lee's suffered 20 percent. For all his reputation as a Southern gentleman, Lee was an aggressive tactician who used up his troops more extravagantly than either the oft-called "butcher," Grant, or the stormy petrel Sherman. Historical images belie the reality. On the other hand, in Lee's undermanned yet highly motivated army, troops might've been more willing to return to duty after a wound and therefore risk becoming a casualty statistic a second time. And it's well to remember that the term *casualties* usually refers to killed, wounded, missing, or captured, but generally not deaths from disease, which of course could, and usually did, occur away from the battlefields. And "missing" is another slippery category and could refer to a trooper who was blown to unrecognizable bits or buried forever under an explosion—or someone who just had enough and deserted.

Regardless of how these nearly thirty-four thousand deaths occurred among African American troops—whether combat or disease—they paid a heavy price for their service. These men had volunteered and been accepted in the army, not as some form of social engineering—although abolitionists were quick to praise the policy—but because they were needed, and they responded. Most of these men were in the infantry, some in the navy. And when they were given combat assignments, they did well: "The colored troops are highly valued here[,] and there is no apparent difference in the way they are treated. White troops and black mingle constantly together and I have seen no single evidence of dislike on the part of the soldiers. The truth is they have fought their way into the respect of all the army." This was the feeling of a white officer in command of black troops, but he was clearly overly optimistic when he said "respect of all the army."

In the year just after the war, as part of its army appropriations bill, Congress authorized the formation of two special regiments of cavalry—the Ninth and Tenth. These were to be composed of African Americans. They also authorized four regiments of black infantry, later reduced to two. These segregated regiments were to be commanded by white officers exclusively. Interestingly, Congress specified that the officers should be a mix of regulars and former volunteers: "Two-thirds of those holding the rank of captain or above, moreover, were to be drawn from the volunteer regiments and one-third from the regular army. Officers of lower rank were to come exclusively from the volunteer services." Whether Congress was making a virtue of necessity is hard to say, for certainly they understood that many of the regular officers who had gone through the war would not be interested in service with a regiment composed of former slaves. They didn't want to do it during the war, and many did not want to do it now that the war was over. They had fought for the Union cause, but they understood that cause in a variety of ways. Not all were strong abolitionists. Perhaps, not even most of them. Many were graduates of West Point, where their classmates were Southerners, many of whom resigned to fight for the Confederacy. They would naturally understand and to some extent sympathize with the attitudes of their former friends. One of

Custer's best friends from West Point, Thomas Rosser, fought for
the South, and when he was captured in the Shenandoah campaign, the
two had a warm and sociable reunion at Custer's headquarters. Their
friendship would continue after the war when Rosser was an engineer
for the Northern Pacific Railroad and Custer and the Seventh Cavalry fought engagements against the Sioux and Cheyenne, who were
threatening the railroad's progress. The bonds of brotherhood formed
at West Point were stronger than the arguments of the Radical Republicans, and once the fighting was over and the Union secure, many
regulars were not in the mood to be told to accept the freedmen on
an equal basis. Custer's attitude toward abolition and the black race
in general was typical of many, if not most, of the regular officers.
"[Custer] believed in elevating blacks, but not at the expense of whites.
He decried recruiting blacks into the military, judging shovels and
hoes as more fitting for them than muskets. And as for black suffrage,
a key plank in the Radical platform, Custer said 'I should as soon think
of elevating an Indian Chief to the Popedom of Rome.'" Custer was
a Democrat, and it's fair to say that his views represented the views of
his fellow Democrat officers. On the other side of the issue, Major
General O. O. Howard, a staunch Christian, felt the discomfort caused
by his abolitionist views: "Howard's problem was that he was not only
an evangelical; he was an abolitionist and a Republican, and his
blending of political and religious moralism in one skin—holding
prayer meetings that condemned slavery, admitting the army's black
teamsters and cooks to these meetings—covered him with contempt.
Hostility to abolition in the army was, as Howard learned, 'bitter and
unmeasured.'" (Howard remained steadfast, though, as a soldier and as
a friend of the freedmen. He was a founder and later president of
Howard University, which was named for him.) Even so, Howard
knew he was in the minority. The army is not a place "for a man who
has nice notions about religion." So said the Duke of Wellington,
who used the word *nice* to mean "fussy and fastidious." "The U.S.
Army was not much different [from the British]. Regular officers were

a tight-lipped, unemotional club; praying soldiers were at best the butt of jokes, and at worst the victims of social shunning."

There was surely another dynamic at work among the Northern regular officers—and many volunteer officers, for that matter. As the Civil War went on with its appalling casualties and misery, it became more and more a war about slavery. What started as a war about union versus secession now increasingly became a war to free the slaves. And regardless of whether a Union officer approved of slavery—and most did not, in principle (although ardent abolitionists were a minority among the regulars), they could not survey the aftermath of a battle, great or small, and not wonder whether the slaves were worth all this blood. As Wellington said, "[N]othing except a battle lost can be half so melancholy as a battle won." The officers who surveyed the horrifying casualties among their comrades and their troops, as well as the enemy troops who, after all, were Americans, too—those officers surely wondered whether the price being paid was too high, and by a large margin. The company captain, who had to write the letters to the families of his men who were killed, certainly and keenly felt the contrast between the actual death of men he knew and soldiered with and the idea of freedom for a race of people he neither knew nor cared about, except in the abstract. The same principle of small-unit cohesion that supported men in the grimmest dangers of combat also multiplied the survivors' grief over the deaths or mutilation of those same comrades. And after the war was over, some soldiers, including officers, certainly retained those feelings and expressed them in resentment, either privately or publicly.

Then, too, there were the escaped slaves who naturally sought out the Union lines during the war. They were what General in Chief Henry Halleck in a letter to Sherman called "the inevitable darkies." These slaves were considered "contraband" by the army and something of a bother and a real logistical burden, especially to Sherman's army, as he penetrated the Deep South and had to live off the land. The slaves who arrived inside the Union lines were hardly in any condition to inspire respect among the officers and men who, being from mainly northern and midwestern states, had little or no prior contact with Africans. To all but the most ardent abolitionist, the slaves would have seemed like ragged aliens who spoke a barely intelligible dialect, and the thought of enlisting them in the army would have seemed at the very least like a strange idea and, at the most, simply preposterous. Nor would the memory of these contacts have dimmed in the minds of most postwar officers—certainly not in only a year.

It was not just the regular officers who were dubious about the blacks. It's not difficult to imagine a group of enlisted messmates sitting around a campfire, after a day of hard marching, cooking up a dinner of bacon, coffee, and hardtack. Rare is the soldier who never mutters, "What am I doing here?" When the dangers and hardships are at the worst, and when there seems to be no end in sight, soldiers ask that question more often and more forcefully. And in the Civil War, when the answer to their questions increasingly became "To free the slaves," many Union soldiers were neither satisfied nor inspired. And if some runaway slaves came into camp, the soldiers would surely ask themselves, "We are away from home, going through this misery and risking our lives and bodies and wellbeing . . . for what? For *them*?" McClellan (a Democrat) was extremely popular with the rank and file, and his men viewed his dismissal as the work of the Radical Republicans: "'It was nothing but the nigar lovers of the North who took [McClellan] from us,' lamented a corporal in the Philadelphia Brigade." The corporal apparently did not consider Philadelphia "the North." Most likely he was referring to New England, in general, and Massachusetts, in particular. McClellan would run against Abraham Lincoln in the 1864 election. Lincoln was well aware of McClellan's views on abolition, but that's not why he fired him. It was because of McClellan's unwillingness to fight, famously saying, "If McClellan is not using the army, I should like to borrow it for a while." On the other hand, politics surely played some role; it usually does. It's interesting to speculate on which of McClellan's characteristics finally cost him his job—his views on abolition, his affection for his army and reluctance to accept casualties, his consistent overestimates of enemy strength, his vainglorious personality, or his tactical mediocrity. Most likely, it was a combination of all of them. That is generally the way of things.

Given this widespread attitude in the army, it's not surprising that recruiting white officers for the new, postwar black regiments went slowly. Custer was offered the job of second-in-command of the Ninth Cavalry but turned it down. He was then given the same assignment in the Seventh Cavalry. But Brevet Major General Benjamin Grierson was happy to take command of the Tenth. As mentioned, Grierson had led the most famous cavalry raid of the Civil War. He took three regiments through the heart of Mississippi as part of Grant's campaign against Vicksburg. Grant called it the most brilliant campaign of the war. Additionally he had the right temperament and attitude for the job: "Tolerant and genuinely fond of his men, he ordered his company commanders not to use the word 'colored' in their reports. 'The Regiment is simply the Tenth Regiment of Cavalry, United States Army.'"

One of Grierson's comrades on his epic raid was Edward Hatch, who was also a brevet major general of volunteers. He was offered command of the Ninth, and he was equally well suited for the job, having amassed a fine record in the war: "Able, decisive, ambitious, and personable, he received Grant's unqualified endorsement to lead the Ninth Cavalry."

Both commanders would stay with their regiments; Hatch until 1889, Grierson, 1890—a testament to their value to the army and their devotion to their duty, which involved plenty of hard fighting on the frontier and plenty of political bickering and professional opprobrium on the home front. It also is a testament to their sense of fairness. Few men who were less sure of their personal values would have stayed that long in the job.

Recruiting troops for both regiments was also a slow process. Grierson, especially, set some initially strict criteria for selection. He told his recruiting officer, Captain Louis Carpenter, to look for "men sufficiently educated to fill the position of non-commissioned officers, clerks and mechanics." That was a tall order, since most of the former slaves were illiterate. It's well-known that most slaves were kept in ignorance for a variety of oppressive reasons, not least to avoid the possibility of abolitionist ideas reaching them in print. In fact, Congress had made a special provision to have a chaplain assigned to each of the new regiments "whose duty shall include the instruction of the enlisted men in the common English branches of education." Normally chaplains were not assigned to regiments but to forts, but this provision recognized the special requirements of the Ninth and Tenth regiments as well as the two new infantry regiments. The army has always generated a lot of paperwork, and the blizzard of reports and requisitions were usually handled by noncoms. But finding men able to do those jobs was slow going, and in the end Grierson was forced to relax his standards.

One recruit, at least, had extensive experience with horse soldiers. Reuben Waller, who became a trooper in the Tenth Cavalry, spent the war with the Confederate Army. After the war, Waller enlisted in the Tenth, because, as he later wrote: "My master was a general in the Rebel army, and he took me along as his body servant and I was with him all through the war, was with him in 29 battles. . . . [W]hile being with Stonewall Jackson's cavalry, I engendered a great liking for the cavalry soldiers." (And in September 1868 Waller and his comrades would have an important rendezvous with Forsyth's scouts.)

Finally, though, both cavalry regiments were filled, company by company. And in the summer of 1867 they were sent to the frontier. Most of the Ninth went to Texas, most of the Tenth to Kansas. The men were sent to the scattered forts in one or two companies, often called "troops" in the cavalry. Soldiers of the Tenth would soon encounter Roman Nose and the Cheyenne, along with Satanta and his Kiowa. They would also encounter the realities of life in a frontier outpost. Most would find it hard to decide which situation was worse.

They would have that in common with the white soldiers who were stationed out there.

The Ninth and the Tenth spent the next twenty years on the frontier, in the thick of the campaigns against the Indians not only in Kansas and Colorado but also in the Southwest. Historians have only recently become interested in their story and the literature on the subject is growing. Suffice it to say here that the Ninth and Tenth did their jobs to the satisfaction of the not easily satisfied General Sherman, who said of them in 1874: "'They are good troops, they make first-rate sentinels, are faithful to their trust, and are as brave as the occasion calls for.'" He could have said the same of many white units, of course. But that is precisely the important point. And while it may be tempting for some to romanticize or overdramatize their contribution or fighting élan, it is true that the black troops were different from their white comrades in two important ways. First, for them the army was neither an escape hatch nor a last resort, as it was for so many white recruits. For the freedmen, the army offered a respectable career. It was a step up, and for that reason the black units did not suffer the chronic and wholesale desertion that afflicted other units. Second, the Buffalo Soldiers were "possessed of the notion that the colored people of the whole country are more or less affected by their conduct in the army." So said the chaplain of the Tenth. Unlike a recent immigrant from Ireland or a drifter from the east, black recruits felt they represented something beyond themselves. That sort of feeling of solidarity must have also strengthened the unit comradery that is the essence of steadiness in combat. Unit comradery and pride in the uniform could also help to sustain the men in the weary hours of boredom and discomfort that were the lot of all frontier soldiers, regardless of race.

LIFE ON A FRONTIER ARMY POST

The politicians in Washington along with their advisers in the army had long been arguing about the best way to deploy troops on the frontier. One major problem was supply. Men and horses had to be fed and equipped. This was not much of a problem east of the Mississippi, because the forts were usually accessible by navigable rivers or saltwater ports or the complex of railroads and decent roads for vehicles, or all of the above. For that reason large installations were manageable—in fact, preferable. It was less expensive to ship supplies in volume to a few major installations. Partially because of this experience in the east, some politicians argued that the best way to employ troops efficiently (in other words, economically) on the frontier was to concentrate them in a series of major forts that could be supplied by riverboats or existing and developing railroads. From those forts the army could then initiate major campaigns against the hostile tribes, who would be impressed and, ideally, overawed by the show of force. Once overawed, they would become more agreeable to the government's proposals and dictates. That was the theory. One flaw in this approach, though, was that impressively huge columns of troops needed equally huge supply trains to go with them on campaign. And even then, they would consume their stores after a matter of a few weeks and have to return to base. What's more, if the hostile tribes were in fact overawed by the sight of a column stretching out for a couple of miles—which they quite reasonably would be—their first thought would be to pack up and disappear—one of their specialties. In fact, they wouldn't even have to see the column—the dust clouds raised by the horses and wagons would be visible for miles. Either way, the Indians would simply wait for the column to turn around and head back to the fort after an expensive exercise in futility. Then the tribes would go back to doing what they were doing before being overawed. And so the strategy of establishing just a few major forts, while perhaps more economical and easier to supply, ran aground on the simple fact that it wouldn't work. As someone observed, the army in that arrangement was like a vicious dog chained to his house. Inside the radius, the dog was formidable. Beyond that, all it could do was bark.

An alternative strategy would be to establish many small posts throughout the West. These would be near both the site of troubles and in some cases near the growing towns and villages that were clamoring for help against hostile marauders. It was felt that the sight of the army would discourage the Indians in the area and give the settlers some sense of peace and reassure them that something was being done to protect them. This strategy could work in theory, and in fact it was the idea that was pretty much finally agreed upon, even though it meant that the much reduced manpower of the army would be stretched very thin. But it also meant that these little outposts, which would be garrisoned by only a company or two at most, were in remote locations—by necessity. And that made the problem of supply much more difficult. Even the largest Western rivers were not reliable avenues of transportation. Some would dry up in spots, others were bedeviled by rapids and shallows, and even the mighty Missouri was navigable only so far, and only at certain seasons. In winters it could freeze to the bottom in spots, but in winters men and animals still had to eat. That meant most supplies had to travel overland by wagon train. That method was slow and dangerous and extremely tempting to the very people the supplies were supposed to help combat. The tribesmen could gleefully fall upon the wagon trains and resupply themselves, while simultaneously denying the materiel to their marooned enemies in blue. It also meant that, because of the risk of spoilage, the supplies sent for the troops could only be the sort of stuff that was either dried, like beans and rice, or preserved—usually in salt, although the process of canning goods came into its own during the war. Still, fresh fruits and vegetables were out of the question. That meant that the tiny forts had to grow their own, or do without. And if they did without, the problem of disease, especially scurvy, raised its very ugly head. And because supply by wagon train was expensive, dangerous, and slow, and because the cavalry horses depended on regular shipments of grain, there was added temptation to man these forts with infantry and have only a minimum of cavalrymen, or none at all. The army was faced with something of a paradox—the very remoteness of the fort (which was only in that place because of the danger of hostile warriors and therefore seemed to *require* cavalry) made stationing cavalry there all the more difficult. Of course, if the outpost was near a civilian settlement that could provide grain for the horses and fresh vegetables and fruit for the men, that would be a significant help. But a civilian farmer who was the sole source of grain for a remote outpost understood the law of supply and demand as well as the next man, and so the staff supply officers who made decisions about these matters back in Washington were presented with a dilemma—send supplies hundreds of miles overland from bases and depots such as Fort Leavenworth, Kansas, or buy food for men and animals locally at inflated prices. There was a third choice—man the forts with infantry and let the men plant gardens and grow their own fruits and vegetables or buy them from local truck gardens. Soldiers wouldn't be able to grow enough oats or corn, but without the cavalry, the problem of grain for horses would go away. But how, then, was the infantry going to deal with the problem of mounted tribes? Once in a while, the local commander would send his infantry patrols out on mules, perhaps pack animals or local rentals. But this was a last resort, and the mules were only transportation to a potential trouble spot. No one expected infantrymen, with their long, heavy muzzle-loading muskets, to be able to fight while mounted on mules. Even the cavalry, who were supposed to be trained to fight on horseback, didn't do it very well and preferred to fight dismounted. Infantry on mules was more of a last resort and no doubt raised a few smiles among the mounted warriors of the Cheyenne and the other tribes. The Cheyenne and their allies had little reason to fear the "walk a heeps," even if (or especially when) they arrived on the backs of mules.

There were no easy answers to the complicated questions of supplying and manning the frontier forts. Perhaps it's more accurate to say there were no *good* answers.

Many of these tiny posts were at the end of roads that were roads in name only. Even well-established roads like the Santa Fe Trail were hardly more than dusty, wide paths through the grasslands and desert. Wagons creaking along with wooden axles grinding against wooden wheels threw up little clouds of dust and sand and had to take things not only slowly but also carefully. Breakdowns meant delay, at the very least. And the draft animals had to eat, too. Horses and mules that spent the day hauling heavy wagons needed more energy than they could get from grass on the Plains. That argued for the use of oxen. As one drover explained: "The ox is a most noble animal, patient, thrifty, durable, gentle, and does not run off. [. . .] The ox will plunge through mud, swim over streams, dive into thickets, and he will eat almost anything." But for all their virtues, oxen were not renowned for being fleet of foot. Then there was the weather on the Plains. Wind could blow up blinding dust storms, and rains could come in torrents and turn the roads into impassable quagmires. Wagnerian thunder and dangerous lightning accompanying the rain could scatter the animals and destroy an evening camp. Dry creek beds and arroyos could turn into torrents from flash flooding—floods that could wash away man, beast, or wagon. Captain Alfred Barnitz of the Seventh Cavalry's diary describes such a storm that hit his camp on the Plains:

> The thunder I cannot describe. Much heavier than cannonading and so very near us. [. . .] The rain fell in torrents. The sight was fearful. The creek upon which we were encamped and which had been very shallow the previous day now was a mighty rushing river, and I think I never saw so strong a current. [. . .] And to add to the terror of the scene, drowning men were floating past us and shrieking for help, but we could not save them. Nine were drowned. Some were saved. The water was rising as fast as a man could step back to keep from it.

Winters were worse. No one could move in the winter without risking snowdrifts, frostbite, and death by freezing. And on top of these natural obstacles was the ever-present threat of Indian attack—although not in the winter, since the Indians went into camp and waited out the weather and waited for the grass to green up in the spring, so that their horses could regain their strength and be fit for hunting and war.

Managing a supply train across the Plains was no work for the weak or fainthearted. The teamsters who supplied the remote forts earned their money. It should be noted that these teamsters were usually civilians, and their wagons and animals owned by civilian companies. Washington had decided in the aftermath of the Mexican War that it was usually better to use civilian transportation companies than to involve the army in a business it knew little about and wasn't very good at. Let the civilians invest in and manage the huge herds of draft animals and fleets of wagons and employees. They were not required on a permanent basis by the army and so could be hired as needed. Horace Greeley described the scene at Fort Leavenworth, the principal supply depot for the trans-Mississippi forts:

> Such acres of wagons! Such pyramids of axle trees. Such herds of oxen! Such regiments of drivers and other employees! No one who does not see can realize how vast a business this is, nor how immense are the outlays as well as its income. [. . .] They [civilian contractors] last year employed six thousand teamsters and worked 45,000 oxen.

Using civilian contractors made sense, but obviously it opened a very large door for graft and sharp dealing—and it was a door that opened on a two-way street, as some politicians quickly understood. Graft was rife. Greeley visited a post in Utah:

> "[T]here have recently arrived here thirty thousand bushels of corn from the States at a net cost, including transportation, of over three hundred and forty thousand dollars, or over eleven dollars per bushel. No requisition was ever made for this corn

which could have been bought here, delivered, for two dollars per bushel. [. . .] Somebody makes a good thing out of wagoning this corn from Missouri. . . . Who believes that that somebody has not influential and thrifty connections inside the War Department?"

A soldier might well think that when he was not getting enough of the right kind of supplies, he was getting too much of the wrong kind and that, in either case, someone was making "a good thing" out of it all.

One very clear solution to the problems of overland supply was the railroad. Not for nothing did General Sherman realize that the railroad was one key, and probably the most important key, to solving the problem of hostile tribes. He wrote to his friend and chief, General Grant: "It's our duty and it shall be my study to make the progress of the great Pacific railways . . . as safe as possible." It's important to emphasize that the object of building transcontinental railroads was not to defeat the Plains tribes. Transcontinental railroads would have been built if there were no Indians on the Plains, anywhere. But the defeat of the tribes would be a salutary by-product of a necessary national development, and Sherman knew it. Railroads would speed the growth of the center. Railroads would solve the fundamental problem of efficiently tying the two halves of the country together and helping the center grow. That growth would then extinguish the very *possibility* of nomadism. Roaming at will would no longer be feasible. And when there was no open land to wander in and no buffalo to hunt, either because they were killed off or died off from lack of grazing space, the nomads would have to settle down like everyone else. They might yearn for the old days—and they would—but the old days would be gone, and they would not be coming back.

Sherman learned the value of the railroads during the war. Then as now, the railroads could rush troops close to the scenes of hostility. They also would cut through the Plains Indians' buffalo grounds and open transportation for the hides that buffalo hunters would strip from the Indians' primary source of life. Sherman could very clearly see that the railroads needed to be protected and their progress not impeded, as they inched westward. As for the Plains tribes, Sherman knew that the end of all this Western expansion was clear; it was only a matter of getting there with the least damage.

But it was a very slow process, and the nomadic tribes would still have to be dealt with, one way or the other. Forts that were built along the growing railroad lines, like several of the forts in Kansas, would fare a little better in terms of supply. But other remote posts would have to be supplied the old-fashioned way—wagons and mules and oxen. The scattering of little forts was the least bad solution to the problem. They would have to do until the progress of civilization eradicated nomadism for good and all. And note, eradicating nomadism was not synonymous with eradicating a race of people. Aside from a few homicidal maniacs and aggrieved and vengeful Western settlers and their politicians, there was no widespread call for extermination of all Indians. No one was complaining about the Pueblo Indians of the Southwest, for example. They were not nomadic and they were generally peaceful. Aside from an 1847 revolt against the American occupation of New Mexico in which they killed Charles Bent, the new governor, they were not aggressive or warlike. And that revolt was a joint venture with local Mexicans who resented the US acquisition of New Mexico during the Mexican War. The nineteen different Pueblo tribes lived in their own towns, farmed their fields, and generally kept to themselves. They might very well serve as a model for the government policy makers who were trying without much success to show the Plains tribes the writing on the wall. The manifest writing.

There were more than one hundred of these small forts in the trans-Mississippi. They were located along travel routes and near to the little settlements that were hanging on to life on the frontier. As mentioned, many of the settlements and therefore the forts were along the railroad that was slowly moving across the country. These little posts were valuable to the settlements not just because they offered some degree of protection, but also because they were markets for the ranchers' and farmers' cattle and produce. In fact, it's fair to say that the local politicians and editorialists were not above exaggerating the risk or severity of Indian attacks in order to ensure the local army post was not abandoned and, even better, to motivate expansion of the post. But sometimes they were located far from the settlements, perhaps because the weather or the resources were better. Tiny Fort Buchanan in southern Arizona was forty miles from the nearest settlement and fifty from Tucson. But it was there because it was near a reliable spring and plenty of wood for fuel and housing. But as a deterrent to the hostile Apache, it was negligible. If that.

Living conditions in many of these remote posts were dreadful. Always to the point, General Sherman said, "[H]ad the southern planters put their negroes in such hovels, a sample would ere this have been carried to Boston and exhibited as illustrative of the cruelty and inhumanity of the man masters." And further: "Some of what are called military posts are mere collections of huts made of logs, adobes, or mere holes in the ground, and are about as much *forts* as prairie dog villages might be called *forts*."

There were few if any creature comforts in the dozens of one- and two-company army outposts. They were stiflingly hot in the dusty summer and frigid in the winter, rather like the soldiers' woolen uniforms. The larger posts, like Fort Leavenworth, were civilized communities, but places like Leavenworth were the exception, especially in the years just after the war. Most of the little forts were built by the men who were sent to man them. The buildings were constructed of whatever local materials were available—timber when possible, adobe bricks, stone in places, mud, and wattles. Many of the buildings were called jacales, which is Spanish for "shack," and were roofed over with brush. Most forts resembled little ramshackle villages—a few huts or tents for the officers and offices, a few larger buildings that served as warehouses, barracks for the men and stables. There'd be a blacksmith shop, a guardhouse, some huts for civilian laundresses (usually wives of the enlisted men), a post hospital, and the sutler's store. If the fort wasn't near a stream, the men would have to dig wells. There might be a pigsty offering the benefits of fresh pork now and then, but those benefits were balanced by the continuous stench and clouds of flies. And there were the outhouses for the men, which added their own odors to the mixture. There were corrals for the animals and maybe a barn, or more likely a ramada, to store hay the soldiers had to cut. Having hay cut and stored on the post meant the animals could be kept corralled or stabled some of the time and therefore would not be wandering on the outskirts of the post, grazing and offering tempting targets for horse thieves of any description. But hay cut from the Plains is still only grass and not a substitute for grain.

Few of the forts had walls around them. The buildings were grouped in a square around a parade ground with a flagpole in the middle. A cannon or two might be located on the square ready to be rushed to the side of the fort under attack. But attacks by hostile tribes were rare. Fort Wallace, which was the westernmost post in Kansas, was an exception. On two occasions the fort was attacked by Cheyenne raiders. One of the officers defending the post during these attacks was Lieutenant Fred Beecher, who shortly thereafter would be Sandy Forsyth's second-in-command. But Wallace, like most frontier posts, had no protective outer walls. And that attests to their relative security. True, they were very good places for accomplished horse thieves to come at night, and if the horse and mule herd was grazing not far off the post, it was a tempting target for mounted raiders. But most of the forts themselves did not experience direct attacks—at least from humans. At Fort Larned in Kansas a rabid gray wolf came into the fort, attacked and badly bit two men in the post hospital and an officer on officer's row before being shot and killed.

For months on end the greatest enemy was boredom. That would be punctuated now and then with patrols to search for hostiles or to follow the trail of raiders who had attacked a lonely ranch house or stage station and then disappeared. Much of the time those patrols achieved little or nothing. They were the real-life version of the Hollywood posses that saddle up and chase after the bank robbers and never catch them. The duty was, in other words, mostly police work for these little one- and two-company forts. Aside from that, their job was simply to be there in case something happened and then to do something about it, if at all possible. Some were connected by telegraph and so could receive information about hostilities in the region. Others would have to rely on dispatch riders from settlements that had access to the telegraph. And, of course, the tribesmen soon understood the function of the telegraph, and when they were in an aggressive mood, they knew what to cut first.

The sutler was a civilian contractor who ran a combination general store and barroom. He sold the simple luxuries that the army did not provide—tobacco, alcohol, some canned foods, candy, cloth for repairing uniforms, and so on. He also operated a bar and was very much the only entertainment to be found, unless of course there was a settlement nearby. And if there did happen to be a settlement in the area, the chances were that it contained the usual collection of barrooms and brothels, worthless characters and hangers-on. When an Episcopal priest arrived in the new mining town of Denver, the first twelve burial services he conducted featured "two [who] had been executed for murder, five [who] had been shot by antagonists, one [who] had committed suicide, one [who] had expired in delirium tremens." The other three apparently died from nothing more remarkable than disease. Old age was not yet an option in frontier mining towns. Tucson had a cemetery in which most of the inmates had been shot dead in a saloon or a street fight. Yet as frontier settlements go, Tucson was fairly well-established (having been a Mexican town originally). But time had not added much to the little town's allure. As one soldier wrote: "If the world were searched over, I suppose there could not be found so degraded a set of villains as then formed the principal society of Tucson. Every man went armed to the teeth and street fights and bloody affrays were of daily occurrence." It was, he said, "a city of mud boxes, dingy and dilapidated, cracked and baked into a composite of dust and filth . . . the best view of Tucson is the rear view on the road to Fort Yuma." And yet Fort Yuma, Arizona, was known to be a pestilential oven in the middle of the desert. There was an old army joke about a sinful soldier who died and was sent to hell. Having served in Yuma and gotten accustomed to the climate there, he sent a message back to his messmates asking them to send him down his blankets. Another soldier stationed in Utah wrote, "[W]e are serving in the most God-forsaken country of the habitable globe, yet . . . with Valley Tan to drink . . . we are all right." "Valley Tan" was the local rotgut. "Tan" was a reference to tanning fluid. "Soldiers, teamsters, and assorted camp followers claimed that Valley Tan 'improved' with each glass—a compliment that loses something of its force, the more you think about it. Indeed, the stuff was described as a liquor that 'smells like gangrene starting in a mildewed silo, it tastes like the wrath to come, and when you take a deep swig of it, you have all the sensation of having swallowed a kerosene lamp.'" While the local Mormon hierarchy did not permit the faithful to drink alcohol, they had nothing to say about making and selling Valley Tan to the soldiers stationed there. It was good business.

Alcohol and desertion were the twin evils of the frontier army. Officers and men shared equally in the boredom and miserable living conditions, and the men took refuge in the bottle or in running off to greener pastures—or any pasture, other than their post. The officers did not desert, but many succumbed to alcoholism. The most famous example is, of course, Ulysses Grant, whose taste for liquor got him tossed out of the antebellum service when he was still a junior officer—a prodigious feat, given the tolerance the army had for alcohol. (Grant actually resigned, but his resignation was requested, so it amounts to getting dismissed.) Grant at the time was a veteran of the Mexican War and a reasonably well-regarded officer, but the boredom and loneliness of being stationed in far-off California accelerated his drinking. He was far from unique among the army's officers who were stationed in remote and often inhospitable places. Captain Alfred Barnitz of the Seventh Cavalry wrote to his wife: "Captain Gillette and Major Beebe are confirmed inebriates, and the same may be said for Col. Keogh—they are seldom sober. The same is true of Col. West. He was drunk all the time we were on the late expedition and had to be hauled in an ambulance." The ranks given are brevets; Myles Keogh was a captain and one of Custer's favorites. Custer was not a drinker and was also disgusted by David Gillette, who submitted his resignation not long after Custer took command. In endorsing the resignation Custer wrote: "He is utterly worthless as an officer and unfit to hold a commission in the army." Barnitz, by the way, was not a Custer sycophant. He detested Custer's imperious style and harsh discipline: "[S]imply because of his recent unfeeling treatment of the enlisted men of the command and shameful discourtesy to officers [Custer] has proved himself unworthy of the respect of all right thinking men."

Even a stereotypical shavetail lieutenant from West Point, who arrived at his new post full of enthusiasm for the job, would almost inevitably lose the edge off his zeal as the months passed by and nothing happened. Being married might help alleviate some of the boredom, but it was not the life for any woman raised in comfortable or genteel surroundings. As one fairly senior officer wrote to his daughter who was considering a young officer's offer of marriage, these little posts were no place for a woman of quality: "How in the world any girl of ordinary sense would think of marrying a line officer I cannot imagine, for they must make up their minds to spend a life of exile, deprivation and poverty."

As for that shavetail lieutenant, another senior officer said: "Take a boy of sixteen from his mother's apron strings, shut him up under constant surveillance for four years at West Point, send him out to a two-company post upon the frontier, where he does little but play seven-up and drink whiskey at the sutler's store, and by the time he is forty-five he will furnish the most complete illustration of suppressed

mental development of which human nature is capable." (Seven-up
is a card game.)

If boredom and alcohol and wretched living conditions and loneliness and only occasional—but very real—danger from hostilities were
not enough, these little forts also were places that attracted disease.
Soldiers on average spent at least three visits to the post hospital
each year. No doubt most diseases were the usual ones, ranging from
alcohol poisoning to venereal diseases to colds and pneumonia to
"the old soldier's disease"—dysentery. But some posts that were near
pestilential environments suffered from malaria. Fleas carried typhus.
And cholera was a danger in any place where water was or could be
contaminated. Camped near Fort Wallace in western Kansas, Barnitz
wrote to his wife: "Only think, seven dead men in an evening (all of
the 7th Cavalry) isn't a small beginning at all considering that this is
reputed to be a remarkably healthful climate. Yes, seven dead men in an
evening and more the following day. [. . .] I would really much rather
see two Indians than one man with cholera, and I am not remarkably
fond of Indians."

Those forts that were along the emigrant travel routes (for obvious
reasons) were exposed to travelers who carried and spread the usual
variety of diseases. As in the Civil War, a soldier on the frontier was
twice as likely to die from disease as from an enemy bullet. And that
assumes the forts were commanded by competent regular officers who
were thought to have, or supposed to have, some understanding of
camp hygiene. There would also be a post surgeon or assistant surgeon
attached, but it's not hard to imagine the quality of a doctor who chose
the army instead of civilian practice and was willing to go to a post at the
back of beyond. (That is perhaps an unfair generalization, though.
Army doctors, like most of their brother officers, had a variety of
reasons for seeking Western service.) Additionally, the general quality
of medical science in the treatment of some diseases was still pretty
primitive. Although regular army doctors who were veterans of the
Civil War certainly had plenty of practice treating wounds, the causes

and treatment of some diseases, like typhus, cholera, and malaria, were not understood until well after frontier forts were a thing of history. People knew what caused scurvy and how to deal with it, but the fresh fruits and vegetables needed to forestall it were often hard to come by. Fort Phil Kearny in Wyoming was built by the troops who manned it, and it was the fort from which the ill-fated Captain Fetterman marched out to the ambush that killed him and eighty other men. But life for those who survived in the fort was almost as risky as going out to meet the Cheyenne and Sioux: "The spring of 1867 was the time the effects of the spoiled flour and bacon showed up. All the men that were at the fort at the time it was established [summer, 1866] got the scurvy. Some lost their teeth and some the use of their legs. In the spring when the grass was up, there were lots of wild onions and the scurvy gang was ordered out to eat them." Having to send men out to dig up wild onions is a sad commentary on the army's treatment of its men on the frontier. It's no wonder desertion was a problem. But it was not that the army neglected its duty, so much, as the very nature of the task they were presented with carried with it almost insoluble problems. The problems were inherent in the geography of the west and the difficulties of supply as well as the attendant evils of civilian and political malfeasance that sent poor-quality supplies to the forts. There was unconscionable profiteering on the backs not only of the Indians, who were promised subsidies and rations that were often not delivered— but also on the troops who were assigned to watch over them. And problems of simple managerial incompetence were constant then, as they have always been. Officers at Fort Wallace were sent wood burning stoves to counteract the frigid Plains' winters, but the stoves were virtually useless, because they were sent without chimney pipes.

To add to the enlisted soldier's catalog of woes, discipline was extremely harsh. No doubt the problem of desertion exaggerated the disciplinary responses, which further exaggerated the problem of desertion. The officers and NCOs and the enlisted soldiers were often out on the end of a very long limb, stuck in inhospitable surroundings.

They endured boredom, poor living conditions, and inadequate food, and every now and then they endured a fight with men who were better warriors and better attuned to their environment. Whereas the troopers had very little training in the arts of combat, the warriors they faced were superbly trained from childhood. And they were highly motivated to fight; it was their raison d'être. The troopers on the other hand were not nearly so interested in combat and engaged in it because it was just part of the job and, more fundamentally, simply to stay alive. Lack of training affected the soldiers' morale, too. "Highly trained men in extraordinarily dangerous circumstances are less likely to break down than untrained men in little danger." It's not surprising that troops who did not know what they were doing—and *knew* that they did not know—would be nervous and unsteady in the alien environment of the frontier—especially when they encountered alien warriors who were trained in just the sort of business the soldiers did not fully understand.

It's small wonder, then, that if they didn't desert, some soldiers malingered or got drunk at the sutler's or got into fights or got into any of the usual troubles. The army's Articles of War gave broad outlines of the appropriate punishments, but the post commander had wide discretion, and punishments varied accordingly. Small infractions like shirking or mild insubordination might result in minor tortures for the soldier—standing for hours on top of a barrel, marching with a heavy log strapped to his shoulders, being spread-eagled in the harsh sunlight or hanging by his thumbs or being locked in a sweatbox. Most officers thought such punishments were necessary to keep their men in line. As one officer's wife explained: "Drastic measures had to be used in those days. The men, both foreign and domestic, were a hard set."

In his diary Captain Alfred Barnitz of the Seventh Cavalry wrote: "Am officer of the day and busy making out a list of the various prisoners. [. . .] I find there are 29 sentenced to break stones (some for 2 or 3 years), 19 under charges of desertion and awaiting trial; six awaiting trial for minor offences and 5 undergoing sentence of hard labor, etc.—quite a formidable array of incorrigible scoundrels, for such they are as a general thing."

In other words, the enlisted men, including the new recruits, were not simply wide-eyed immigrants or apple-cheeked farm boys or compliant former slaves. There were plenty of hard cases among them—criminals and the usual catalog of men escaping either legal or domestic woes. So although the frontier soldier's life was harsh, many of the men were equal to the hardships and challenges—until, that is, they decided they'd had enough and went over the hill. Captain Barnitz wrote: "Tomorrow they (of my company) will be paid, and I will not be surprised if some of them disappear shortly afterward. They have not been paid for six months, and meanwhile they have been sorely distressed for the want of many little necessities, even needles and thread, postage stamps and stationery have been beyond their means of purchasing of late."

If a court-martial could be organized in the case of serious crimes, the court had wide discretion in deciding punishment. When George Custer was on Reconstruction duty in Texas, he chaired a court-martial that sentenced two men to be shot, one for mutiny, the other for desertion. The "mutineer" was a popular sergeant of volunteers whose crime was nothing more than a technicality. He had circulated a petition to have a tyrannical officer transferred. (Note that the sergeant was a veteran volunteer soldier who was waiting to be mustered out in the immediate postwar period.) In a scene better suited to a Russian novel, Custer had both men lined up, seated on their coffins, facing a firing squad. At the last second, before ordering *Fire!*, Custer had the condemned sergeant led away and reprieved. Then he ordered the deserter shot. Even from the perspective of history, Custer's treatment of the mutineer was unforgivable and led to a growing belief in the army that Custer was something less than his glittering and self-polished image.

As mentioned, many of these posts were built by the troops who were initially sent to the area. The precise location was generally selected by the commanding officer, and his criteria could vary depending on environmental factors that might be at variance with military considerations. The officer who selected the location for Fort Buchanan in Arizona was more concerned with the availability of wood and water than proximity to the settlements he was there to protect. He also had an understandable aversion to the lawlessness in Tucson. It was hard enough maintaining a disciplined and reasonably healthful post without the added allurements of saloons and brothels. What he did not know, however, was that the site he chose was not far off from some ciénegas—standing water that bred malarial mosquitoes.

When a location was chosen, the troops went to work to build the post, and they used whatever local materials were available and applied whatever skills they brought with them, however scanty. West Point officers, who were trained very well in civil engineering, might be less adept at the problems of building with adobe bricks. But they got the job done, such as it was. It's fair to assume that the majority of enlisted men were familiar with hard work and manual labor, but that does not mean they liked it or were at all happy about learning that army life on the frontier more resembled a chain gang than a military mission against the nation's enemies. As one enlisted man complained:

We are obliged to perform all kinds of labor, such as all the operations of building quarters, stables, storehouses, bridges, roads and telegraph lines, involving logging, lumbering quarrying, adobe and brick making, lime burning, mason work, plastering, carpentering and painting etc. We are also put out at teaming, repairing wagons, harness and blacksmithing, and sometimes wood chopping and haymaking.

And note that that kind of labor continued after the fort was built. It was an essential part of what was apparently the army's primary mission on the frontier—simply being there.

With the lure of the western goldfields, the wretched living conditions, the poor and erratic pay, long hours of manual labor and the harsh discipline, it's a wonder that any soldier stuck it out. Perhaps it was fortunate for the army that so many recruits were recent immigrants. Life in the old country must have been pretty terrible to make the army on the frontier seem like an upgrade. As for the officers, well, some of them might surrender to alcohol and indolence, but most remained true to their calling, as did many if not most of the noncoms and regular army lifers. Given the conditions, the devotion to duty and the professionalism of most of the officers, noncoms and troops is remarkable. A traveling journalist summed up the situation: "'If there be any who deserve the sympathies of those who enjoy comfortable and secure homes in the settlements, they are the officers and soldiers condemned to the isolation of duty on the Plains.'"

The contrast in attitudes between the Cheyenne and the ordinary soldiers regarding life on the frontier could hardly be more stark, or dramatic. The Cheyenne were fighting to stay there; one-third of the enlisted soldiers risked harsh, even capital punishment, just to get away from there—and did. True, there were officers like Forsyth and Custer who appreciated the vast spaces and the freedom they represented— officers who relished being in command in a hostile and yet strangely beautiful world. How many ordinary soldiers felt that same way is hard to say, but it's likely that very few of them experienced the joy of the Cheyenne warrior. When the Cheyenne surveyed his domain, he saw and tasted freedom—and adventure. When the enlisted soldier, black or white, first looked out on the emptiness, he probably felt something more akin to loneliness, with perhaps a trace of uneasiness. The Plains were unlike anything else he had ever seen. They were empty and foreign. Ireland was never this brown and limitless; neither was Mississippi or Ohio. Like Moses in Exodus, a soldier was a stranger in a strange land. He could look in every direction, across all points of the compass and see—nothing, nothing but rolling grasslands and the horizon. "Oh, Bury Me Not on the Lone Prairie" was not only an old folk song; it was a commonly held emotion. One of the grave markers in the old Fort Wallace cemetery reads, *Ludwig Frey, Age 35. From Prussia. Died of dysentery, 8-26-1869. Buried 8-27-1869. Relatives unknown.* It is a lonely place. Even today you can stand at this grave site and look in every direction and see almost exactly what the soldiers saw as they buried Ludwig Frey—nothing but the Plains and the horizon and the sky—on the edge of western Kansas.

The doctor who treated Frey was post surgeon Captain Theophilus Turner. He was Fred Beecher's best friend. When he arrived at Fort Wallace, Turner went looking for a horse to buy. He needed one to ride, of course, but there was another reason. "There is nothing to love out here," he said.

Like it or not, the Cheyenne warrior and the army soldier were joined together in this drama on the prairie. One was enjoying it, with perhaps an unsettling premonition of what the future could bring, perhaps a sense that this Cheyenne summer might not last much longer. The other just wanted to get through it intact. And then get away.

There was a third category of actors—the civilians. And among the civilians, there were groups whose interests were rarely compatible—not with the Indians, not with the army, not with each other. They were the politicians, the businessmen, the settlers, the miners, the philanthropists. They may have spoken a common language, but they rarely saw things in the same way. But taken all together, they were the hordes coming west, either figuratively or literally. They were the people who presaged an end to the Cheyenne summer—some in one way, some in another.

3

THE CIVILIANS

"THE MINERS, FORTY-NINERS . . ."

General Sherman's brother John was a US senator from Ohio. Surveying the westward movements and thinking about what might be done about it all, he said: "If the whole army of the United States stood in the way, the wave of emigration would pass over it to seek the valley where the gold was to be found." He said this in a statement to the US Senate in 1867. The country's destiny was manifest for anyone to see, and it was no more organized and directed than a riot or a flood. And just about as stoppable. And usually leading the mob were the miners. Or, more broadly, the prospectors.

As mentioned earlier, there would have been no possibility of westward emigration if not for the Louisiana Purchase and the Mexican War (and the attendant Gadsden Purchase). These (along with Oregon Treaty with the British) provided the entirety of the trans-Mississippi, and importantly, this vast territory was federal land—to be administered and dispensed as the federal government saw fit. Territories would be organized and territorial governors appointed. Then came the discovery of gold, most famously of course in California in 1848, just as the luckless Mexican strongman Santa Anna was signing away California and all the Southwest. Gold fever prompted mass migration across the country. Subsequent gold and silver discoveries throughout the West—New Mexico, Arizona, Colorado, Montana, and Nevada— sparked new frenzies that surged and ebbed, surged again and again, periodically, almost until the last year of the century. The 1898–1899 Yukon and Klondike were the last major rushes. When it was all over, it was well past the time the Plains tribes had become reluctantly resigned to the end of their nomadic culture.

George Bent, the half-Cheyenne, half-white son of trader William Bent, described the reaction of his mother's people to only one of the surges of gold fever, this one in Colorado:

The Indians watched these mad proceedings of the whites with astonishment, but they were still further amazed and alarmed when the real rush began in the spring of '59. Even before the snow was melted on the Plains and the ice had broken up in the streams, parties of eager gold seekers began to make their appearance. [. . .] Wagon trains, bands on horseback, and ragged parties afoot, they poured into the mountains in a ceaseless stream. Even the Smokey Hill and the Republican routes were used by parties. [. . .] [The Cheyenne] did not understand this rush of white men and thought the whites were crazy.

In short, miners often led the way west. But it was clear to anyone who thought much about it, that the discovery of gold or silver, or even the rumor of discovery, could set off a stampede to the West, and that the best and most reliable way to make money from mining was not to grab a shovel but to sell the miners everything they needed, along with lots of things they didn't. Following close on the miners' heels, therefore, were the shopkeepers to sell the picks and shovels, beans and bacon. Probably at the head of the line were the saloon keepers and soiled doves to help the miners forget their disappointments or spend their newfound wealth. Doctors also drifted west to look after gunshot wounds, bones broken in the diggings, or miseries acquired from soiled doves or rotgut whiskey. Much like many of their colleagues in the army, the Western boomtown doctors were not the cream of their profession, but they were better than nothing, probably. Then there were the town builders and real estate agents and of course the lawyers and newspapers to register claims and print the legal notices, as well as news of the latest strikes or the most recent barroom shooting or Indian atrocity. It was astonishing how quickly the little boomtowns attracted itinerant printers who started a daily newspaper with their portable presses. And if the boomtown failed and became a ghost town, the printers would pack up and move to the next strike. Samuel Clemens was one of the hopeful miners for a while, but when he found it was a lot of work for very little profit, he went into the newspaper reporting business. (And when Sam could not find any news, he made some up, to the enduring benefit of posterity.) Life insurance agents also arrived to point out that digging for gold in the mountains could be dangerous. It was only prudent for the sturdy miner to consider what would happen to the folks back home, if he had fatal accident or, worse, ran into Indian treachery. "If something happened to you . . ." was then, as now, their operative line. Occasionally, a missionary or a parson would show up and put up his tent and have a revival meeting, although with the vast majority of hard-case miners, there was precious little to revive. And if there was a critical mass of miners' families, a school might even sprout, if a schoolmarm or itinerant Ichabod Crane could be lured to the settlement.

The new settlements were rough places, of course, and so law and order became a consideration. People had to take it into their own hands, because regular law and order was often slow in arriving, even with territorial governors in place. Either a local marshal could be appointed, or if that didn't work for some reason, a vigilance committee would be formed to track down and hang any criminals who preyed on the miners, or otherwise made a violent nuisance of themselves. Mark Twain encountered one of these—the notorious Jack Slade—at a stage stop on the way west: "The coffee ran out. At least it was reduced to one tin cupful. Slade offered to refill it, but although I wanted it, I politely declined. I was afraid he hadn't killed anybody that morning, and might be needing diversion." Slade was later hanged by a vigilance committee in Virginia City—a mining town in Montana.

In short, the miners were most often the head of the Western comet, but everyone else was the very long tail. And when disappointed miners went back home with their hopes and clothes in rags, others came west to replace them, and the lawyers, saloon keepers, gamblers, and bar girls were there to welcome the new arrivals. So too the local politicians who knew a good thing when they saw it and were among the first to shake hands with the new arrivals and explain how things were done there and, perhaps, offer to sell them a newly surveyed town lot; it would be a fine place to build a stately home, once they had struck it rich.

And that was one of the ways the West grew. There were other ways, of course, but gold fever was highly contagious, and the only people who seemed to be immune to it were the Indians. It was just about the only white man's disease they never caught.

From the Federal government's point of view, these gold discoveries were a very good thing, especially in the years after the Civil War. The war had run up an enormous national debt—enormous by nineteenth-century American standards, anyway. And that debt was denominated in gold, meaning that the banks and investors, both domestic and foreign, who bought the US Treasury bonds that were issued to finance the war, paid for them in gold specie. They expected therefore to receive their regular interest payments and ultimately their principal in gold. The government sold these bonds, because it needed gold to finance the huge demands placed on it by the suddenly swollen army and navy. There was initially no national paper currency. All government payment and receipts for taxes (tariffs and excises during the first part of the war) were in gold or silver coins. Specie.

Part of the problem was that the federal government relied on tariffs and excise taxes to generate income. There were no income taxes. And income from those tariffs and excise taxes was not nearly enough to support the suddenly huge expenses of the war. The government turned to borrowing, mostly from banks. But banks don't have money, basically—they borrow money from depositors and investors and then relend that money, while taking a spread and building on their initial capital. Therefore, when the Union armies began to suffer defeats, and it looked like the South might prevail, depositors and investors began withdrawing their gold from the banks, and banks became increasingly reluctant to invest their limited capital in loans to the government. Overseas investors also began to shy away from US government bonds. As a result, the Treasury was drying up. "Chase has no money and tells me he can raise no more," so said by a despairing Lincoln referring to his secretary of the treasury, Salmon Chase. The revenues from tariffs and excise taxes for the first year of the war were $55 million. The estimated cost of the war was $532 million. Something had to be done, either in the field of finance or on the field of battle. Small wonder then that Lincoln was impatient with his generals. A few victories might calm the nerves of the banking and investor communities, both here and abroad. But a few headline grabbing, investor soothing victories were not forthcoming.

Lincoln and his advisers looked around for answers and fairly quickly arrived at two primary solutions. First, they passed an income tax law and established the Bureau of Internal Revenue to collect the taxes. Second, they created the greenback dollar—a paper instrument. At the outbreak of the war there was no federally issued paper money. All paper money in circulation was issued by state banks, and that paper was nothing more than a receipt that could be redeemed for gold or silver at the issuing bank, or its branches. "Roughly seven thousand

varieties of bank notes were in circulation. Some were issued by legitimately chartered state banks, but many were of dubious quality or
simply counterfeit." Farmers and storekeepers outside the commercial
area of the issuing banks were reluctant to accept payment in paper
from a bank they didn't recognize. And rightly so.

Out of sheer financial desperation the federal government not only
created the greenback but also passed a law stipulating that greenbacks
must be accepted for any and all transactions throughout the country. It
was the national currency, and it had value only because Congress said it
had value. The greenback was not backed by anything, other than green
ink. Not gold, not silver. The inevitable result was inflation, because
although a shopkeeper was legally required to accept payment with a
greenback, he didn't have to accept it at face value. A sack of potatoes
worth one silver dollar might go for three greenback dollars, and no one
was going to be able to do anything about it. Take it or leave it. "The wit
of man has never discovered a means by which paper currency can be
kept at par value except by its speedy, cheap certain convertibility into
gold or silver." This was the view of Congressman George Pendleton of
Ohio; he was not alone in thinking that. As a result of this iron law
of economics, inflation during the war ran to 25 percent in the North.
It's a wonder it wasn't higher. In the South, the Confederacy created
the "blue back"; the notorious Confederate paper money. Inflation there
ultimately got to 9000 percent. By the end of the war the South was in
ruins; there was no economy. Hence Reconstruction.

But . . . the greenback along with the income tax succeeded in
papering over the federal difficulties in paying for the war. But when
the war was over, there was still the national debt—a debt in the form
of bank loans and Treasury bonds that had been bought by institu-
tional investors, as well as by ordinary citizens in denominations as low
as fifty dollars. (It was estimated that by the end of the war 5 percent
of Union families owned Treasury bonds—quite a large percentage
given the fact that no one but institutions had previously invested in
these instruments.) All that debt was denominated in gold and would

have to be repaid in gold. Greenbacks would not do the trick. The national debt at the end of the war was $2.6 billion.

Where would the gold come from? From the mines, of course. Lucky miners who struck it rich sold their gold to the Treasury in exchange for greenbacks. They worked through intermediary banks or agents, each of whom took a commission for doing the exchange. And then the miners went on a spree, or perhaps even bought that town lot they had been shown. Maybe they did build their mansion, maybe in a brand-new city, like Denver—a city that rose in the midst of the gold strikes on Cherry Creek, while George Bent's people watched and wondered what the excitement was all about.

BLACK HILLS

The Black Hills of southeastern South Dakota and eastern Wyoming were, and still are to some extent, the jewel of the Plains. They were also a symbol of tremendous significance to both the white civilization and the Plains Indians, primarily the Cheyenne and Sioux. For both the whites and the Indians, the Hills represented wealth. But, as usual, the two peoples defined wealth in very different ways.

Roughly 1.2 million acres, and 70 miles wide by 110 miles long, the Black Hills rise up from the Plains like a dark island, dark because of the thick covering of pines. The ways in are few and difficult, like cracks in the wall of a natural fortress. But once into the Hills you find that the dense pine forests are punctuated with elk meadows and steep mountains and clear streams. The Hills are still unspoiled, in spots, and it's not hard to imagine what they must have looked like before the invasions of the late nineteenth century. Intrepid historian Francis Parkman was there in 1846 when he was a young man:

Yet wild as they were, these mountains were thickly peopled. I found the broad dusty paths made by the elk as they filed across the mountain side. The grass on all the terraces was trampled down by deer; there were numerous tracks of wolves, and in some of the tougher and more precipitous parts of the ascent, I found footprints different from any that I had ever seen, and which I took to be those of the Rocky Mountain sheep. I sat down upon a rock; there was perfect stillness. [. . .] I was in a hunter's paradise.

Clearly when Parkman says "thickly peopled," he is not talking about humans.

But there were humans there. The Plains Indians had gathered there for more than a hundred years to trade and meet Mexican traders coming up from the south and French traders from the north and east. But peaceful trade was only a leitmotif of the Hills. The real story was war between the tribes, because they all understood that the Hills were a resource unlike any other on the Plains. The game there did not migrate—elk and deer, and smaller game as well as valuable fur bearing animals, like beaver and marten—were there year-round. Whereas the buffalo on the open Plains were more numerous, obviously in herds of thousands, they also had a frustrating way of disappearing now and then on their migrations. And they would sometimes wander into territories claimed by other tribes, perhaps stronger tribes, who violently resented incursions by alien hunting parties. In the Black Hills the game was always there, and there was plenty of it. Accordingly, the Sioux battled and finally expelled the Kiowa and Crow tribes and fought for a while with the Cheyenne over the territory, before making agreements with them that would create a lasting alliance against the white encroachers. The Sioux call the Black Hills their "meat pack," and claimed the territory by right of conquest—a natural law that they and all the tribes perfectly understood and accepted as an undeniable reality.

What's more, the forests and mountains in that area were not only a source of food year-round, but also a refuge from the bitter winters of the Plains. It was cold there too, but the mountains and valleys and forests of the Black Hills offered shelter from the arctic winds that blew unimpeded on the treeless Plains.

The Black Hills were often described as sacred to the tribes who fought over them and used them. Whether *sacred* is the proper word, the Hills were definitely treasured as a resource, and they acquired a level of meaning or symbolism not unlike the symbolism of the open Plains. The Plains meant freedom; the Black Hills meant wealth, prosperity, and refuge from the storms. And the Indians were well aware of the aesthetics of the Black Hills. The natural beauty was there for anyone to see, and the Sioux and Cheyenne could see it and appreciate it as well as the next man.

Thus the Sioux and the Cheyenne were willing to contest any advances the whites might make into that richest—and most reliable— of the Plains hunting grounds. True, there were some half-wild trappers who ventured into the Hills, many of them mixed blood Frenchmen who were married to Indian women. And they either kept a low profile and survived from season to season, or they didn't. But they posed no real threat to the Indians. The real threat came from rumors about that puzzling, virtually useless metal that drove white people crazy—gold. Parkman's guide and companion in the Black Hills, a French Canadian trapper named Reynal, said: "Many a time when I have been with the Indians I have been hunting for gold all through the Black Hills. There's plenty of it here, you may be sure of that. [. . .] [But] it won't do for a white man to be rummaging too much about these mountains . . . I believe that it's no good luck to be hunting about here after gold." Reynal was married to an Oglala woman and perhaps felt somewhat secure as a fur trapper in the Hills. But he was not the only one to talk about gold in the Hills. The rumors persisted through the decades, and at various times white prospectors tried to probe the Hills to find out if it could be true. But it was not until 1874 that the Seventh Cavalry under Custer made a reconnaissance in force into the Hills. Custer brought a pair of civilian miners with him, and they discovered the truth of the matter. Yes, there was gold there.

But up until that fateful incursion, the Sioux and their Cheyenne allies successfully fought off any attempts to enter the Black Hills. They were part of the broader hunting grounds that the Sioux and Cheyenne and their allies the Arapaho were desperate to protect. But once gold was discovered a wave of miners washed into the Hills. Neither the Indians nor the army could keep them out. Soon there were four thousand prospectors roaming the Hills, and in the wake came the fellow travelers and hangers-on who always followed the miners. The Black Hills merely proved what Senator Sherman had said—nothing could stop people who were driven to find El Dorado.

CIVILIANS: EAST AND WEST—NEVER THE TWAIN . . .

The spectrum of attitudes toward the Indians and particularly the troublesome Plains Indians, was broad, with many subordinate clauses. But the two extremes were clear—virulent hatred at one end and pious paternalism at the other. These two attitudes naturally resolved into two diametrically different policy ideas: war to the knife versus peaceful "negotiations." Moreover, these two points of view tended to have a geographical flavor. The war party generally resided in the West, where the troubles existed. The peace party generally resided in the East, where the troubles did not exist, except at second- and third-hand in the pages of the newspapers.

The Plains Indians were the most fractious and therefore became more or less the face of the Indian problem. Other tribes, whether peacefully minding their own business in the pueblos or on their reservations, were not much discussed. The Pawnee and the Crow, among others, were on the side of the whites because of their hatred of common enemies and so were not considered part of the problem. The Navajo had been defeated in war and, after a disastrous experience at New Mexico's Bosque Redondo, were permitted to move to a reservation in their Arizona homeland and seemed resigned, if not content, to a pastoral and semi-agricultural existence. Now and then an individual might cause a disturbance, but as a tribe the Navajo were basically finished with fighting the white man. It was the Cheyenne, the Sioux, the Arapaho, the Comanche, the Kiowa, and the Apache who were causing most of the difficulty. Most were nomads of the Plains, although the Apache were a mountain-dwelling people of the Southwest and northern Mexico. They were not engaged in a territorial struggle with the whites. Few white men other than miners had any interest in the rugged mountains of the Southwest. The Apache had always lived primarily by raiding the peaceful tribes, like the Pima and Papago, as well as the Mexican villages and haciendas. When they started raiding the southern travel route and the newly arriving Americans who were settling in the valleys, war became inevitable. But it was not about the right to follow the buffalo. The Apache didn't do that.

In the latter half of the nineteenth century the concept of the Noble Savage had some residual currency, but the popularity of the notion existed mostly, if not exclusively, in the East. This was a romantic, or more accurately, sentimental belief or idea that the Indians were somehow harmless wandering philosophers, primitive but uncorrupted, sprung bodily from Jean-Jacques Rousseau's imagination, simple people who had been living blamelessly in the wilderness and worshipping nature in a kind of colorful pantheism cum Thoreau-vian isolation and contemplation. That is—they had been living that way until they were disturbed by the chaotic and unwelcome contact with white rapacity—a contact they resisted and continued to resist with the approval, or at least the sympathy, of humanitarians and men of goodwill. This compassion and sensitive understanding were possible largely because the whites who more or less believed this resided far from the scenes of mayhem, far from the loneliness and hazards of the frontier. And while the attitudes of the eastern philanthropists were denounced by critics as simple-minded and dangerously—even harmfully—naive, advocates could argue that distance gave them perspective and objectivity. They were not subject to the virulent prejudice of the turbulent settlers of the West who may or may not have legitimate grievances but who were all too often also motivated by lust for Indian lands or by poisonous racial hatred.

It's hard to believe that many people actually subscribed to the Noble Savage idea, but it's not hard to believe that a great many wanted to. And a great many believed that there might be at least *something* to it. They were attracted to its imagery and to the thought of a people living a peaceful communitarian life in nature, in a kind of Western version of Brook Farm. The nineteenth century was awash in sentimental notions and utopian dreams, and many were attracted to works such as Longfellow's 1855 poem, *The Song of Hiawatha*. Few people seriously read Longfellow these days, but at the time the epic poem was a bestseller and spawned many works of art and imitation— and some parodies. Longfellow said the story was taken directly from the legends of the Ojibwa as collected by an amateur ethnologist named Schoolcraft, who also served as an Indian agent in Michigan for several years. Hiawatha was indeed a noble character. He was not unlike the Culture Heroes that most, if not, all tribes revered—the semi-divine giver of wisdom who taught the people how to live. The Cheyenne hero Sweet Medicine was similar. Both, in fact, introduced corn to the people and showed them how to cultivate it. So if Longfellow's work is in the romantic tradition of the mid-century America, he was at least starting from legends that were common. But it was in the presentation of the story that Longfellow's verse fell into the Noble Savage genre and helped spread it within certain mostly eastern circles. James Fenimore Cooper, of course, was in the same literary camp. Or village, perhaps.

Not only did Hiawatha have a series of adventures with demons and demiurges, he also married a beautiful maiden, called Minnehaha, or Laughing Water, who subsequently died in a satisfyingly melodramatic manner. The scene spawned paintings and illustrations in a kind of overwrought Pre-Raphaelite style. Importantly, Minnehaha was a Dakota maiden, and Hiawatha was an Ojibwa—two tribes who actually hated each other in the manner of the Montagues and Capulets. The story of star-crossed lovers always goes down well with large segments of the public. It's not hard to be dismissive of such stuff, but the poem is at least readable and you would have to have a very hard heart indeed not to feel a little sorry for Hiawatha when he loses Minnehaha and later when he paddles off into the sunset. Milan Kundera wrote that kitsch is the denial of reality. Well, of course. But still . . .

But the tribes that drew all the attention—the Plains tribes—were nothing like the storybook imagery that was so attractive to the Eastern reformers and their fellow travelers.

Both Mark Twain and George Custer, two odd bedfellows in many ways, agreed on scorning the sentimental notions that come under the rubric the Noble Savage, and blamed it in part on popular fictions, such as those produced by Cooper and Longfellow. Mark Twain, in particular, was keenly aware of the effect popular literature and art could have on the culture and politics. He was more than half serious when he blamed the Civil War on dreamy romantic notions of a chivalry that never was but was ardently imagined, wished for, and imitated by the Southern cavaliers and their ladies. "Sir Walter Scott had so large a hand in making Southern character as it existed before the war that he is in great measure responsible for the war." And Twain's contempt for the mawkish poetry of the time is evident in Huck Finn's visit to the Grangerford farm. He had no sympathy for the Noble Savage idea, largely because he had traveled the West, and, more important, because he saw the innate absurdity of that popular imagery and iconography. He also had a dim view of the human race in most, if not all, its manifestations. As he once said the Almighty "invented man because he was disappointed with the monkey." That applied to white and red, alike. As he wrote in *Roughing It*:

The disgust which the Goshoots gave me, a disciple of Cooper and a worshipper of the Red man . . . set me to examining authorities to see if perchance I had been overestimating the Red Man, while

viewing him through the mellow moonshine of romance. The
revelations that came were disenchanting. It was curious to see
how quickly the paint and tinsel fell away from him and left him
treacherous, filthy and repulsive—and how quickly the evidence
mounted that whenever one finds an Indian tribe he has only
found Goshoots, more or less modified by circumstances and surroundings. [. . . .] They deserve pity, poor creatures; and they can
have mine—at this distance. Nearer by, they never get anybody's.

The Gosiute were a particularly poor and degraded tribe in Utah and
bore little if any resemblance to the Plains tribes. Twain encountered
them during his stagecoach trip to the Western gold diggings. So it's
fair to say that Twain was not judging Indians from a representative
sample. Regardless, his relentless skewering of sentimental fantasies—
about everything in nineteenth-century culture—generally applied not
so much to the Indians but to those who succumbed to the silly fictions.
And while Cooper and Longfellow had rather lofty literary reputations,
their popularity, and sales, attracted lesser writers who adopted the
Noble Red Man tropes in dime novels and periodicals. And so the idea
trickled down. Bret Harte, another Westerner, wrote about the popular
novels and stories of the day: "What flowers of rhetoric surrounded the
picturesque savage! How perfectly we were to believe that he invariably
addressed us in the abstract, as 'the Pale Face,' that he seldom spoke in
three consecutive sentences without an allusion to the 'Great Spirit,'
that his daughter was the model of womanly grace and beauty."

Custer, who knew something about the Cheyenne and Sioux and
the others, was equally contemptuous of the storybook Indian. And
although not a Western civilian, his assessment of the Indians in the
West accurately reflected the views of the settlers, almost to a man. In
fact, Custer's opinion verged on the mild side by comparison to some:

Stripped of the beautiful romance with which we have been so
long willing to envelope him, transferred from the inviting pages

of the novelist to the localities where we are compelled to meet with him, in his native village, on the war path, and when raiding upon our frontier settlements and lines of travel, the Indian forfeits his claim to the appellation of the "*noble* red man." We see him as he is, and, so far as all knowledge goes, as he ever has been, a *savage* in every sense of the word; not worse, perhaps, than his white brother would be similarly born and bred, but one whose cruel and ferocious nature far exceeds that of any wild beast of the desert.

Both men clearly believed, or rather understood, that there was a direct correlation between distance and the "moonshine of romance"— the greater the distance, the more appealing the moonshine. Both men were also keenly aware that the Indian's "white brother" was capable of the same sort of barbarism. Custer's phrase "not worse perhaps than his white brother would be similarly born and bred" shows a level of understanding or sophistication not normally associated with the man. But he had, after all, been through the Civil War and had seen what Man *qua* Man was capable of.

Custer's other phrase, "'Savage' in every sense of the word," conveys the fact that the word was commonly used not only to describe a level of human ferocity, but also—or alternatively—a stage in a culture's development. And it had nothing to do with nobility. A savage state was not necessarily murderous, indolent, and useless, although it often was, but rather it was a phase of development just below the civilized. A savage might even be a decent sort of person, but he could not invent the steam engine or printing press or anything else along those lines, because he was uneducated and unenlightened. Science and mathematics were a closed book to him, and all nature—instead of being a fascinating laboratory for investigation (as well as a storehouse of resources) was alive with spirits and mysterious forces that directed his life, and both awed and terrified him. He had little or no understanding of medicine beyond the use of a few herbs, and he believed illness was caused by spirits that might be exorcised by incantations. He did know, of course, that a bullet or arrow wound could not be cured by chanting and shaking a gourd rattle, but he had little else in the way of remedies. He might very well worship the sun, but he had no idea that the earth was orbiting, and he could not even be sure that the sun would rise again, if not propitiated by some ritual. He could neither read nor write his spoken language—(although among Indians, the Cherokee became an exception, but the Cherokee were one of the so-called Five Civilized Tribes.) The savage man was quite literally ignorant of almost everything the civilized person respected, including science, the arts and, most notably, Christianity. He had no notion of progress. Or, rather, *Progress*. And, as regards the Plains tribes, even the advanced warriors of the Cheyenne, all of this was quite true.

It was also believed that most, if not all, cultures throughout history inevitably went through this stage as they progressed naturally from primitive to savage to civilized. So to call someone a savage, while clearly condescending, was not necessarily insulting. Obviously, Noble Savage was not opprobrious. Rather, the term was used simply to identify him as a member of a culture that was not completely evolved and might very well be stuck in place, unless shown the way to the next stage of development, which was civilization. The kindliest Quaker missionary could use the term *savage* simply to identify the category of people. But if that savage also happened to be a murderous berserker, the word might take on added meaning. Army captain John C. Cremony described the famous Apache chief, Mangas Coloradas this way: "He combined many attributes of real greatness with the ferocity and brutality of the most savage savage." Adjective and noun. The word meant both a state of cultural development and/or a pattern of detestably violent behavior. Accordingly, a white man who acted in a similar fashion could also be called a savage, even though he sprang from a civilized culture. And a savage who was educated properly could become civilized. In fact, that was the goal of many white politicians, philanthropists, and not a few army officers.

Others, like Custer, were dubious about the prospects of civilizing the Indian. He understood the thinking behind the effort, but thought success was unlikely. "Civilization may and should do much for him, but it can never civilize him. . . . He cannot be himself and be civilized; he fades away and dies. Civilization such as the white man would give him deprives him of his identity." It seems that Custer and Satanta saw things in a very similar way. Nor was Custer's observation a curt dismissal of their culture as worthless. In fact, he also says: "To me Indian life with its attendant ceremonies, mysteries and forms is a book of unceasing interest." He understood a little of the Plains Indians' way of life; he appreciated and shared many of their enthusiasms and interests—and their distaste for hierarchical authority. After all, his alter ego was "Nomad," and his troubles from his time at West Point until the end at the Little Bighorn stemmed from high spirits, love of freedom, and his tendency to obey orders selectively. His own writings suggest strongly that a part of him sensed that the Plains Indians were not so much backward and inferior as they were profoundly *different* from settled white civilization, as though the two peoples had at some point in the mists history come to a fork in the road, and the whites had gone one way and the Indians, the other. And the roads would never converge. The Indians in fact described the unappealing civilization being offered to them as "the white man's road." Custer was also fully alive to the fact that "the blessings of civilization [came] with its vices thrown in without stint or measure." He would fight the Indians, because that was the job—and he liked his job—but he did not have the same maniacal hatred of Indians felt by many of the western settlers and politicians.

In an irony Mark Twain would have appreciated, the Indian, especially the Cheyenne, would never agree that he was stuck in some backward phase of cultural development. When he thought about it at all, he believed he had reached the pinnacle of development, had progressed as far as possible. After all, if the afterlife was exactly the same as this life, how much better could things get here and now?

True, the *wihio*—the white man—had interesting inventions and useful tools, because he was clever—a characteristic that went hand in hand with his deviousness. But aside from cleverness, *wihio* had little to recommend him to the Cheyenne, except as targets. Besides, there were far too many of them. Indeed, the most warlike tribes, like the Cheyenne and Sioux, considered themselves superior beings. It was perfectly in line with their warrior culture. The individual who achieved great deeds in war expected and received the acclaim of the group and was fully justified in expressing his pride. And he did. Small wonder, then, that he considered himself superior to the ragged immigrants who were plodding across the Plains or the sweating construction crews who spent their day pounding spikes and hauling rails, or the sod busting farmer who spent his days looking at the rear end of a plow mule. What kind of man would willingly spend his time doing that? Certainly not a warrior.

Significantly, Longfellow's Hiawatha ends with the hero introducing Christianity to the Indians. That went over well with the reading public, too. It was a satisfying combination of imagery—the noble and heroic red men discovering the true religion. It was not much different in tone and imagery from the Victorian paintings of Sir Galahad kneeling before a vision of the cross.

Introducing Christianity to the tribes was a major plank in the platform of the reformers inside government and, more important, among Indian advocates and church leaders outside official circles— *more important* because the reformers were sincere in their humanitarian campaigns, whereas the government bureaucrats wanted to do something primarily to make the annoying problem go away. To the Christian reformers it seemed a matter of simple logic—if the Indians could be converted into loving their neighbors, they would stop killing each other and the white people who were living next door. Putting it that way, it was hard to disagree. What's more, and more realistically, organized religion, and certainly Christianity, almost universally operates in a settled *place*. It requires churches and schools.

A diocese or parish is a place with boundaries and an administration: ministers, deacons, sextons, choir masters, Sunday schools. And while there are wandering missionaries or revivalists to spread the word to the far flung, once the word is accepted, the converted naturally settle down into congregations and cease their rambling. Thus, introducing Christianity to the Plains tribes was not only the right thing to do for their immortal souls and their transition into civilization, it was also a good strategic solution to the problem of nomadism. And if you eliminate nomadism, you eliminate violent squabbling over land and resources. And ideally if you can add the Protestant work ethic to the mixture, you have a workable formula for peace. QED. It would also be much easier to administer the government's largesse, if the Indians would agree to stay in one place, so there was a logistical benefit to be achieved. Taken all around, Christianity had the look of a comprehensive solution, both spiritually and practically.

That was the theory, and it's fair to say that those who espoused it were sincere and wanted to see an end to the violence afflicting all parties in the west. And, importantly, they were sincere Christians who were quite convinced of the rightness of their beliefs *and* in the belief that it was what the Indians desperately needed to emerge from savagery.

Interestingly, there were some largely anonymous tribes who almost fit the desired mold. Here again, the Pueblo tribes lived by themselves, farmed their land, and didn't seem to bother anyone. Some were even Christians, of a kind, courtesy of the Spanish conquistadors and their wandering priests.

Unfortunately, the Plains tribes had little interest in Christianity. Not only did they have their own well-evolved religion with its attendant myths and legends, they had little use for a religion that preaches peace on earth, goodwill to man. And even if they had not noticed that many white Christians hardly practiced what they preached—and of course they must have—they were quite content with their own theology. As Captain Cremony wrote:

[Earnest Christians urge us] to take the red man by the hand as we have done to his negro brother, and guide him gently, kindly toward a better state in this world and the hope of salvation hereafter. I admit that these are very persuasive and forcible arguments, but reverend sir, the red man resolutely refuses to come. He disdains to take my hand, he flouts my proffered sympathy, and feels indignant at my presumption in offering him my aid to improve his condition. He conceives himself to be not only my equal, but decidedly my superior.

VOLUNTEERS VERSUS REGULARS

The Eastern reformers who were eager to introduce civilization to the tribes were also skeptical of the idea and expense of maintaining a standing professional army and were quick to decry its excesses or failures. They had watched the Civil War unfold with volunteer soldiers doing the majority of the work (simply because of the need for great numbers), and they could not see why the Western issues could not be handled better and more humanely by local action. And less expensively. And here again the reformers were sincere, but wrong.

General Sherman put it bluntly: "There are two classes of people, one demanding the utter extermination of the Indians and the other full of love for their conversion to civilization and Christianity. Unfortunately, the army stands between and gets cuffs from both sides." But that situation explains why Custer thought that "the army was the Indian's best friend."

The great frustration for the regulars was that they knew the volunteer citizen soldiers of the West were likely to be the most rapacious and violent, in part because they were the very ones whose friends, families, and properties were suffering from Indian attacks. They were also many of the people who cast covetous glances on the lands that the Indians valued and occupied. The regular army had no interest in that. They were merely passing through trying to do a difficult and dangerous job. This is not to say they were saints; far from it. But it is to say that their ambitions, incentives, and opportunities were different from the settlers. What's more, many of the civilian men who wandered west and might volunteer for Indian hunting would hardly be welcome at a Boston poetry reading. Many were little better than riffraff, gamblers, criminals, and drunks. As journalist Henry Stanley wrote of Julesburg, Colorado:

> I verily believe that there are men here who would murder a fellow creature for five dollars. Nay, there are men who have already done it and who stalk around in daylight un-whipped of justice. Not a day passes but a dead body is found somewhere in the vicinity with pockets rifled of their contents. But the people generally are strangely indifferent to what is going on.

No greater proof of that need be offered than the massacre of the Cheyenne village at Sand Creek, Colorado in 1864.

The attack was perpetrated by the Third Colorado Regiment of Volunteers, a regiment of temporary (one-hundred-day volunteer) civilians drawn from the sweepings of the Denver saloons and commanded by a homicidal preacher turned volunteer colonel named John Chivington. Not only was Chivington a Methodist minister, he was a genuine hero of the earlier Civil War battle at Glorieta Pass, New Mexico, when his troops helped defeat and turn back a rebel force bent on invading the Colorado goldfields. As colonel of the Colorado Volunteers he turned his attention to the Plains tribes that were causing trouble in Colorado: "Coloradoans had suffered little bloodshed but they had lived through a summer of stark terror, and Denver had nearly strangled as a result of raids that had choked off the flow of food and merchandise from the East." There were conflicting reports of peace negotiations with the Arapaho and Cheyenne, and the situation was confused by the usual combination of local politics,

Indian decentralized authority, regular versus volunteer army disagreements. The result was an opening for Chivington to act, and
he did. He attacked Black Kettle's village, even though Black Kettle
thought he was under the protection of the army and was in that
place to discuss peace terms. Chivington ordered that no prisoners
be taken and massacred upward of two hundred people, two thirds
of whom were women and children. (George Bent who was in the
Cheyenne camp along with this brother, Charlie, placed the number
killed at 137. Others place the numbers higher.) Chivington then
paraded the Third Colorado through the streets of Denver, displaying Cheyenne body parts and scalps to the general approval of
the gawkers and even the local editorialists. The mutilations carried
out on the bodies of the victims were varied, grotesque, and obscene.
Chivington was exultant. But the Cheyenne never forgot. That was
hardly surprising.

Chivington and his ilk represented the extreme wing of the Western
settlers' attitude toward the Indian problem. Their solution, simply
put, was extermination. Chivington was quoted by one of his subordinates succinctly stating his position: "[H]e believed it to be right and
honorable to use any means under God's heaven to kill Indians that
would kill women and children and 'damn any man that was in sympathy with the Indians.'" Chivington left the volunteer service shortly
after the massacre and was reviled in many circles nationwide, but he
was never punished. But Chivington spoke for himself and the rabid
minority of opinion. His atrocity outraged much of society, and few
who condemned him and his men differentiated between his short-term
volunteers and the regular army. They all wore blue coats. Chivington's
action hardened opinions that were already critical of "the army."

Reporter Henry Stanley expressed a more temperate view, which
was the general opinion of the majority: "Extermination is a long word
and a long task, and civilization cannot sanction it." And elsewhere:
"[E]xtermination which is often urged by the vindictive Western men,
is alike as impolitic as it is barbarous."

As for the regular army, Captain Barnitz wrote: "General Smith [. . .] has written a wonderful letter to Major Elliott [of the Seventh cavalry] telling him to 'kill innumerable Indians—spare none but the women and children.'" This is not to say that women and children were not killed in regular army attacks; they were. But it is to differentiate the *policy* of the regulars from the *policy* of the volunteers, such as Chivington and his ilk. When a village is attacked—especially by cavalry— by either whites or other tribal enemies, casualties will happen in the confusion, the dust, the noise, the manic excitement and fear of the battle. Not all shots—in fact very few of them—will be well aimed and almost none will be made calmly. Friendly fire will wound or kill people from both sides. People of all sizes and conditions will be hit. George Bent describes a Cheyenne attack on an army patrol:

As we rushed in among them, the air was thick with dust and powder smoke; you could not see a dozen yards and the shots and yells deafened the ears. As we went into the troops I saw an officer on a big bay horse rush past me through the dense clouds of dust and smoke. His horse was running away with him and broke right through the Indians. [He] had an arrow sticking in his forehead and his face was streaming with blood.

Furthermore, Indian women were not shy about picking up a weapon and using it against an attacking enemy. And any soldier encountering that situation would not hesitate to shoot. Or if he did hesitate, it might have been the end of him. But as a general rule, the regular army did not order or sanction the killing of women and children, and there is ample evidence of written orders to that effect.

Of course, the Cheyenne reacted to the Sand Creek massacre. Historian Robert Utley wrote:

As the survivors of Chivington's strike straggled into the other Cheyenne camps on the Smoky Hill [river], runners bore war pipes to all the Sioux, Cheyenne, and Arapaho bands of the central Plains. Through January and February 1865, they spread death and destruction along the overland route, burning virtually every ranch and stage station on the South Platte, twice sacking the town of Julesburg, ripping up miles of telegraph wire, plundering wagon trains, running off cattle herds, and completely cutting off Denver from the East.

George Bent, who participated in his share of Cheyenne raids, wrote:

The result was panic in Colorado. There was only enough food to last a few weeks, and prices jumped to famine rates, and even then there was little on the market. Besides that, the stage line was broken up and no coaches were running; every station for a distance of nearly a hundred miles had been burned and the stock run off; the Overland telegraph had been destroyed. [. . .] All of this trouble was the result of Colonel Chivington's "great victory" at Sand Creek.

Interestingly, the attitudes of the Plains tribes mirrored the white spectrum. There were chiefs who had glimpsed the inevitable and were willing to make the best deal they could. Red Cloud and Spotted Tail for two were powerful Sioux spokesmen who finally agreed to peace terms after Red Cloud's War of 1866–1867. Black Kettle among the Cheyenne was another who consistently counselled an end to hostilities. He escaped the Sand Creek violence only to be killed four years later by Custer's attack at the Washita, in Oklahoma. But then there were the inveterate enemies of the whites—men like Satanta and Roman Nose as well as whole groups, such as the Cheyenne Dog Soldiers who were having great success doing what they enjoyed doing. They saw no reason to give up the rapine and plunder against the pathetic white hordes who were obliging targets as they traveled through their territory or against the railroad construction crews and stagecoach stations. There were riches and glory to be gathered there. Then there was the rich lands of eastern Kansas that were being rapidly converted into ranches and farms. They, too, were ripe for plucking.

The attitudes by both whites and Indians were hardened—especially what may be called "the war parties"—by the same mechanism: attacks against the poorly defended villages and settlements, the killing and mutilation of innocents, the kidnapping of women and children. In the case of the hostile Indians, the attacks were against the ranches and stage stops and even the little towns, such as Julesburg, Colorado. George Bent described the Cheyenne and Sioux attack at Julesburg; he was there as one of the warriors:

> The shelves in the store were packed with all sorts of groceries and canned goods. The Indians took whatever they wanted. [. . .] The big warehouse belonging to the stage company was also plundered. From it the Indians secured all the flour, bacon, corn and sugar the ponies could carry.

They also stole a herd of beef cattle. Some of the warriors wanted to burn the warehouse and stores, but the chiefs advised against it by saying they'd probably want to come back some day for more provisions. Normally the warriors would not have listened to the chiefs, but they had to agree the idea made sense. And in fact they did come back a second time.

The escalation of violence on both sides had no discernible end point.

FETTERMAN

Their most successful battle of the Indians' war against the whites was the defeat of Captain Fetterman and his troops near Fort Phil Kearny in Wyoming. Fort Phil Kearny was built by the army in 1866 along with Fort C. F. Smith in Montana. Both forts sat astride the Bozeman Trail, which was a road that led off from the Oregon Trail from Fort Laramie, Wyoming, and headed northwest to the new gold diggings around Bozeman, Montana. Both forts were built by the troops sent to man them, and they did a good job of it. Fort Phil Kearny was one of the few Western posts to be surrounded with log ramparts, and it was fairly secure, as long as the troops and their families stayed inside or nearby. But many of the Sioux and the Cheyenne bitterly resented this new road and the parade of emigrants who were using it to get to the gold diggings, and they were attacking wagon trains and smaller groups and bringing travel to a halt. (Although one intrepid Texas cattleman, Nelson Story, ignored the army's warnings and in 1866 drove a thousand head of longhorns north to the Montana diggings, where he figured, correctly, that fresh beef would be welcome.) Frustrated by the constant harassing attacks against emigrants and against his fort and working parties, Colonel Henry Carrington, the fort's commander, sent Captain Fetterman to disperse a group of raiders who were showing themselves defiantly and attacking a woodcutting detail. It was December 21, and the Indians were deviating from the usual plans of suspending aggressive warfare and going into winter quarters. Fetterman's command consisted of forty-nine infantryman, twenty-seven cavalry, three officers, and two civilians. The infantry and cavalry were mostly poorly trained recruits who had spent the previous months building the impressive stockade and very little time training to fight their adversaries. Carrington was a colonel in the Eighteenth Infantry, and he interpreted his mission as building a fort . . . and then occupying it. His job was, in his mind, to establish a presence and then simply to remain there. He apparently believed that his position alongside the Bozeman Trail would be sufficient to the task of protecting it. This understanding was in some ways consistent with the army's policy of establishing forts throughout the troubled areas of the frontier in the belief, or hope, that mere presence would discourage Indian hostility and in case of trouble provide a base for responding to emergencies. And in fairness to the army and to Carrington, the tribes were sending mixed messages. Some like Red Cloud were angry about the road. Others were less concerned and claimed to want peace. Still others lived in areas that were far from the Bozeman road and so didn't much care about it. Some like Roman Nose were inveterate opponents of the whites, period. And some like the Dog Soldiers were not only inveterate opponents, but aggressive warriors happy to have a war to fight and plunder to collect. As usual among the highly decentralized politics of the Plains tribes, there was no single spokesman and no single point of view or policy. Such a thing was unheard of and unwanted. Government agents sent to Fort Laramie to negotiate with the tribes muddied the picture with either poor or mendacious analyses of the situation, claiming absurdly that "Most cordial feelings prevail" among the Indians. Given the confused nature of the political and military situation, it's not surprising that Carrington was a little muddled about the object of his mission. But he clearly did not regard his fort and his troops as a *means* to a broader strategic end, but rather simply as the end, itself. He had spent the Civil War behind a desk and was not by nature an aggressive soldier. Moreover he was an infantry officer, and although the infantry might be "the queen of battle" in normal war, here in the West it was usually relegated to garrison duty and guarding plodding supply columns and emigrant trains.

Carrington's subordinate, Captain Fetterman, was a supremely confident officer. Unfortunately, his confidence was not based on experience, but on his contempt for the Indians. He once said he could march through the entire Sioux and Cheyenne nations with fifty troops, and here he had eighty. So much the better. It's hard to believe that, when he surveyed his little command, he thought they made a very impressive force. But they were soldiers in uniform, and he must have felt that would be enough. The infantry were armed with Civil War muzzle-loading muskets; the cavalry had Spencer repeaters that they borrowed from the fort's band. Fetterman sallied out, blithely disobeyed Carrington's orders and marched over a ridge and out of sight. Apparently unaware of the common Indian decoy tactics, he chased after a small group of riders who led him into the proverbial jaws of a trap. He and his command were overwhelmed and annihilated in a matter of minutes. Some reports say that among those waiting in ambush was Roman Nose. If so, he was no doubt bedecked in his protective headdress. He hardly needed it. (George Bent says Roman Nose was not there. That is probably more likely. Roman Nose was reported to be active in almost every Cheyenne fight with the whites.)

When Carrington went to see what happened to his troops, he found an appalling scene of mutilation:

> Eyes torn out and laid on rocks, noses cut off, ears cut off, chins hewn off, teeth chopped out, joints of fingers, brains taken out and placed on rocks with other members of the body; entrails taken out and exposed, hands cut off, feet cut off, arms taken out from sockets; private parts severed and indecently placed on the person [usually shoved in the victim's mouth] eyes, ears and mouth penetrated with spearheads, sticks and arrows; ribs slashed to separation with knives, skulls severed in every form, from chin to crown, muscles of the calves, thighs and stomach, breast, back, arms and cheek taken out. Punctures upon every sensitive part of the body, even to the soles of the feet.

The troops who collected the bodies that had frozen stiff in the December snow were of course terror-struck and shocked by the scene. Even the mules who hauled the wagons were spooked. Later Carrington said he was told the mutilation was an expression of the Indians' religious view: when a man went to the next life missing important parts, he could not participate in the regular joys of life there and would, like Tantalus, spend eternity in a state of frustrated longing. Perhaps. But that fanciful belief did not in any way ameliorate the emigrants' or the army's horror and anger at the butchery.

It's worth remembering here that the Plains Indians lived by hunting and, therefore, by butchery, quite literally. The sight of blood, entrails, and organs was nothing new to them and not in the least shocking. They treated other enemies in a similar fashion; they didn't single out the whites for this special treatment. There's another aspect to it, too—for the Cheyenne, at least, there didn't seem to be any fuss made about a dead body, even the body of a respected warrior. More often than not they would leave a man lying on the prairie to be eaten by scavenger animals and birds. True, if the family or friends wanted to prepare the body and wrap it in the best buffalo robes and place it on a scaffold, that was an option, too. But that was not much different from leaving him where he lay when killed, for the scavenging animals would soon pull down the scaffold anyway, and until then, the carrion birds would use it as a platform. The survivors knew that perfectly well. As mentioned earlier, the Cheyenne felt that being killed on the battlefield was the best of all deaths, and having paid "the debt they owed to God," no more needed to be said or done about it. None of this is meant to minimize the grotesque nature of the Fetterman mutilations, and even someone who understood what lay behind it would still be revolted. But it is to say that the Cheyenne looked at the death of a warrior differently. What happened to his body after death didn't seem to matter much to them, no matter who it was. This suggests Carrington's theological interpretation of the mutilations is open to question, at least as far as the Cheyenne were concerned. It's impossible to know for sure, because there were reportedly well over one thousand Indians engaged; there were undoubtedly many different reasons behind the mutilations—probably a mixture of religious feeling, simple rage, adrenaline-fueled combat euphoria, contempt for the white soldiers, desire to terrorize others who found the scene, and, almost certainly, a bit of macabre humor. And certainly there was the memory of the similar mutilations of the Cheyenne at Sand Creek. Revenge was a powerful motive for the Cheyenne at all times, and their memory of the specific horrors of Sand Creek was clear and vivid.

Whatever their motivations, the Indians certainly succeeded in sending a terrifying message, for the news of the battle and its aftermath spread throughout the army and the frontier. From that point on, if they hadn't known before, the soldiers knew now what lay in store for them, if they lost a battle with the tribes. And the thought of what would happen if they were captured was the stuff of nightmares. Saving your last bullet for yourself became more than a cliché for writers of pulp frontier stories. Custer wrote:

> Colonel Fetterman and Captain Brown no doubt inflicted this death upon themselves or each other, by their own hands, for both were shot through the left temple and powder was burnt into the skin and flesh about the wound. These officers had often asserted that they would never be taken alive by the Indians.

In fact, the Cheyenne rarely, if ever, took adult male prisoners; they killed them all. Mutilations were performed on the dead. Unlike some other tribes, most notably the Apache, the Cheyenne did not seem to be interested in torturing prisoners, although Captain Alfred Barnitz talks about the Cheyenne women as "fiendish" in their treatment of captives. But the generally reliable half-caste, George Bent said:

> Cheyenne Indians never torture prisoners. Harsh treatment by captors was considered a disgrace to the tribe and always resented as such. In a fight the Cheyenne always killed the men at once, taking no prisoners except women, girls and young boys, all of whom were well treated and adopted into the tribe.

"Well treated" is a matter of opinion, as some of the women captives who were rescued could attest. During one attack on the Cheyenne village of Tall Bull, the soldiers and Pawnee scouts rescued a bleeding Swedish woman who had been captured during a raid on a settlement in Kansas. "Tall Bull had taken her for a wife and when the soldiers charged the camp he tried to kill her, but only made a flesh wound in her breast." For women who were captured, rape was inevitable. Army reports invariably noted that women were "outraged"—a nineteenth-century euphemism.

The truth is, there was no way to know for sure whether the grisly remains of Fetterman and his troops were the result of torture or whether the soldiers were mutilated after being killed. But it is certainly true that the aftermath of the fight regenerated and perhaps cemented Western white opinion that the tribes were ruthless savages and that the West, and the world, would be better off without them. And that included many in the army.

The raids and fighting raged on. In the summer of 1867 Henry Stanley wrote:

> Between Bishop's Ranch and the Junction cut-off, eighty miles from Denver, there are no less than ninety-three graves, twenty-seven of which contain the bodies of settlers killed within the last six weeks. Dead bodies have been seen floating down the Platte.

Strike and counterstrike. It is not surprising that the white emigrants or settlers whose ranches were being attacked and families murdered should seethe with hatred and want revenge. It is not surprising that the Cheyenne whose families were attacked, murdered, and grotesquely mutilated should seethe with hatred and want revenge. And it is not at all surprising that these attitudes hardened as the conflict rolled on and escalated.

The regular army, undermanned and overstretched, did not want war with the tribes. The regulars, who had no personal stake in the issue other than doing their jobs, were far less rabid in their attitudes toward the Indians and believed that the Indian problem would be handled more humanely and efficiently if *more* regulars were available and assigned to the West, and that the volunteer and ranger units never took the field. In the eyes of the regulars, Sand Creek was sufficient proof of that. True, the army had some hard cases enlisted in the ranks, but those men were subject to a harsh discipline of the kind potential volunteer troops would not tolerate, or even sign up for. But the politicians and the taxpayers did not want to hear any of that, and if they did hear it, they did not care to believe it.

It was not that the army officers were pacific, exactly, but that they knew they didn't have enough of the right tools to fight a war properly. As Captain Barnitz wrote:

> It needs not less than 40,000 men to make a speedy end of this Indian business, and we haven't a fourth of this number, and our troops are scattered in parties too small to accomplish anything through an area of about 10,000 square miles.

As currently constituted, the army could only be a constabulary force in an immense country better suited to the natives than to the troops, who were strangers to both the country and the tactics of the enemy. What's more, the army felt aggrieved to be in the middle of the political and philosophical arguments over what to do about the Indian problem. (Ironically, the same sort of arguments were being held in tribal councils, too.) It was seemingly impossible to satisfy the civilians, Western or Eastern. There was never enough action to satisfy the Westerners, and there was usually too much action for the taste of the Easterners. Even Custer, probably the most notorious of the cavalry firebrands, at least by reputation, understood that the army had a thankless task that offered almost no chance of success or reward, certainly nothing like the Civil War honors:

> [F]ame and glory? How many military men have reaped laurels from their Indian campaigns? Does he [the regular officer] strive to win the approving smile of his countrymen? That is indeed [. . .] a difficult task. For let him act as he may in

conducting or assisting in a campaign against the Indians, if he survives the campaign, he can feel assured of this fact—that one half of his fellow citizens at home will revile him for his zeal and pronounce his success, if he achieves any, a massacre of poor defenseless, harmless Indians; while the other half, if his efforts to chastise the common enemy are not crowned with satisfactory results, will cry: "Down with him. Down with the regular army, and give us brave volunteers who can serve us in other ways besides eating rations and drawing pay."

He goes on to say: "I have yet to make the acquaintance of that officer who, in time of undisturbed peace, desired a war with the Indians."

Periodically through all this strife there were calls for peace negotiations—primarily from the white reformers. The two events—Sand Creek and the Fetterman fight—seemed to divide white opinion into two camps, each suspicious of the other and each accusing the other of imbecility and incompetence. Sand Creek was roundly and justifiably denounced by almost all Eastern political and unofficial parties. That included the army who were quick to point out that these men were volunteers. But then came Fetterman, and the bureaucrats in the Indian Bureau had the temerity to blame the army for the disaster, saying that the Sioux and Cheyenne were angry because they were prevented from buying firearms from traders (licensed by the Interior Department's Indian Bureau) and so could not hunt. The Indians were said to be on the verge of starvation all because of the cruel and shortsighted position of the army. In response, the army pointed out with perfect truth that the Plains tribes had gotten along quite well with their traditional weapons and that they were far from being on the verge of starvation and were in admirable fighting condition. Only a lunatic would arm the very people you were fighting with. Further, Sherman was so incensed at the Fetterman disaster that he let his temper get the better of him and said: "'We must act with vindictive earnestness against the Sioux even to their extermination, men, women and children.'" Never much of a politician, the fuming Sherman walked into the trap laid by the Indian Bureau and its advocates who said that such intemperance proved that the army could never be trusted to manage Indian affairs. The politicians were quick to extrapolate Sherman's anger at the hostile Sioux, specifically, to mean all Indians, generally.

There were Indian peace advocates, but given the decentralization of Indian politics even within a single tribe let alone inter-tribe, the calls were less vocal or at least less audible. The attack on Sand Creek damaged Cheyenne chief Black Kettle's reputation, and his earlier calls for peace with the whites seemed more than ever a foolish and dangerous idea. Besides, there were too many tempting targets.

It's worth remembering that the territory being contested was gigantic, and so the army more or less divided it into a northern and southern campaign sectors. While the Indians roamed freely between the two, the army viewed it as two different fronts. The southern Plains were the homes primarily of the Kiowa, the Comanche, the Plains Apache, and the southern Cheyenne and some Sioux. The northern Plains were home to the Sioux and northern Cheyenne along with the Arapaho, but all of these tribes mingled freely through the North and South. Of course, there were many other tribes in both areas, some of them hostile, others more or less allied with the whites.

In 1867 Sherman ordered General Winfield Scott Hancock to take the field. Hancock, a hero at Gettysburg, was a handsome image of a general. Some newspaper reporter had dubbed him Hancock the Superb. Hancock agreed with that description and was in a belligerent mood, despite the fact—or perhaps because of the fact—that he had no knowledge of Indians, either fighting them or dealing with them. But of course he was not unique in his inexperience. He would take the field with a force of fourteen hundred troops, which included seven companies of infantry, a battery of artillery, and eleven troops of the Seventh Cavalry under Custer, who was to get his first taste of Indian fighting in this campaign. Hancock's goal was to show the flag and to assess the mood of the Indians and to do something about it if they proved fractious or aggressive. He had been told by government agents that the Indians in the South, which included Kansas, were mostly pacific and that the chiefs wanted peace. Whether that was true, the fact remained as always that the chiefs had only the power to persuade, and their persuasions were being largely ignored. Instead, the young warriors, and especially the Dog Soldiers, were raiding along the travel routes.

Hancock and his impressive outfit arrived at a large Sioux and Cheyenne village on the Pawnee Fork of the Arkansas River (in southwestern Kansas). Hancock's massive force terrified the Indians. The women and children quite naturally feared a repeat of Sand Creek and fled. They had no understanding of the difference between regulars and volunteers, nor would they have cared if they did. Fourteen hundred soldiers were a terrifying sight, so they ran away, while the men palavered with the army to distract them. In the night the men escaped, too. Hancock was furious. He sent Custer and seven troops of cavalry to follow the retreating Sioux and Cheyenne warriors as they went north. The Sioux and Cheyenne, using their normal tactics, split into ever smaller bands to the point that Custer and his men finally had no one to follow. Meanwhile, the bands of escaping Indians raided the Smoky Hill travel routes, and when Custer arrived he found the trail dotted with burning stage stations, empty corrals, and mutilated civilians. Hancock meanwhile decided that the abandonment of the village represented bad faith at the very least and an act of war at the worst, and so he put the abandoned village to the torch—over the objections of the Indian agents who were on the scene. The destruction included 111 Cheyenne lodges, 140 Sioux lodges, and all of the camp equipment abandoned by the fleeing women—in other words, the vast majority of their food and belongings—everything they could not carry with them, when they fled.

Hancock achieved little except to create a public relations disaster for the army as well as to confirm the hostile warriors in the belief that *wihio* could never be trusted. Talks of peace were not only fruitless but counterproductive and wasteful. Let the old men talk, if they wanted.

That's what old men did. Warriors went on the warpath. And besides there were too many rich pickings to be had. The warriors, such as the Dog Soldiers, didn't need an excuse to go raiding, but they had one, anyway, and that played into the hands of the civilians who preached the need for negotiations that would lead to a peaceful solution. They knew what that solution would look like, and it was now a matter of selling it to the tribes and elbowing the army to the sidelines while more rational people talked.

Meanwhile, farther north, along the Bozeman Trail, other Sioux and Cheyenne, primarily under the leadership of Red Cloud (to the extent that anyone ever followed a chief), kept up their attacks against the two forts—Phil Kearney and C. F. Smith, in Montana. Hoping for a reprise of their success against Fetterman, the Indians attacked working parties at both forts, and in both cases in fights (subsequently called the Hayfield Fight and the Wagon Box Fight), the soldiers defended themselves and inflicted heavy casualties on the Indians. The soldiers had recently been armed with new Springfield single-shot breech-loading rifles that fired .50 caliber metallic cartridges. These so-called trapdoor rifles allowed much faster reloading than the old Civil War muzzle loaders. (The 1866 models were forerunners of the later .45 caliber 1873 models that were became the standard infantry rifle for the next two decades.) The Indians tried frontal assaults against the troops who had taken shelter behind wagons in the one fight or in a makeshift corral in the other. The Indians suffered from the unexpected volume of fire, and in both cases they were driven off.

The two forts remained a profound irritant to the Indians, but the Bozeman Trail was still virtually closed to unescorted civilian travel.

PEACE COMMISSION

The summer of 1867 was a time of change in the policy of the government. Hancock's campaign in the southern Plains had done nothing but infuriate the tribes and set them raiding even more violently on the settlements and travel routes in Kansas. The Bozeman Trail was still effectively closed, and the newly built forts were little more than hostages to fortune and to Red Cloud's Sioux, the Cheyenne, and the Arapaho. Peace advocates saw the opening for a change of policy and in July Congress authorized the Peace Commission to investigate causes of the strife and to recommend solutions, including treaties with the hostiles. The commission consisted of senators John Henderson, Benjamin Tappan, and John Sanborn; Indian Affairs commissioner Nathaniel Taylor; and generals William Sherman, Alfred Terry, and William Harney.

Even the simplest-minded white politician realized that the basic Plains Indian problem was nomadism and an economy that was built on hunting migratory animals. That way of life required space—and a certain kind of space. It required huge grasslands that were reasonably flat and fertile and that were watered by rivers. That sort of country was not only ideal for buffalo but also for roads, railroads, farms, and ranches, which, in turn, inevitably spawned towns and cities. Those two ways of life—nomadism and settlement—were incompatible, and that incompatibility could not be negotiated away. It was fundamental. Therefore the Indians must go somewhere and stop wandering after buffalo and bothering the settlers who were building the roads and townships and farms and ranches. Even the warmest-hearted Indian advocate understood that the change may be sad and unfortunate but it was unavoidable. A nomad might regret the loss of his wandering life the way an old man regretted the loss of his youth; both regrets were understandable, but both were the result of inevitability.

The good news to and from the government—the reformers, Indian advocates, and bureaucrats—was that there was somewhere for the nomadic Indians to go and something to do once they got there. The government had the answer, and it was always the same one—reservations. Regardless of how many forms the federal government's plans for the Indian question took and how many different politicians offered opinions, the basic idea for dealing with the Indian problem always came down to reservations. But no matter how large a reservation might be (and initially they were very large indeed and only gradually dwindled as the lands became increasingly coveted), a reservation by definition has boundaries. And boundaries are fundamentally inconsistent with nomadism and a migratory hunting culture. It is inconceivable that even the dullest politician or government agent did not understand that. A reservation is simply another word for *settlement*. The proposals to the tribes therefore had to—and did—offer incentives to give up their traditional way of life and accept this new arrangement that was sure to be not only unpalatable but also antithetical and obnoxious to the Indians. There had to be sweeteners.

A great conference was held at Medicine Lodge Creek on the southern border of Kansas. The peace commissioners met the leaders of several tribes. Senator Henderson made a speech to the assembled chiefs that contained the essence of the deal they were offering the tribes:

> We [the government] would give them all the comforts of civilization, religion and wealth, and now we are authorized by the Great Father to provide for them comfortable homes upon our richest agricultural lands. We are authorized to build for the Indian schoolhouses and churches, and provide teachers to educate his children. We can furnish him with agricultural implements to work, and domestic cattle, sheep and hogs to stock his farm.

It's important to mention that during these conferences the speeches made by the commissioners were honest in the sense that they spelled out precisely what the future would be—or rather what the choices were. The buffalo were dwindling. The settlers were advancing and multiplying. As much as the Indians might want to go on the way they always had, it would soon be impossible. The government was perfectly clear about that, and there was really nothing they or anyone could do about it. The settlers would come and continue coming, and like the miners, they would not be stopped. Could not be stopped. The government was therefore offering a package that however unpalatable to the wandering nature of the tribes was, their only alternative to a few years of war followed by surrender with diminished numbers—and numbers that would continue to dwindle, from poverty and starvation. Henderson said:

> You say you do not like the medicine houses of the whites, but you prefer the buffalo and the chase and express a wish to live as your fathers did. We say to you that the buffalo will not last forever. They are becoming few now, and you must know it. When that day comes, the Indian must change the road his father trod, or he must suffer and probably die. We tell you that to change will make you better. We wish you to live, and we will now offer you the way.

That was certainly plain enough—and accurate. There really was no choice; there was only the possibility of fighting a delaying action, an action the Indians would certainly lose eventually at the cost of much blood and destruction on both sides.

Churches and schools. The Indians called them "medicine houses," and wanted no part of them. "We don't want any. I want to live and die as I was brought up. I love the open prairie, and wish you would not insist on putting us on a reservation." So said Ten Bears, a Comanche chief. If he was not an appointed spokesman for the other chiefs, he certainly said what the rest of them thought. They understood what schools and churches meant—a profound assault on the tribes' religion and their entire body of cultural thought and practice. Nor did the idea of becoming farmers have any appeal. As mentioned, the Cheyenne and some other tribes might have some sort of tribal memory of days when they were semi-agricultural, but they were long past that phase and did not want to return. There was nothing in the government's proposal that had any appeal aside from the promise of "wealth" in the form of regular subsidies of food and presents, such as blankets and useful tools and even, in some cases, money. Now and then they were offered guns and ammunition under the fig leaf that there were only to be used for hunting. This was more attractive to the Indians, but it did not go down well with the army, for obvious reasons. Even so, the deals offered to the Indians were very thin gruel. But it was thin gruel or nothing. Worse, the arrangements would be managed by agents appointed by the government. The agents would be the middlemen between the government and the tribes. That arrangement was tailor-made for inefficiency at best, and corruption at worst.

Finally the commissioners had their way, or at least seemed to, and a treaty was concluded with the southern tribes. Called the Medicine Lodge Treaty, the agreement concentrated the tribes on two large reservations in western Oklahoma. They separated the Kiowa and Comanche from the Cheyenne and Arapaho. The treaty also called for thirty years of annuities as well as schools for the children and aid in establishment of farms. "In return for this the tribes would relinquish all claims to territory outside the reservations." The chiefs from the five principal tribes signed the treaty—"touched the pen."

Captain Barnitz, who was there at the negotiations, said afterward:

[T]he Cheyennes were with great difficulty persuaded to sign the treaty. They were superstitious in regards to touching the pen, or perhaps they supposed that by doing so they would be signing away their rights—which is doubtless the true state of affairs as they have no idea that they are giving up or that they have ever given up the country which they claim as their own, the country north of the Arkansas [River]. The treaty amounts to nothing and we will have another war sooner or later with the Cheyenne, at least, and probably with the other Indians in consequence of misunderstanding of the terms of present and previous treaties.

Major George "Sandy" Forsyth, commanding officer of the Beecher Island scouts.

Lieutenant Frederick H. Beecher, second-in-command.

"Medicine Bill" Comstock, frontiersman, rancher, gunman, scout for the 7th Cavalry and for Fred Beecher. Killed by the Cheyenne in the summer of 1867.

Artist's rendering of the Cheyenne attack against Fort Wallace, summer of 1867.

Officers outside Fort Wallace Adjutant's office just after the Cheyenne attack. Seated in the center is Captain Albert Barnitz, 7th Cavalry. Standing to Barnitz's left is Fred Beecher holding his Henry rifle. The rude construction of the office and the canvas covering of the roof are typical of frontier forts.

ABOVE AND OPPOSITE: Roman Nose. No known picture of Roman Nose exists, but this artist's reconstruction is as accurate as possible, both in the design of his face paint and his war bonnet. *Both photos taken by the author at The Fort Wallace Museum.*

Dr. J. H. Mooers in his Civil War uniform. Mooers was a civilian when he volunteered to join Forsyth's scouts as a surgeon. He "always wanted to see a real live wild Indian."

S. E. "Jack" Stilwell, the nineteen-year-old scout who went for help along with Pierre "Avalanche" Trudeau.

Artist rendering of two of the scouts hiding in the tall grass of the island.

Reuben (Ruben) Waller,
Company H, 10th Cavalry, and
one of the first of the relief party
to reach the beleaguered scouts.

Dr. Theophilus Turner and Fred Beecher—good friends at Fort Wallace. Turner was among those in the relief party.

Thin gruel or not, the offers of the federal government negotiators were roundly denounced by the Western settlers. The celebrated British journalist Henry Stanley traveled widely in the West just after the war (in which he fought as an adopted American). It was Stanley who later reported Senator Henderson's speech to the assembled chiefs at Medicine Lodge, and his travels and interviews along the roads through the central plains gave him an unvarnished picture of Western attitudes toward the Indians in the summer of 1867:

[W]e determined to proceed personally to the scene of hostilities. On our arrival at Bishop's Ranch we commenced to hear of the actions of the ubiquitous Indians. The great highway of the gold regions was strewn with emigrants thitherward bound, who were well armed with the best and most effective arms, and on the qui vive against any sudden attack of the redskins. Along the bluffs are the Indian videttes, patiently watching weak posts and helpless emigrant trains. When the opportune moment arrives, from every sand hill and ravine the hawks of the desert swoop down with unrivalled impetuosity, and in a few seconds the post or camp is carried, the tent or ranch is burnt, and the emigrants are murdered. It is generally believed here that, if the present suicidal policy of the Government is carried on much longer, the plains settlers must succumb to the unequal conflict, or unite in bands to carry on the war after the manner of the Indians, which means to kill, burn and destroy Indian villages, innocent papooses and squaws, scalp the warriors and mutilate the dead; in fact follow the same course as the red men, that their name may be rendered a terror to all Indians. From conversations with the ranch men and freighters on the prairie, we are of the opinion that the time is not far distant when we may hear of such a confederation of whites organized for such purposes. It is a desperate remedy and yet it seems the only one likely to affect the sanguinary savage.

Not to put too fine a point on it—extermination. Stanley represented a milder point of view:

To make a war of extermination would involve vast expense; besides, it is not an enterprise becoming of a great nation. Everything points to the coming destruction of the aboriginals of North America, but we should not hasten their doom, if it be possible to avoid it. There ought to be a large tract of land given them, where they may hunt the buffalo, the antelope and other game, as of old. We should keep them there and when any of the inhumanities with which they are charged are again committed, let them be punished, man for man, blood for blood, injury for injury, and so by doing we may avert their speedy destruction, and avoid the terrible murders and massacres which every now and then visit these western military posts and frontier settlements.

The following year, the Peace Commission negotiated a similar treaty with the Sioux and Cheyenne in the North. This was called the Treaty of Fort Laramie and essentially offered the same sort of deal to the northern tribes:

The treaty laid before the Indians at Fort Laramie also defined a reservation on which would concentrate the Sioux and the other northern tribes—nearly all the present South Dakota west of the Missouri River. It granted hunting rights on the Republican River and in Nebraska and Wyoming, north of the Platte. [. . .] [It] reserved the Powder River country as "unceded Indian territory" on which no white man might trespass without Indian consent.

In exchange for this massive amount of land to roam in, the Sioux and Cheyenne said they would cease raiding the settlements and attacking travelers. But adding further chagrin to the army, the treaty

commissioners agreed that the two newly built forts—Phil Kearny and
C. F. Smith in Montana—would be abandoned. The Indians would
be allowed to burn them down, which they did, gleefully, while the
departing troops were still in sight along the trail south. The Bozeman Trail would then be unprotected. While this seemed to maroon
the gold diggings of Montana—cut them off from supplies and new
hopefuls—the fact was that the Union Pacific Railroad was inching
ever closer to Salt Lake City, and from Salt Lake City there was a trail
to Virginia City, Montana—a center of the diggings. This trail was
shorter than the Bozeman, which therefore became unnecessary. The
miners would simply go a different way. And they could go much of
the way in the comfort of a railroad train. And so while the abandonment of the two forts embarrassed and disgusted the army, it did not
pose a problem to the continuing development of the goldfields and
therefore the furthering development of the frontier. The huge section
of land set aside for the tribes also included the Black Hills, and so its
ever-abundant supply of game would be protected from gold-hungry
prospectors—at least for the time being. But in fact it would be only
seven years before the question of Black Hills gold would again to
trouble the tribes, the army, and the civilians.

From the army's point of view, though, the Treaty of Fort Laramie
might have one important benefit. It drew a kind of east-west line
across the North, above the travel routes, and if civilian white men
were not permitted in the treaty area without tribal permission,
Indians operating outside of it could therefore be considered hostile
and subject to punishment. In theory, this would solve the always-
thorny problem in guerilla war—identifying the enemy. The tribes
had long been accused, and correctly, of raiding in the summer and
then returning to their agencies in the winter to live off government
largesse, such as it was. And of course there was the more fundamental
problem of the young warriors who could not be controlled and who
were asserting their identity as warriors by doing what warriors do.
Many not only raided during the summer but stayed out all winter,

too, preferring the freedom of a winter camp to the sight of a soldiers' fort and the unappealing taste of beef. Others were happy to make a raid on a ranch or a stage stop and then wander innocently into a fort's trading post to buy tobacco. They understood how guerilla war works. So the hope that treaty lines would clarify who was, and who was not, the enemy was really a vain hope, and no doubt the army knew it. But at least now they would have some legal justification for their actions and could deflect civilian complaints about what they did, what they did not do, and how they went about doing whatever it was they did. But Sherman and his colleagues surely realized that nothing the army did would ever completely satisfy the settlers in the west—not as long as there were Indians roaming and raiding. As for large segments of the Eastern population, well, the army was at best an unnecessary expense and at worst a gang of trigger-happy Cossacks.

RESOURCES

While there was intense political disagreement between the various parties about the Indian policy, the various white perspectives did seem to agree on one thing—the Plains Indians not only did not use the natural resources but they also prevented others from using them. And it was a criminal waste. The *Yankton Press & Dakotian* editorialized:

This abominable compact [the Treaty of Fort Laramie] with the marauding bands that regularly make war with the whites in the summer and live on government bounty all winter is now pleaded as a barrier to the improvement and development of one of the richest and most fertile sections of America. What shall be done with these Indian dogs in a manger? They will not dig the gold or let others do it. [. . .] They are too lazy and too much like mere animals to cultivate the fertile soil, mine the coal, develop the salt mines, bore petroleum wells, or wash the gold. Having all these things in their hands, they prefer to live as paupers, thieves and beggars, fighting, torturing, hunting, gorging, yelling and dancing to the beating of old tin kettles.

It was not merely gold in the Black Hills. As the editorial notes, the Hills were also known to have fertile and well-watered meadows for farmers to plow or ranchers to graze their cattle. And the endless forests were prime for lumbering. They were a rich natural resource of the kind that the advancing civilization coveted and knew what to do with. Thus the Black Hills symbolized something to the white man that was very different from their meaning to the Indians. To the whites, and especially the settlers and miners, the Hills were a vast resource to be developed, and to let those resources sit idle under the lazy occupation by the tribes was a crime against enterprise and a glaring symbol of the imbecility and ineptitude of the government's policies toward the Indians. Lieutenant James Calhoun of the Seventh Cavalry succinctly expressed the white civilization's point of view:

Man is the noblest work of God. In this wild region man will ultimately be seen in the full enjoyment of happiness obtained by honest labor. For the hives of industry will take the place of dirty wigwams. Civilization will ere long reign supreme and throw heathen barbarianism into oblivion.

The white civilization's attitude toward the Black Hills and, in fact, the entirety of the frontier, could hardly be expressed more succinctly.

Where white opinion got it wrong, however, was in thinking that the Indians did not value or use the natural resources. They hunted the game animals and trapped the fur bearing animals for trade; they cut the timber for lodge poles, and they grazed their horses on the grasslands of the Plains or in the mountain meadows of the Black Hills. They did not dig for gold because they did not value it, and perhaps the thought of digging around in the streams and mountains was distasteful for aesthetic or quasi-religious feelings. They knew gold could be used to buy things they did admire from the whites—guns, ammunition, metal tools, even horses. But they saw no reason to go grubbing about in the dirt to find it. After all, there were much easier ways to acquire the white man's tools and livestock—ways that were both more satisfying and consistent with a warrior's ethic—simply raid or attack and kill the people who had what you wanted. It was both righteous and productive. Nor were the Indians lazy in their uses of the resources. Hunting can be a pleasurable recreation, when you don't have to be successful. It's a different matter when your life depends on success. And if the game does not cooperate and populate your neighborhood, you might have to travel days over often difficult terrain to find it. Then having killed the game it is not always an easy matter to butcher it and carry it home to your camp—which might well be many miles away. So the Plains Indians were not exactly idle lotus eaters. True, they had lost the taste for farming, but they had not lost the memory of the work it entailed, and they had realized that hunting big game and gathering fruits and berries was a far more agreeable way of life than raising corn and beans and hunting rabbits and skunks. Besides, farming had always been women's work. What's more, while relying on the hunt to sustain you involved some risk and uncertainty, there was nothing certain about farming for a living, either—especially not on the Plains, as immigrant farmers were soon to learn. To the tribes' way of thinking, there was no inherent virtue in work qua work. The Protestant work ethic had not reached them, or if it had through some wandering missionary, it had not made an impression—other than the Cheyenne version of "surely you jest."

At first glance the two treaties seemed to find a middle ground between the fact of a nomadic hunting culture and the idea of a reservation. The treaties would allow for a peaceful transition period. Basically, if the reservations were large enough, hunting could still go on, and when the buffalo inevitably died off, the Indians would have become accustomed to a settled way of life and would have eased into the business of farming or ranching. Perhaps, too, the children would have learned the right lessons from the medicine houses and would be ready to assume their role in the cultural integration of their people. That was the assumption or the hope. The fact that the Indians seemed to agree more or less with this reasoning meant that Indians did not reject the ideas behind the treaties out of hand, which proved that the terms were at least palatable. Maybe they could work. That hopefulness overlooked the fact that many of the chiefs did not completely understand what they were signing, and a few, who may have understood, had no intention of complying and were merely getting the whole thing over with to collect the gifts that accompanied the signing.

In the north, the Treaty of Fort Laramie pretty much gave Red Cloud and the northern tribes all that they wanted. True, there was a theoretical reservation, but it covered the territory the tribes valued most and spent the most time in. The Black Hills were protected, and so was the Powder River Country. The hated forts on the Bozeman Trail were gone and the emigrants would be finding new ways around that country, as they went to the gold fields. Red Cloud could tell himself this was a victory, and it was. But there was something else at work in Red Cloud's agreement. He had seen the devastating effects of the new Springfield breech-loading rifles at the Wagon Box Fight. A frontal attack on the soldiers resulted in severe casualties. The Roman Nose tactic of "emptying their rifles" did not work against these new weapons; the fire was continuous and lethal. The warriors charged gallantly and were shot down from behind a well-prepared defensive position. The same thing occurred at the Hayfield Fight in Montana. Red Cloud said afterward that he had "lost the flower of his fighting warriors at the Wagon Box fight." And he had apparently lost a little of the heart for continuing the fight. Both fights were symbolic of the two cultures—one relying on unit discipline and technology, the other on traditional tactics meant to glorify the individual. (The ending of Mark Twain's *A Connecticut Yankee in King Arthur's Court* comes to mind.) In any event, Red Cloud could retire with his laurels to his reservation, and that's what he did. The other major Lakota chief, Spotted Tail, did the same. Both knew, of course, that the other bands, the other warriors, the other war leaders would do as they liked about continuing to fight. That was their business and only natural.

It's worth wondering what the commissioners really thought of their work. Assuredly the generals would have been as skeptical as Captain Barnitz. But at least they were seen trying to negotiate, and that was something of a public relations victory for the army, which needed one. The politicians would feel more hopeful of genuine peace, since their stock in trade was compromise, and they would have felt they'd reached just such a result. And at the very least, the politicians could tell themselves that had been seen doing something. Time would tell whether that something was the right thing to do, but for the time being there was reason for satisfaction and even cautious optimism—perhaps a politician's most natural and comfortable state.

In any event, the treaties were in place. But now that the tribes had agreed, more or less, the question became—who should be in charge of administering the terms of the agreement?

THE INDIAN BUREAU

The tribes had no written law; in fact, they had no writing of any kind. To the whites, that was one of the many indications and conditions of their savage state. As such, they had no concept of legal title to land or real property. Therefore, when they spoke of "our land," the Plains tribes, especially, were really only referring to the hunting grounds and territory they liked to roam over and from which they were able to expel their enemies among the other tribes. As mentioned, they understood the law of conquest, and, having defeated their enemies and occupied their territory, that was sufficient for them. If a more powerful tribe came along an expelled them, well, that was unfortunate, but that was how the world worked. After all, the Cheyenne and the Sioux were on the Plains, because the Ojibwa had forcibly evicted them from the Great Lakes regions. Nor did an individual consider he owned any real estate, personally. This is not to say that the Indian disdained personal property or wealth. He was keenly aware of the value of his horses and other material possessions. He may choose to give them away now and then, but it was precisely because he valued his possessions that his charity became significant and praiseworthy. The idea of personal real estate, however, was foreign to him. People can romanticize this attitude as reverence for sacred earth and so on, and there may be something to that. But more fundamentally, the idea of owning a few acres personally was an absurdity to a nomad.

But that was not how the white civilization's world worked. For them there was law, and from law came property rights. From the very beginnings of the country, there was disagreement and discussion about what that meant for the Indians who were in the way and on the land that the ever-westering frontier was encroaching upon. The Indian concept of land ownership was unworkable and incompatible with civilized law. Even as far back as John Quincy Adams in 1802 the question was raised, rhetorically: "What is the right of the huntsman to the forest of a thousand miles over which he has accidentally ranged in search of prey?" To a culture based on the rule of codified law, that question was rhetorical.

But what to do about these people who were there, if only now and then, for hunting or temporary camping? Legislators and jurists were forced with a choice—either apply the law of conquest, which is essentially the way the individual tribes acquired the land in the first place, or devise a more humane way around the problem. Chief Justice John Marshall strove to find a palatable solution by ruling that the tribes were "domestic dependent nations"—a kind of quasi-legal entity within the broader legal entity of the country. And if they were "nations," however domestic and dependent, the federal government could legally negotiate *treaties* with them. (The federal government could not legally make treaties with individuals, groups, or tribes; only other nations.) The Indians were in a territory according to the laws of conquest—or because no one else had been there before—and their presence there was the basis of their title. And because they were nations "of a kind," the leaders of the tribe, who were assumed to represent the rest of the tribe, could negotiate and make treaties on a variety of matters—including their title to the land the tribe occupied or claimed. As part of the treaty negotiations, the federal government could offer emoluments in exchange for the "extinguishment" of the title to the land the Indians occupied. If the government wanted to acquire only a part of that land, that could be arranged, too. Viewed that way, the remaining "reserve" was not so much a place where the Indians were isolated, but rather the remainder of the broader territory that they signed away in exchange for cash and annuities. In that case, there would also have to be established boundaries that separated the land that was sold from the land that was retained. And where there are legal boundaries, there is the possibility of trespass.

A legislator looking for ways to explain things to his own conscience and constituents could say that the idea was really no different from a person dividing his farm, selling one half and living on the other. The "farmer" in this case did not originally know that he owned the place, but through negotiations he learned that he did and that he could sell off pieces of it in return for cash or other gifts. Of course, the situation could become sticky if the newly aware farmer had no interest in selling, as in the case of some Eastern tribes, most notably the Cherokee. But that was a separate problem and did not invalidate the basic premise behind the idea of treaty negotiations to extinguish Indian titles.

So the seeds were sown for ensuing decades' worth of legal and moral difficulties, because the whites brought with them not only a legalistic mind-set that believed in treaties but also an unexamined assumption that the tribes, as nations, had a hierarchical structure and government that would allow one chief, or perhaps a senate of the tribe, to ratify and then enforce a treaty. Ironically, the whites were bringing the standards and practices of civilization to their dealings with people whom they regarded as uncivilized savages (a tautology), and expecting it all to work. But if people noticed the irony, they were not troubled by it.

It is easy to be cynical about this process, but the government did have the alternative of simply snatching away the land by conquest and putting the indigenous people to the sword or simply expelling them to find some other place of refuge—until that land, too, was wanted. In some cases, of course, expulsions happened. But that was not the preferred way. It was felt that the nation's honor required a more humane and legally acceptable way to accommodate the inevitable western movement of civilization. Of course, not everyone agreed. "Treaties were expedients by which ignorant intractable and savage people were induced without bloodshed to yield up what civilized people had the right to possess." So said a governor of Georgia who favored a blunter instrument to solve the problem.

Depending on your point of view, the idea of treaties was either a moral fig leaf or well-intentioned attempt to avoid a more violent solution and to deal fairly with the Indians. But it's hard to escape the feeling that the titles, on which the treaties were based, were conjured out of whole cloth. In a sense, the titles were like the greenback dollar during the Civil War: the titles came into existence—and then had value—because the government said they did. As such, they could be traded, like the paper dollar. They could be sold. And they were.

Initially the Bureau of Indian Affairs, or the Indian Bureau, was established as part of the War Department, but in 1849 it was transferred to the Department of the Interior. The Indian Bureau was therefore staffed by civilians. The purpose of the bureau was to negotiate treaties with the tribes, in part to extinguish their titles, and then to manage the terms of the treaties and deliver the goods and annuities that invariably attended the treaties. Civilian agents would be assigned to certain tribes in certain regions and would be the tribes' conduit to and from the federal government. Additionally, civilian traders would be federally licensed and given the exclusive right to deal with the agency wards.

The concept of domestic dependent nations was abandoned in 1871. But by then the machinery of the Indian Bureau was well oiled and the bureaucrats and politicians operating it were well entrenched and powerful. So, too, was the fundamental belief in the value and efficacy of negotiations with the tribes. And underpinning the belief in negotiations was the enduring ignorance of the Indian culture—ignorance that led bureaucrats and politicians to assume a chief spoke for the tribe and could compel adherence to an agreement. Or, as was more likely in some cases, the ignorance was a sham, because some of the agency bureaucrats must have known full well that the chiefs had little authority to enforce the terms of an agreement. But negotiating treaties was understood to be the only alternative to all-out war. That policy was also good public relations for the bureau. And so, if and when a peace treaty was violated, because the Dog Soldiers wanted to sack a frontier settlement or attack a stage line, the bureaucrats and the politicians could shrug, sadly. They had done their best to negotiate a fair treaty and then to perform their duties under its terms. They could say that they negotiated in good faith, and maintaining the appearance of good faith was an important object for anyone dependent on the public for his job.

These treaties were couched in legal language and included surveyors' map coordinates—none of which made any sense to the chiefs who were expected to agree. At peace councils, such as Medicine Lodge, the treaty terms with all their precise terminology were translated to the assembled chiefs by interpreters who were usually half-caste members of the tribe, or frontiersmen who had picked up the language by association. There was really no other way to learn any of these difficult languages. So it's fair to wonder exactly how fluent these translators were, especially given the need to translate legalese. And even if they had the fluency of a Cicero, how could they translate a legal term into a language that had no idea of law and therefore no corresponding vocabulary? At treaty negotiations involving multiple tribes, such as Medicine Lodge, there were necessarily several different translators to explain the treaty terms to each of the chiefs from the different tribes. And in fact there were more than principal chiefs, for each one had colleagues from his tribe who also needed to understand the terms. The situation was farcical. (One oddity: at the Medicine Lodge conference, the Arapaho translator was a woman named Mrs. Virginia Adams. She appeared in "a crimson petticoat and a small coquettish velvet hat decorated with an ostrich feather." How she came to be in that role is something of a mystery.)

If the chiefs did not fully understand the treaties they signed, it's not surprising. And if they signed simply to put an end to the interminable droning of the political negotiators and their translators (so that they could finally get hold of the gifts), well, that's not surprising, either. And if they despaired of ever explaining the treaty to their people and therefore simply decided not to bother, well, that too is not at all surprising. Just gathering the various wandering bands of an entire tribe together for a council was not an easy task and usually only happened once a year or so for religious festivals and ceremonies. And of course the chiefs knew that whatever they said would not affect the young warriors. They would be lured to the warpath by the thought of plunder and glory. That was traditional and to be expected. Furthermore, many chiefs, such as the wily Satanta, would have had no interest in enforcing compliance on their warriors, even if they could. He, and others like him, were capable of shifting their position as expedient and were as happy as their younger acolytes to sign a peace treaty, collect the spoils and then return to the warpath, themselves. The conferences for them were an ideal means to dupe the credulous white commissioners into supplying the weapons and supplies the tribes needed to continue fighting. To think otherwise is to patronize the chiefs as a group of naive innocents who were being sold a bill of goods in exchange for trinkets and promises. In many ways it was the legalistic commissioners who were being deceived, as they rolled up the signed treaty documents and congratulated themselves on their negotiating ability. There is an element of "peace in our time" about these negotiations. And it's easy to imagine the more experienced army officers staring gimlet eyed at the assembled Indians and politicians and thinking it was all a sham. Others, like Hancock the Superb who met with the Cheyenne during his failed campaign, were likely to raise smiles among the chiefs when he said, "Every tribe ought to have a great chief, one that will command them. For any depredations committed by any one of his tribe I shall hold the chief and his tribe responsible." No doubt they were thinking, *Yes, that is what you want, but that is not how it works. But if those are your intentions, we would be foolish to stay here. And after we leave, we wish you good luck in trying to find us.* And in the morning they were gone, leaving an empty village to be burned by the surprised and angry Hancock.

In his May 1867 report on the Fetterman disaster, frontier scout Jim Bridger wrote about the Sioux, northern Cheyenne, and Arapaho who had made the attack and were still aggressively hostile:

> Friendly Indians report that they [the hostiles] are being supplied with ammunition by half breed traders connected with the Hudson's Bay Company. There is no sense sending commissioners to treat with them. [. . .] They would be willing to enter into any temporary treaty to enable themselves to get fully supplied with powder with which to carry on the war. The only way to settle the question is to send out a sufficient number of troops to completely whip the hostile Sioux, Cheyenne and Arapaho and make them sue for peace."

Other chiefs, like the tragic Cheyenne Black Kettle, were fairly constant in their desire for peace and in their belief that negotiations could actually lead to peace. There was no single spokesman for any tribe, much less a single spokesman for an entire assembly of tribes— Hancock's demands notwithstanding. And there never was a consensus among the tribes, or even within individual tribes, as to what to do about the whites. Accordingly, though the army tried now and then to arrest chiefs and warriors (Satanta for one), there was really no one to hold accountable for breaches of peace terms that were improperly understood to begin with, inadequately explained to the whole tribe and fundamentally at odds with the culture of the warrior, anyway, and therefore ignored. So unanimity of understanding, assent, and compliance, was a pretty much a chimera.

This is not to say that peaceful negotiations were a bad idea. It is simply to point out the inherent difficulties of the process and the fact that, although negotiations and treaties could have worked, often they did not. In some cases, failures were due to the fundamental, almost unbridgeable differences between the cultures. In other cases, it was because the people involved in the process were dishonest and willing to exploit the ignorance of the other side to gain material advantages.

CORRUPTION

The army was never happy with the Indian Bureau. Senior officers and junior officers in the field alike had long argued that the bureau was a sink hole of corruption in which jobs as Indian agents and post traders were sold to the highest bidders in return for political favors, straight cash and continuing kickbacks. That was true. In fact, as structured and managed, the bureau was tailor-made for corruption. Custer wrote:

It seems almost incredible that a policy that is claimed and represented to be based on sympathy for the red man and a desire to secure him his rights, is shaped in reality and manipulated behind the scenes with the distinct and sole object of reaping a rich harvest by plundering both the government and the Indians. To do away with the vast army of agents, traders and civilian employees which is a necessary appendage of the civilian policy,

would be to deprive many Members of Congress of a vast deal
of patronage which they now enjoy. There are few, if any, more
comfortable or desirable places of disposing of a friend who has
rendered valuable political service or electioneering aid than
to secure him the appointment as Indian agent. The salary of
an agent is comparatively small. Men without means, however,
eagerly accept the position; and in a few years, at furthest, they
almost invariably retire in wealth. Who ever heard of a retired
Indian agent or trader in limited circumstances? How do they
realize fortunes upon so small a salary? In the disposition of the
annuities provided for the Indians by the government, the agent
is usually the distributing medium. Between himself and the
Indian there is no system of accountability, no vouchers given or
received, no books kept, in fact no record except the statement
which the agent chooses to forward to his superintendent.

Custer may not have been a universally popular man within the army
or even within his own regiment, but he was articulating the nearly
universal opinion of the regular army. The army was charged with
fighting the battles against Indians who were furious at being cheated
and shortchanged by the system, and they reviled the system as dangerous to their lives and careers. It was bad enough having to fight
the inveterate warriors such as the Cheyenne Dog Soldiers who went to
war because it was their métier. But to poke the hornet's nest of tribes
that wavered between peace and war simply to enrich cronies and
political benefactors was a bridge too far. The army argued that the
Indian Bureau should be transferred back to the War Department. In
so doing, the civilian malfeasance that led to so many troubles with
the tribes would be removed.

Viewed objectively, the army had a very strong case. This is not to
say, again, that the army was composed of humanitarians or reform-
minded Quakers, but rather that it had a structure based on strict
hierarchy, accountability, and very clear reporting channels. There was

oversight on almost all aspects of army life. What's more, army quarter-masters were accustomed to dealing with logistics, with the process of requisition and delivery. One of the Indians' chief complaints against the Indian Bureau was that the supplies they were promised did not arrive in the quantity and quality that they expected, and sometimes they did not arrive at all. Having no experience with paperwork, invoices and bills of lading, no ability to read, the Indians had no way of knowing the extent to which they were being cheated and had no recourse for complaint. They could only see that the promised annu-ities that did arrive were not the things they were promised, in either quality or quantity. Or both. To whom should they bring their list of grievances? The Indian agent who was responsible for distributing the faulty goods? The army's supply systems were far from perfect, of course, and the vast distances supply trains needed to travel made logistics a constant management problem. But the army was far better organized, experienced, and motivated to deliver against the terms of a treaty than the agents of the Indian Bureau who, as Custer says forthrightly, were there to get rich. Most of them, anyway.

For their side, the politicians and the beneficiaries of patronage defended themselves to the Indian apologists and pacifists and to the general public by asking a rhetorical question—was it wise to place the welfare of the Indians in the hands of the army—that same crowd that could be responsible for outrages such as Sand Creek or devastating attacks on innocents, such as Hancock's destruction of the Cheyenne and Sioux villages? Framed that way and placed in the context of the widespread civilian distrust of a standing regular army as well as revulsion over occasional bloody fights with the Indians, the answer was easy. And public relations were not the strong point of the army's senior men; witness General Sherman. When up against a politician making a political argument, the army's generals were no match. For the duration of the Indian Wars and beyond, the Indian Bureau remained in the hands of the civilians and the Department of the Interior. (It is still there.)

There was little or no oversight, apparently, in the Indian Bureau, and there were plenty of incentives not to know what was going on—or to keep what was going on in the dark. The nineteenth century, especially after the Civil War was awash in corruption throughout all levels of government, and the Indian Bureau was just one more example among many.

Family members were frequently on [Indian] agency payrolls. A daughter in one case was paid as the reservation school teacher, although she did no teaching. Appropriations for construction of agency buildings were a fertile source of cash. In one instance an agent received $10,000 to build a school; he build a small log cabin for $200. Invoices and receipts were easy to forge, or in the case of Indians who were illiterate, it was simple enough to get one of them to make his mark on a receipt. The census of Indians on a reservation was yet another source of easy money. An agent at the Spotted Tail (Sioux) agency submitted a census listing 9170 Indians when in fact there were only 4775. By virtually doubling the size the population he thereby received twice the amount of subsidies. And it would not be too farfetched to think that after keeping and selling the one fictional half, he skimmed some of the subsidies actually delivered to the Indians. Shipping companies were paid mileage, and it was easy enough to convert a hundred mile trip into something considerably longer. Who in Washington knew the wandering roads and distances out on the Plains? [And who even cared?]

Walter Burleigh, an agent for the Yankton [Sioux] Agency in 1865 before leaving to run (successfully) for Congress, accidently left behind a document that detailed only one of undoubtedly many similar transactions during his tenure:

W. A. Burleigh received payment in gold, $15,000
W. A. Burleigh sold gold for 100% premium, $30,000
W. A. Burleigh paid per capita $5 to 2000 persons, $10,000

Amount pocketed by W.A. Burleigh, $20,000
Amount paid to Hon. Secretary of the Interior, $10,000
Amount paid to Commissioner of Indian Affairs, $5,000
Amount paid by W. A. Burleigh to self, $5,000

Since the greenback was at a significant discount to gold, Burleigh was able to sell the gold for twice the amount of paper dollars, some of which he distributed to the tribe (two thousand persons at $5.00 each), some of which he used to bribe his political bosses, and some of which he kept. (His statement that he paid $10,000 to the Honorable Secretary of the Interior is fine piece of an unintentional irony.) Small wonder that the politicians in Washington wanted to maintain control of the Bureau. Further, like the soldiers, if the Indians needed gold specie to buy from the appointed traders, they would have to rediscount their already discounted greenbacks, so that the value of their contracted subsidy was reduced to a fraction of what they were owed. (The two thousand reservation Indians should each have received $7.50 in gold but instead ended up with $2.50 in purchasing power. What's more they had no alternative to the politically appointed trader who could adjust his monopoly prices as he liked—to say nothing of the quality of his goods. As a result the greenbacks the tribe received were worth less in purchasing power than those same greenbacks were worth to the politicians who received them; the politicians and agents operated in competitive markets and so could shop around for the best prices. In short, one greenback dollar was worth more to a corrupt politician than to the reservation Indian who received it as part of his promised treaty annuities.

It's worth noting that Agent Burleigh was so brazen in his fraud that he even wrote and then kept this memo to himself. He obviously had no worries that he'd be found out or prosecuted. Nor was he. In fact, the county in North Dakota in which the capital, Bismarck, is located, is named for Burleigh.

Custer comments wryly: "It's a common saying in the west that next to, if not indeed before, the consulship to Liverpool, an Indian agency is the most desirable office in the gift of the government."

Even worse from the army's point of view—and that of the Western settlers—was the sale of modern weapons to the tribes, on the debatable theory that the Indians needed them for hunting. During General Hancock's abortive campaign, Custer describes an early encounter with the Cheyenne:

It was nothing less than an Indian line of battle drawn directly across our line of march, as if to say, Thus far and no farther. Most of the Indians were mounted, all were bedecked in their brightest colors, their heads crowned with the brilliant war bonnet, their lances bearing the crimson pennant, bows strung and quivers full of barbed arrows. In addition to these weapons, which with the hunting knife and the tomahawk are considered forming the armament of a warrior, each one was supplied with either a breech loading rifle or revolver, sometimes with both— the latter obtained through the wise foresight and strong love a fair play which prevails in the Indian Department, which seeing that its wards are determined to fight, is equally determined that there shall be no advantage taken, but that the two sides shall be armed alike; proving, too, in this manner the wonderful liberality of our government which not only is able to furnish its soldiers with the latest improved style of breech loaders to defend it and themselves, but is equally able and willing to give the same pattern of arms to their common foe.

As the army saw it, the formula for chaos was clear: the Indian Bureau made treaties, after which, appointed Indian agents administered the terms of the treaties, including and especially the gifts and annuities supposedly guaranteed. The agent then skimmed the annuities and delivered less than was promised to the Indians. The Indians suffered from the shortfall, resented being cheated and lied to, had no one to complain to, and finally went on the warpath and attacked travel routes, stage stations, ranches and settlements. Whereupon, the army had to take the field against them—with limited or the wrong kind of resources and not enough well-trained men. That was virtually the unanimous feeling among the professional officers, who might otherwise agree on very little. And that has more than the ring of truth. As General George Crook said: "'A tardy and broken faith on the part of the general government' was the cause of most Indian unrest and hostility."

All tragedy seems to have an element of inevitability. When examining the settlement of the West and the role of the Indians in it, the only reasonable conclusion is that the end of the Indian nomadic culture *was* inevitable, and that the tribes ultimately, although reluctantly, agreed and ceased their wandering. It is hard to see how it could have been otherwise. But it was definitely not inevitable that the treaties they signed in either good faith—or something less than that—should be violated by politicians and bureaucrats who paid off their cronies with patronage and looked the other way, while holding out their own hands for more. There was nothing inevitable about that. It was simply criminal, legally and morally. Not for nothing were these private and public figures together known as the Indian Ring, and the Indian Ring was unquestionably a gang of crooks who were responsible for much of the unrest among the tribes—unrest that cost the lives of emigrants, soldiers, and Indians alike.

On the other hand, it's well to remember that the corruption of the Indian Bureau and the systematic cheating of the Indians were not the only causes of war with the Plains tribes. As the estimable novelist Patrick O'Brian says: "In history we must look for multiple causality." The tribes gloried in war and defined themselves in terms of combat. They acquired their wealth by raiding and killing both their tribal enemies and the newly arrived, far richer, whites. It is too easy to ascribe the violence in the settlement of the West to the evils the whites inflicted on the tribes. That is not only facile but dishonest in its dismissal of other causes. Most, if not all, of the white emigrants killed by marauding Indians were merely trying to get to the other side of the country and had no particular interest in the Plains and no interest whatsoever in the Indians. It is also too easy to romanticize the warlike tribes as freedom fighters resisting an oppressor. They were defending their land as they understood the concept, because the land was where their wandering prey animals lived. In that sense, it was a war to preserve an unpreservable nomadic culture and to continue an economic system built on a fast dwindling resource. But they were also raiding places like wretched little Julesburg, simply to steal the merchandise from the warehouse of the stage station—and for the joy and prestige of attack and victory. The warriors would not have drawn distinctions about any of it. Raiding was natural, and plunder came with it. The plunder was useful, but it was also a trophy. George Bent writes about the first attack on Julesburg: "One old warrior took a great fancy to the big sugar bowl and tied it to his belt. I saw him afterwards riding off with the big bowl dangling from his belt behind him."

Killing the enemy, whoever he might be, was righteous and honorable, and there really needed to be no more discussion about it. They would not have thought that an attack against the soldiers was striking a blow against the army of an oppressive aggressor; it was simply an attack against an enemy, little different from an enemy tribe. They would not have considered an attack against emigrants as an attack against trespassers from an alien culture; it was an opportunity to gather riches and for the glory of it. They would not have viewed an attack against the warehouses of the stage company as gathering of materiel so as to carry on the righteous fight. It was simpler than that. It was all a piece of the warrior's métier. War was often a means to an end, certainly; but it was also—and always—an end in itself.

THE SMOKY HILL

The routes to the West were initially blazed by traders and pioneer emigrants. The Santa Fe and the Old Spanish Trails brought trade traffic to and from the Southwest and Mexican territories, both before and after the Mexican War. The Oregon Trail took pioneers to the Northwest.

And then came the discovery of gold, first in California, then in territories throughout the West. Those discoveries accelerated dramatically the westward movement and created the need for additional roads west and additional modes of transportation—first the stagecoach and wagon trains of freight, and soon thereafter, the railroad.

Geography, of course, dictated the best routes west. Mountain passes were the only way through otherwise impassable barriers. Rivers provided water, albeit sometimes unreliably, but they also pointed the way through and around difficult terrain. So it was with the Smoky Hill River, which flows east and runs in a fairly straight line across Kansas. When gold was discovered in Colorado, the fastest way for Eastern prospectors to get to the diggings was by following the Smoky Hill. But there were problems with the route:

> The Smoky Hill route was considered dangerous by frontiersmen, as the western two-thirds of it were through a semiarid region where most of the streams flowed only in wet seasons and both grass and game were scarce. But in their eagerness to get to the diggings before all the claims had been staked, the more improvident, feckless and greedy among the gold rushers ignored the old timers' warnings and flocked westward along the Smoky Hill.

A lot of them didn't make it. And "because so many unprepared easterners had died of thirst and starvation" while heading for the goldfields, the Smoky Hill route was eventually abandoned for the longer but somewhat safer route in the north. The more northerly "Overland" route ran through western Nebraska. At Julesburg, Colorado, one branch headed down along the South Platte to Denver, while the other went north and west, partially through Wyoming and then down to Salt Lake City, on to Virginia City, Nevada, and finally to Sacramento, where it met riverboats to San Francisco. This was the route operated by the Overland Company, which hauled freight to the booming mining camps. The company also operated stagecoaches for passengers, express packages, and, importantly, mail. That was the line supervised in part by the gunman Jack Slade. That was also the route Mark Twain took on his way to the silver mines of Virginia City, Nevada. While safer, the route to Denver was quite a few days longer than the old Smoky Hill route.

As the mining camps grew and the merchants arrived and the camps became towns and settlements, the need for freight shipments also grew. The freight along the Overland Trail moved by ox-driven wagon trains at a pace of around twelve miles a day. So not only was it inadequate to the demand for increased volume, it was slow.

Into the breech stepped David Butterfield, a Colorado businessman who, it was said, could "charm a bird out of a tree." He decided to build and operate a freight and passenger service along the old Smoky Hill route. Oddly, Butterfield was no relation to John Butterfield, who had built and operated the southern Ox Box stage line that carried the first transcontinental mail service before the Civil War. (John Butterfield's son, Daniel, was a general in the war and distinguished himself primarily by composing the bugle call "Taps.")

The freight and stagecoach business was complicated and required significant investment. But David Butterfield was up to the challenge. He raised three million dollars from New York financiers to get his company up and running. Then he "bought twelve hundred fine Missouri mules and two hundred huge prairie schooners, assembled harness, feed, building materials and constructed bridges and relay stations." His survey of the old route (assisted by the army) located water at reliable intervals. And he solved the problem of speed by using mules to haul freight wagons instead of plodding oxen. The year was 1865, and the business naturally and quickly expanded to include stagecoaches for passengers. Butterfield bought twenty new stagecoaches, two hundred high-quality horses, and set about building stage stations along the Smoky Hill road. The Smoky Hill road became the Butterfield Overland Company line. (Since both major trails used the term *overland*, it can be confusing, so it's perhaps better to refer to Butterfield's line as the Smoky Hill.)

Mules were used to draw both freight wagons and stagecoaches, but horses were preferred for coaches. Mules were used where terrain was difficult. But no horse or mule was good for much more than fifteen or twenty miles of hard—and fast—work per day, which meant in turn that stagecoach stations had to be built where a change of animals could be stabled, fed, and otherwise cared for. And just because a stage stop must be located at a certain interval on the route did not mean that nature would conveniently provide reliable water or grazing at that spot, or even nearby. So, either wells had to be dug or water transported. Even if the road and station were immediately alongside the Smoky Hill, it was a temperamental stream. If it wasn't flooding due to sudden storms, it was drying up after weeks of drought. Captain Barnitz writes of the August weather along the Smoky Hill River route:

> Have had a hard and tiresome march today—over the hot plains—the torrid plains—prairie fires surging everywhere in the distance , and clouds of dust rising among the column—for it has only rained twice . . . and the heat has been fearful at times, and the grass looks as though it has been dried in an oven, and the streams are all dry—even the Smoky is dry—not a drop of water to be found except by digging in the dry sand of the channel, and it (the water which we obtain thus) isn't very delicious— tastes as though it had been filtered through several mud holes (which is a fact).

Stagecoach lines like the Smoky Hill used essentially two types of vehicles—the elegant-looking Concord coach (so called because it was designed and built in Concord, New Hampshire) and the homely, canvas-sided celerity wagon that was lighter and capable of traversing rougher terrain. The Concord had a unique suspension system designed to make it a little more comfortable for passengers. The body of the coach rested on straps called thoroughbraces, and the bottom of the coach was rounded on the sides and fore and aft, so that the coach had more of a rolling action than a jarring up and down motion. The celerity, or mud wagon, had no such luxuries.

A stage line also needed men at each station, all along the route—men who could maintain and repair the equipment, service the horses and coaches, and protect that section of the line against marauders—of whom there were plenty: red, white, and brown. Those same men were needed to repair the road when storms and flash floods washed away ramps in and out of arroyos, or carved new miniature canyons across the road. When the road ran through narrow canyons where rockslides could close them off, someone had to be there to clear away the debris and rubble. And in winter there were snowdrifts to contend with.

Experienced men to drive the coaches were obviously essential, and it was no mean skill to handle a team of six galloping coach horses, especially when the road was little more than a track through the prairie, and the danger from raiders was always present. Horses were generally preferred to mules because the large, well-cared-for stage horses could generally outrun the Indian ponies. Mules, though, were better in deep sand, so that different stations needed different animals depending on the terrain and the threat from raiders. Drivers had to be able to handle both, and a mule's reputation for stubborn independence and occasional laziness was well earned. Many drivers came from New York, a state that had an extensive stagecoach system. Almost all drivers were from the East, for similar reasons. (The aforementioned John Butterfield got his start as a coach driver in New York.) Guards, station keepers, and hostlers were another story. They were recruited from the small army of hard men who had drifted west. Mark Twain describes them this way:

> The station keepers, hostlers, etc. were low, rough characters . . .
> a considerable sprinkling of them might fairly be described as
> outlaws—fugitives from justice, criminals whose best security
> was a section of the country which was without law and without
> even the pretense of it. [. . .] Now and then a division agent was

really obliged to shoot a hostler through the head to teach him some simple matter that he could have taught him with a club, if circumstances and surroundings had been different.

Twain's brief acquaintance Jack Slade was notorious as a stage company department manager on the northern Overland line. He did not hesitate to hunt down and kill bandits who threatened or attacked his section of the line. There was no other law to speak of, and Slade was happy to take it into his own hands. One of his victims was Old Jules Beni, a criminal who gave his name to Julesburg, Colorado. Old Jules had originally established it as a trading post for travelers along the Oregon Trail. Jules was widely suspected to be part of a gang that attacked the wagon trains heading to Oregon, and his trading post was a useful means of evaluating which trains were worth robbing. For a while he was the manager of the Overland stage station that came to Julesburg, but Jack Slade fired him. Old Jules then ambushed Slade with a pistol and shotgun, but he didn't finish the job. Slade somehow recovered, hunted Jules down, tied him to a corral post, and cut off his ears before filling him with bullets that were carefully placed to make him last a little. It was said that Slade kept the ears and wore them now and then as a decoration on his watch chain. So the story goes. It may have been only one ear. Hard men. Slade was finally fired by the Overland Stage Company for shooting up one too many barrooms, whereupon he went north to his unhappy appointment with the vigilantes in Virginia City, Montana.

A stage line also required regular supplies of grain. Like their cousins in the cavalry, hardworking draft animals could not survive on grass alone. And the prairie grass wasn't always reliable. Not only did it dry to a crisp in the summer droughts, but the tribes often set fire to it, both to drive game animals and to frustrate army patrols. (Custer's 1874 reconnaissance in force into the Black Hills almost came to grief, because on the way home he'd run out of grain, and the Sioux had fired the grass. A number of his horses died; the column just barely made it back to base.) The need for grain and a reliable supply of hay meant the stage station not only had to have stables for the animals, quarters for the men, and accommodations for the travelers, but also barns for storage. Grain needed wagons to haul it and farmers to supply it. As usual, when there was a need, there was someone willing to fulfill it. Hence ranches and farms and towns sprouted along the travel routes. That happened pretty quickly, especially in eastern Kansas; but less so, in the west. But it did not happen overnight. For a while, those stage lines, roads, and stations were lonely outposts of civilization that depended on shipments of grain and supplies for their existence. Scattered along the routes would be the equally isolated forts of the army, also dependent on wagon supply trains. Knowing the forts were there was cold comfort for the isolated station keepers. Everyone involved knew that Indian raiders could swoop down upon a lonely stage stop and destroy it, before the army could even be alerted. Quite obviously, the army could not afford to build and maintain enough forts to protect all the stage stations, most of which were only fifteen or so miles apart. Even if some stations were connected to the forts by telegraph, Indian raiders understood how that worked. These stage stations were ideal targets for Indian raiders. On one hand, they were the deeply resented harbingers of white encroachment. On the other, they were little storehouses of wealth—horses, weapons, even some supplies. They were not well defended and offered opportunities for revenge, prestige, and plunder. And almost every one of them was entirely alone. There were only four forts all along the entire Smoky Hill route in Kansas. Fort Wallace, from which Forsyth and his fifty scouts left, was at the far western end. And it was still under construction in 1868. So if the stage companies hired some rough and dubious characters to man the stations, perhaps it was not that bad an idea.

Living conditions for the station employees were no better than at the tiny forts. Aside from the cottonwoods that grew in occasional groves along the rivers, there wasn't much timber on the Plains. And of all woods, soft cottonwood is probably the least useful for building anything. Stone was available here and there but competent stonemasons were even scarcer. Building materials could be shipped in, but as often as not, the wretched little stations were made mostly from sod. There was plenty of that.

If the living conditions for the station employees were marginal, they were little better for the passengers. If it wasn't the danger of attacks by Indians or gangs of horse thieves and highwaymen, there was the sheer discomfort of travel by stage. One traveler wrote:

> The condition of one man's running stages to make money while another seeks to ride for pleasure are not in harmony to produce comfort. Coaches will be overloaded . . . passengers will get sick, a gentlemen will gallantly hold the baby, children will cry . . . passengers will get angry, the driver will swear. The sensitive will shrink . . . and the dirt is almost unendurable . . . Stop over nights? No, you wouldn't. To sleep on a sand floor of a one story sod house or adobe hut, without a chance to wash, with miserable food, uncongenial companionship . . . won't work. A through ticket and fifteen inches of seat, with a fat man on one side, a poor widow on the other, a baby on your lap, a bandbox over your head, and three or four persons immediately in your front, leaning against your knees, makes the picture, as well as your sleeping place for the trip. [. . .] I have just finished six days and nights of this thing, and I am free to say, until I forget a great many things now very visible to me, I shall not undertake it again.

The mention of terrible food makes it impossible to pass over Mark Twain's story about a man who stopped in a remote stage station. He was offered dinner by the manager: "'There's mackerel and there's mustard to go with it,' said the manager. 'But I don't like mackerel,' said the traveler. The manager looked surprised but said, 'Well, then help yourself to the mustard.'" Twain doesn't bother explaining how fish got to the remote station; it was probably salted. If not, it had to be well past its prime and would need the mustard. But Twain wasn't about to ruin a good story with extraneous details.

THE MAIL

Passenger travel to the West was one thing. But there was also a need for regular, frequent, transcontinental mail services, all the way to California.

Because of its rapid growth and wealth, due primarily to the gold discovery, California had become a state in 1850, and San Francisco had become a major commercial center. Denver, too, was growing rapidly, for much the same reason, and Colorado was clamoring to become a state. Mining camps and communities were springing up in Montana, Idaho, and Nevada. Regardless of the differences between Westerners and Easterners about a number of thorny issues, not least the Indians, it was obvious to everyone that the two sections of the country had to be connected—not necessarily in their attitudes, but in their ability to do business; they had to be able to communicate efficiently.

The transcontinental telegraph had been completed in October 1861, and it was fine for short messages, assuming there was no damage to the wires, by weather or human agency. But there also had to be a way to transmit legal documents and reports, to say nothing of letters home from miners and settlers—letters that might contain money orders, or desperate requests for one. Banks had to communicate with their correspondent banks for the transfer of funds. Most legitimate financial transactions didn't (and don't) involve movement of cash, except in someone's pocket or in a strongbox carrying payroll. Usually, large commercial transactions require bank-to-bank money transfers on behalf of their customers; banks transfer funds by means of their accounts with each other. When a bank customer on the West Coast wants to send money to a beneficiary in New York, he instructs his West Coast bank to debit his personal (or corporate) account, whereupon his bank sends a message to its New York bank (its correspondent) which in turn debits the sending bank's account and pays out to the beneficiary. The West Coast bank keeps the sender's money in exchange for the debit of its East Coast account. And both banks charge a fee for the service. Most money, in other words, moves by information flow. (A check, after all, is simply an instruction telling the bank on which it is drawn to pay the designated beneficiary, and checks obviously move by mail.) The telegraph was useful for some of that business, but other business required physical documents, such as letters of credit, stock certificates, legal papers of all kinds, including checks, and they all needed reliable mail service. And gold and silver—which did move physically—needed express services to transport the wealth from the mines. (Hence, the birth of Wells Fargo and American Express, to name two.) Finally, the paper money that was due to the long-suffering, thirteen-dollar-a-month soldier needed to travel to the distant forts; a check would do that soldier no good, when he had no bank in the area to cash it for him.

In short, the nation and the nation's business required regular, reliable two-way mail and express service. Even before the war, the government was being pestered by Western interests to do something about it. The settlements were getting mail now and then via short-line stagecoach or ships going round the Horn, but it was intermittent and slow. The celebrated Pony Express was only a stopgap for sending small amounts of mail. A transcontinental railroad would eventually be built, but it would be a long while before it was finished. Stagecoach services would have to carry the mail until the railroad could be built. And even when a transcontinental railroad was completed, stage lines would still be needed to branch off the main lines to connect to other frontier places that were developing.

In the late 1850s the federal government decided that a transcontinental mail delivery system would be built. It would not be federally owned or managed, however, except at certain points of origination and termination. The job of carrying the mail would be contracted out to private companies.

The project was put out for bids. Five private companies presented proposals to the postmaster general. Naturally, the companies would continue to augment their income with passenger service, but the especially attractive business lay with the mail contract and subsidies. Unlike the passenger business, the revenues would be reliable and large.

The eastern terminus would be St. Louis, and the western, San Francisco. But the best way to connect those two was a matter for debate and proposal. As it turned out, each of the five bidders proposed different routes west, although four tended to concentrate on central routes. Some proposed to use existing roads in the central corridor. Others proposed to build new routes and stations. But whoever won the bid would be undertaking an enormous investment of time, money, and energy.

Unlike the other four bidders, John Butterfield proposed a southern route that would swing down from St. Louis and follow the Thirty-Fifth Parallel through New Mexico and on to Los Angeles before heading north to San Francisco. Postmaster General Aaron Brown, a Southern sympathizer from Tennessee, was well aware that a transcontinental railroad must soon be authorized by Congress, and he knew that the stagecoach mail road would serve as the forerunner and precedent for the railroad route. He also knew that a stage line with regular schedules would stimulate business and growth all along its route. Accordingly, as a Southerner, he favored John Butterfield's proposal, but only if Butterfield would agree to an even more severely southern route that would take the road to the Thirty-Second Parallel—down though Oklahoma and at angle across Texas to El Paso and across southern New Mexico and Arizona to Southern California and then up to San Francisco. Postmaster General Brown said with a straight face, and some degree of truth, that the northern routes, like the Overland Trail, were subject to brutal winter weather that often blocked the mountain passes, whereas the southern route, while longer, had much better weather and flat desert valleys that wound around the mountains but did not require going over them. It would be reliable twelve months of the year, whereas the snows on the Plains and in the Rockies could close it down for months. The southern route was ultimately called the Ox Bow, because of its severe southerly dip.

John Butterfield was also a friend of President James Buchanan, and his proposal was accepted. The Northern sympathizers howled and called the route "one of the greatest swindles ever perpetrated on the country by the slave holders." There was a caveat, however—Butterfield had to have his stage line up and running within a year—a seemingly impossible task, because unlike some of the central routes there were no existing trails to speak of on the Ox Bow route, and there were no stage stations whatsoever. Perhaps it didn't matter to Brown whether Butterfield succeeded or not, as long as the precedent for the southern route was established. Someone else might come in afterwards and finish the job. But the road would be surveyed and established and would pave the way for railroad tracks ultimately to be laid alongside.

Butterfield, against all odds, did finish the job on time, even though he was starting essentially from scratch. Within a year he had built the line with 139 stations (growing to two hundred), all built and equipped and manned, and he had regular, twice-a-week, two-way coach travel along the entire 2,700-mile route. It took twenty-five days to make the one way trip. A reporter for the *New York Herald*, who was the first passenger to cross the country on Butterfield's Overland Mail, described the achievement as "superhuman." He also described it as "roughing it with a vengeance," and suggested that gentlemen might be better off not wearing "white pants or kid gloves."

Then the Civil War erupted. The southern mail route had to be abandoned for obvious reasons, and delivery of the mail shifted to the established central Overland routes. As mentioned, the northerly Overland Trail ran from Fort Leavenworth through Nebraska and along the South Platte and then to California via Salt Lake, with a branch line down the South Platte to Denver. The main road and its major branches ran through the Plains Indians' hunting grounds, and the tribes resented the intrusion even as they welcomed the increase in targets. What's more the Sand Creek massacre in 1864 had embittered and infuriated the Cheyenne, especially. Further, the other Butterfield, David, was by 1865 operating on the Smoky Hill route, which ran straight through Kansas Plains and into Colorado. The result was an increase in violence along both central travel routes. As George Bent wrote:

> The war was now raged with great fury through all the middle Plains. Stations on the great overland routes were attacked, stock was driven off and agents killed. Isolated settlers were attacked and driven off, and detached settlements were deserted. The troops as usual were powerless, and Sherman himself said the "fifty Indians could checkmate three thousand troops." In fact, the troops could reach the Indians only when it suited the latter to risk an engagement, and this happened but seldom."

As a result of the continuing violence along the central routes and not least because of the interruption of mail service, the peace commissioners at both the Medicine Lodge meeting (1867) and the Fort Laramie conference (1868) had a primary objective—to create a safe corridor for travel and transportation in the center of the country. That corridor was already dotted with stage stations, little settlements and, increasingly, the construction crews for the railroad. But they were subject to regular and frequent attacks, and the treaties were designed to stop the raiding by concentrating the tribes to the north and the south of the central travel corridors. As mentioned, the tribes at both conferences eventually agreed to the proposals in exchange for a variety of promises, gifts, and annuities. The northern tribes agreed to stay in the Dakotas, Wyoming, and Montana, and the Southern tribes to stay in reserves that were south of the Arkansas River. If everyone lived up to the terms of the two treaties, the central travel corridor would be safe. Mail, freight, and travelers would continue to flow.

There were mixed feelings about the Medicine Lodge and Fort Laramie treaties and doubts about whether they would accomplish anything. Similar treaties had been signed with the warring tribes, and those had had the same object—to protect that central travel routes.

A series of treaties with all the warring tribes in the autumn of 1865 had restored peace. In the south the Kiowas, Comanches, Kiowa Apaches, Cheyennes and Arapahos had agreed to withdraw to the territory south of Kansas and east of New Mexico. In the north all seven tribes of the Teton Sioux . . . had agreed to leave the warpath and "withdraw from the routes overland already established or hereafter to be established through their country."

Few, if any, of the tribesmen paid any attention to those earlier treaties. Would the Medicine Lodge and the Fort Laramie treaties be any more effective? Only the peace commissioners who were there at the signing could tell you if they really believed they would. No doubt they were hopeful, because certainly the financiers who put up millions were putting pressure on their political cronies to do something about the attacks. The investors had to be outraged when they read about their company's wagons and stations being burned, livestock run off and employees killed. All of those valuable assets, men included, would have to be replaced, even as business came to a halt, literally. The nervous politicians could respond by saying they had, in fact, done something. They had gotten the chiefs to sign some papers.

The army had no illusions about those pieces of paper. It's worth remembering what Captain Barnitz said about the Medicine Lodge Treaty:

[T]hey [the Indians] have no idea that they have ever given up the country which they claim as their own, the country north of the Arkansas. The Treaty amounts to nothing, and we will certainly have another war sooner or later with the Cheyenne at least and probably with the other Indians too, in consequence of misunderstanding of the terms or the present and previous treaties.

In the summer of 1868 the Cheyenne, with George Bent and his brother alongside, were raiding the stagecoach lines in Kansas and Colorado, while the chiefs of the northern tribes, Red Cloud among them, were trying to decide whether they wanted to sign the Fort Laramie treaty. They finally did, but it didn't change much, if anything. The attacks continued. The central travel routes were just as dangerous as they were before the treaties were signed.

IRON HORSE

In 1862 Congress passed legislation establishing the Union Pacific and the Central Pacific Railroads. Both railroads were stock corporations and proposed to build the first railway across the Western frontier and thereby link the eastern states with California and the territories of the West. The railroads needed congressional approval first and foremost to gain the rights of way across federal land. It should be remembered that vast sections of the West were federal property, as a result of the Louisiana Purchase and the Mexican War. The railroads also needed—or wanted—federal money. And since a transcontinental railway was obviously in the nation's interest, the government was willing to be partners in the enterprise, not only by granting rights of way, but also by providing subsidies, loan guarantees, and grants of huge swaths of land on both sides of the right of way. The West would gradually be transformed to individual ownership, in part because the railroad had a stake in land development and in part because of the Homestead Act, also of 1862. As the railroad construction crept through the rich farming and ranching lands of the Plains, settlers would be attracted, towns would be built, much of it on land sold to the settlers by the railroad from their portfolio of land grants. Small towns would become bigger towns as the good citizens who were there first advertised the virtues of their homes and invited others to come and share the good things. Newspapers would spring up to assist in this process, which was called "booming." And it worked. It was real estate development on a national scale, but executed locally, town by town—and with the able assistance of the railroads.

With the Civil War raging, the southern Ox Bow route for the railroad was obviously out of the question. And so the Union Pacific proposed to follow pretty much the same route as the Overland stagecoach northern route. It was only reasonable, since emigrants had followed that route for years as the best way through and around natural obstacles. Of course, the engineers would have to survey the actual roadbeds, and there would be some engineering hurdles to surmount, but the general direction of the road was simple enough to decide upon. The Union Pacific would build west from Omaha, the Central Pacific east from Sacramento. They would meet somewhere in the middle. (In Utah, as it turned out.)

Though the Union Pacific more or less followed the emigrant and stagecoach trails, building the line involved some tricky engineering, and the resulting road contradicted the notion, if there was such a notion, that the road would be a simple matter of laying track through the flatlands of the Plains. For example, the Union Pacific road crossed the pass in the Laramie Mountains at an elevation of more than eight thousand feet (above sea level). And having climbed the pass, the train necessarily had to descend the other side:

West of Sherman's Summit [Wyoming] the train ran at four miles an hour crossing the 700 foot long, 126 foot high wooden Dale Creek trestle in three minutes. The bridge was like "scaffolding erected for the purpose of painting a house . . . and more than one passenger breathed more freely and gave audible expression of relief once the cars passed over in safety." Just afterward came the descent of 1000 feet in 20 miles. It would be a year before George Westinghouse's airbrake first became available, and the railroads still relied on men stationed on every other car who manually slowed the train by turning a brake wheel—the "Armstrong system," as it was wryly called. [. . .] One traveler wrote: "The axle boxes smoked with friction . . . The wheels were nearly red hot. In the darkness of the night they resembled disks of flame.

Another railroad, the Union Pacific Eastern Branch (later called the Kansas Pacific) was chartered under the Railway Act. It would start in Kansas City and more or less follow the Smoky Hill line of the stagecoach. It would terminate in Denver, and from there the Denver Pacific would connect to the Union Pacific at Cheyenne, Wyoming. From Cheyenne, the Union Pacific would go on to meet the eastbound construction of the Central Pacific at Promontory Summit, Utah. They would officially be connected in May 1869, when the golden spike was pounded in.

All in all, a stupendous project. And both lines were through the central corridors that the treaties with the tribes were designed to protect.

FINANCING A RAILROAD

The deal offered the Union Pacific is the most famous and representative of the arrangements Congress and the railroad companies made with each other. The government agreed to pay the Union Pacific for the cost of construction. Payment would be made as construction proceeded and according to a degree of construction difficulty. The railroad would receive $16,000 for each mile of track laid over level terrain, $32,000 for each mile in the foothills, and $48,000 for each mile laid through the mountains. These achievements were to be certified by an inspector before payment was issued. The federal government issued thirty-year bonds at 6 percent to finance the project. Additionally, the company would be granted not only the necessary rights of way through federal land, but also huge plots of land on both sides of the tracks. Titles to adjacent land would pass after certification of a completed section of track. As mentioned, the company could sell this land to settlers, or it could use the land as security to issue mortgage-backed bonds to institutional and individual investors, alike. (It may be remembered that during the Civil War, individual investors developed a taste for buying small denomination government bonds; before, institutional investors were the only investors in government debt. Now, railroad bonds also seemed a safe bet.) If the land happened to hold valuable deposits of minerals, so much the better. The railroad could develop those resources or sell the property at a premium to mining companies and investors. The railroad could also sell stock to raise additional capital.

This multifaceted arrangement suited all the interested parties. The government would get the vital communication with the Western states and territories; the mail would go through quickly and regularly. Express shipments from the gold fields would be fast and more secure. Products could be shipped in both directions—Western ranchers and farmers could get their goods to markets safely, cheaply, and quickly, while Eastern manufacturers could send the materials and machinery and manufactured goods to the West, as it developed. Beef one way, shoes the other. Also, Western settlement would gradually populate the frontier and solve the Indian problem. The deal with the government was equally beneficial to the railroads. They could sell land they did not pay for, and therefore, in theory, partially self-finance the construction of the railroad. They could lay down a mile of track, receive a payment, sell some adjacent real estate and then use the money to go on to the next section. Though it has some earmarks of a Ponzi scheme, there was no risk to the railroads, because the investor in this case was the federal government. The money would continue to flow as work was completed. (Indian attacks were therefore not only dangerous to the construction crews but also hazardous to cash flow.)

As part of their real estate development business, the railroad sent agents to Europe to promote the idea of coming to America to get cheap land in the rich farming country of the Plains. The reliable and competent peasants of northern and central Europe were especially desirable. (The woman rescued from Tall Bull's camp came from a settlement of immigrant Swedes; she spoke no English. And readers of Willa Cather's estimable stories will recognize some of the descendants of these immigrants to the Plains.) If the idea of personally farming or ranching did not appeal, more prosperous investors could buy land cheaply from the railroad and then speculate in real estate, reselling at a higher price or subdividing and developing the land. Or they could develop the mineral resources—dig the mines and build the mining towns to house the workers. There was a lot to fire the imagination of an entrepreneur.

The Homestead Act of 1862 supported the settlement, too. The federal government retained sections of land interspersed with the grants to the railroads and offered these (as well as other sections of federal land) to anyone who could settle on them and last it out for five years. Even the poorest sharecropper in the east might realize the dream of having his own section of land (160 acres), as long as he could survive Indian attacks, drought, brutal winters, grasshopper swarms, crop failures, disease, backbreaking work, loneliness, and bad luck. If he and his family could do that for five years, they would own the property, sod house and all. Viewed objectively, it was no easy bargain, and the homesteaders who survived earned their land, and then some. But it was a pretty fair deal for all concerned, because the homesteaders didn't need money to acquire their land—just energy and courage.

The arrangement between the government and the railroad, however, was not such a fair deal, though it seemed to be on paper. The structure of the deal was tailor-made for corruption. And the insiders were quick to notice. (In fact, they knew in advance and negotiated the deal accordingly.) The deal paid the railroad for each mile of *track laid*. That was a built-in incentive to take the long way around and perhaps add a few ox bow curves where a straight line would suffice. The temptation would be hard for some to resist. And if you got paid twice as much money per mile for laying track in the foothills as opposed to a flat plain, decisions about roadbeds might be unduly influenced. And after all, what constitutes a foothill? Payment would be made only after a mile of track was certified by an independent inspector. But more often than not the inspector was concerned primarily that the track was simply there. Whether it was well laid or not was another question and often not the inspector's concern. As an example on the Northern Pacific Railroad, which crossed Minnesota under similar terms of government financing, a bridge that had been certified as completed so that payment was made, collapsed. "Contractors were paid by the completed mile, so they took short cuts in both piling and fill—using inadequate piling and filling with wood and brush." And of course it was easy enough to bribe inspectors to certify whatever the railroad needed to certify in order to receive Federal cash. If the brother of a contractor specialized in building bridges, the contractor might be tempted to suggest going straight across the pond or lake instead of going around it. There was little if any government oversight. The government could hire independent inspectors, but who would inspect the inspectors. As the poet Juvenal said: "Who will guard the guards themselves?"

The railroads were being built through the frontier wilderness, much of it, and few if any congressmen wanted to undertake the journey to inspect the railroad's progress. And if one or two did want to go, they would be escorted around by railroad executives and shown what everyone wanted them to see. It's not at all surprising that the government took a fleecing; indeed, prominent members assisting in the shearing. The government did not carefully oversee the management of its bureaucracy; it did not oversee the Indian Bureau's distribution of annuities, and it did not oversee the details of railroad construction. What's more, many in the government did not want to know, because they were receiving bribes from the railroads in general, and the Union Pacific in particular.

There was another problem, too—the federal government had grown to enormous and unmanageable proportions:

> By the end of the Civil War more than fifty thousand citizens were employed in the federal bureaucracy. [. . .] Criteria for employment and promotion were usually unstated, but competence and training beyond a minimum were not usually prerequisites for continued tenure. Rather, federal appointments were used to reward political supporters and contributors small and large.

Some of those people were in the Indian Bureau. Others were working for the congressmen. But with all that manpower, no one seemed to be watching the railroads, although it is interesting that the government could find enough money to pay for fifty thousand bureaucrats, but kept the regular army at less than half that number—and complained about that—to the point that Sheridan and others had to hire civilians to do some of the work and had to find the money by fiddling the books. And it's doubtful that any of the federal bureaucrats worked for thirteen dollars a month—the salary of a private in the army.

Speaking of fiddling the books, it was obvious to all involved that the Union Pacific Railroad would need to be finished and fully operational before it could begin to generate enough freight and passenger business to become profitable. Merely running buffalo hides and local produce back and forth along freshly laid track would not be enough. Investors would have to wait years before they saw any return, either in terms of dividend from profit or appreciation of their stock based on anything more than speculation. That included not only the smaller investors in railway bonds and stocks, but more importantly the insiders who owned the majority of the Union Pacific—and their clients in government. (Of course, stock speculators could and did manage make money from market fluctuations, but the gains, or losses, in a railroad's stock price had nothing to do with the profitability of the company, because the unfinished railroad was not profitable and would not be until it was completed—if then.)

There was a way around this problem, though—a way to accelerate the flow of cash to the railroad owners and interested parties. A railroad under construction at best broke even mile by mile by balancing the costs of construction against the government payment. The construction companies hired by the railroad to do the actual work got paid by the mile, too, and therefore earned money in the here and now. And because their profit margin was built into their bids for the work, construction companies could become immediately profitable for their investors. And if the shares of *that* company traded on the public markets, profitability meant higher share prices—in addition to stock dividends, which in turn meant even higher share prices.

The obvious way to accelerate return on investment to the railroad insiders, therefore, was to get involved in the construction business. Hence the Union Pacific insiders created the Crédit Mobilier—a shell construction company that was apparently completely independent of the Union Pacific, but in fact was owned by the Union Pacific insiders. Crédit Mobilier submitted bids for construction to the Union Pacific, which then awarded them the contracts. Crédit Mobilier, which was really nothing but a few people in an office shuffling paper, subcontracted the actual work to small construction companies. Crédit Mobilier would also buy and sell construction materials, so that the subcontractor used Crédit Mobilier rails and ties and whatever else was required. The subcontractor would do the work and get paid after the mile was certified. When the mile of track was finished and certified, Crédit Mobilier submitted an invoice to the Union Pacific for the completed work and the materials, but at a grossly inflated cost. In other words, the Union Pacific received a bill, not from the subcontractors, but from Crédit Mobilier alone, and there was no accompanying breakdown of the subcontractor's costs or invoices.

> The Union Pacific in turn submitted the invoices to the federal government which had agreed to finance the railroad's construction to the tune of roughly $50 million . . . in addition to granting the Union Pacific twenty million acres of land on which to build the line and to sell as real estate. The actual costs incurred in construction were in the neighborhood of $30 million.

These figures are very general and the actual numbers are a little murky, for understandable reasons. Some estimates have the numbers almost double.

The $20 million profit from inflated invoices (or however much it was) not only lined the Union Pacific insiders' capacious pockets but also filled a very large trough from which elected politicians and bureaucrats alike could feed.

Although the mechanics of the fraud were a little more complicated, in concept it was the simplest sort of scheme and would have been spotted immediately, if anyone was paying attention. But no one was. Or, more accurately, no one wanted to. The directors of the Union Pacific, who in fact owned Crédit Mobilier, in turn gave stock in the company—Crédit Mobilier—to influential politicians. The stock was publicly traded, the shares were given gratis to the politicians or sold to them at par, and since the shares on the market at one point reached four times their par value, they could be sold immediately at an enormous profit. If a politician who bought them at a discount felt a little queasy about the ethics of the deal, he could hold them to sell later and have what's now known as "plausible deniability" in achieving a capital gain.

> One of the principals (of Crédit Mobilier), both a director of the company and a Member of the House of Representatives,

was Oakes Ames of Massachusetts, who thinking to forestall adverse action by Congress when it discovered what was going on, passed out shares of Crédit Mobilier stock to members of both the House and Senate [....] In extenuation Ames argued that giving shares to Congressmen was 'the same thing as going into a business community and interesting the leading men by giving them shares [. . .]A Member of Congress has the right to own property in anything he chooses to invest in. [. . .] There is no difficulty in inducing men to look after their own property.

And the executive branch was not immune. In 1868 "Ulysses S. Grant's first vice president was Schuyler Colfax; Colfax had taken Crédit Mobilier bribes and was disgraced and replaced in the 1872 election by Henry Wilson of Massachusetts. Wilson was subsequently accused of taking similar Crédit Mobilier bribes."

As Mark Twain said, "To be sure, you can buy now and then a Senator or a Representative, but they do not know it is wrong, and so they are not ashamed of it." Well, maybe they had some idea it might be wrong, but they could live with it.

Also living comfortably with questionable practice were the newspapers. The railroads had well-conceived public relations campaigns that involved advertisements in the major newspapers. The ads extolled the virtues of the railroad in general, its successes in moving forward across the frontier, the rich nature of the land that was being opened up and available for purchase at a very reasonable cost. These glowing advertisements also helped to prop up the stock and bond prices and attract and reassure new investors. And since newspapers lived on advertising, they were expected to find positive stories about the railroad and the opportunities in the west. And they were able to find those stories, and they published them.

The Crédit Mobilier scheme was finally uncovered in 1872 and created a great scandal among people who expressed their shock at what was going on. But by then the transatlantic railroad system had been finished, and one of the owners of the east-building Central Pacific, Leland Stanford, had pounded in the golden spike. A few years later he and his wife, Jane, would found a university "to promote the public welfare by exercising an influence in behalf of humanity and civilization."

Assigning the army to protect the security of the construction crews and surveyors was another form of government subsidy. The senior officers of the army were unhappy and frustrated about their man-power levels, but they were generally in agreement with this particular assignment. It was a top priority—a strategic necessity.

"To [the Union Pacific and Kansas Pacific] and to others to come, Sherman looked for the ultimate solution to the Indian problem, and he regarded no mission more urgent than affording protection to the construction workers." It's worth reiterating the line he wrote to Grant in 1866: "It is our duty and it shall be my study, to make the progress of construction of the great Pacific railways . . . as safe as possible."

It is more than fair to say that the railroads could not have been constructed anywhere close to schedule or with anything close to an acceptable expense without the protection of the army. At the very least, construction would have been slowed to a crawl by Indian attacks, workers would have been hard to recruit and many more civilian workers would have been killed. The development of the Western towns along the railroad routes—one of the desired objectives of the government and the railroads—would have been slowed con-siderably. Even with the efforts of the army, Indian attacks on survey and construction crews and on finished roadways and related instal-lations were galling. But without the army's constant patrolling from its handful of Western outposts, the damage would have been even more severe. On the other hand, the use of the army to protect the railroad project meant that those troops could not be used elsewhere, and that aroused the ire of Western ranchers and miners and emigrant trains and stagecoach lines and all those westerners not associated with the railroads who were being attacked while the army was otherwise employed. Their losses were an opportunity cost to the government measured in property and blood—and political turbulence. Moreover, it meant that outraged civilians would turn to volunteer units during times of emergencies.

There was no choice, though. The railroad was not only the key to settlement, it was also the corresponding key to the problem of the recalcitrant nomads. Most people agreed about that—the tribes, not least of all. Custer once suggested running a railroad line from the Canadian border to the Mexican border. Since there was little if any reason to do that aside from its effect on the tribes, his idea only emphasizes the seriousness of the railroad's threat to the Indians of the Plains, especially. If Sherman didn't agree with Custer's north-south idea, he certainly agreed with the strategic necessity and impact of the railroads. Sherman's experience in the Civil War taught him the value of the railroad as a means to moving huge armies and supplies quickly. In the West, where the army was anything but huge, the railroad meant moving small resources quickly to the scene of trouble, or at least close to it. It also meant faster shipment of supplies to the isolated forts that had been depending on slow wagon trains for their food, ammunition, and medical supplies—and for recruits to replace the troops who had deserted or died.

Some may wonder why the railroad would have such a drastic effect on the buffalo and therefore on the nomadic culture. After all, couldn't the buffalo and Indian ponies merely step over the tracks and go on their way? But of course it wasn't the tracks; it was the settlements that came along with them. Settlements were the poison pill of the nomad and the buffalo. And there was also the infamous and disastrous impact of the professional hunters who killed huge numbers of buffalo and shipped the hides to market, by train. It seems unlikely that raw hides could have been shipped by plodding wagon trains, and certainly not in the quantity that the railroad cars could carry. (William F. Cody—Buffalo Bill—and more than a few others also had jobs shooting buffalo to feed the railroad construction crews; at least they were using the meat.)

The surveying crews and the construction crews and their wretched little way stations were under constant danger from attack. The trains, too, were targets. Naturally, as the construction crews worked their way west, the locomotives and freight cars ran back and forth the full length of track to keep the workers at the farthest end supplied with construction materials, food, and other supplies. One of the more spectacular attacks against the Union Pacific train involved George Bent's band, as he traveled with the Cheyenne chief Turkey Leg:

Turkey Leg's band struck the Platte near Plum Creek and along about four miles from the railroad station, a party under the direction of Spotted Wolf took out a culvert and ditched a west bound freight train. The train came along in the night and when it went off the track the Cheyennes killed as many of the train crew as they could find. Then they broke open the box cars and began plundering. When daylight came the goods were strewn over the ground—bolts of silk and calico, sacks of flour, sugar, coffee etc., boxes of shoes, barrels of whiskey, and all kinds of stuff. The Indians broke in the head of a whisky barrel and many of the warriors got very drunk. Taking hold of the end of a bolt of calico or silk, a young man would mount his pony and gallop wildly across the prairie. [. . .] Some took hot coals from the engine and scattered them in the empty boxcars, setting the train into a blaze. After packing as much of the goods as they could on their ponies, the Cheyennes moved on south toward the Republican [River].

The Kansas Pacific (Union Pacific—Eastern Division) had fewer dramatic engineering feats to accomplish as it crept across the Kansas Plains. And by the summer of 1868 the Kansas Pacific had reached within thirteen miles of Fort Wallace, Kansas—the westernmost post in Kansas and only a few miles from the Colorado border. In eastern and central Kansas the towns and settlements along the Kansas Pacific grew up quickly, but there were also isolated stations along the route that were there merely for water and maintenance. And western Kansas was still open and dangerous country. Captain Barnitz, whose troops were patrolling the western sections, describes one such outpost about fifteen miles from Fort Hays, Kansas:

> About one mile west of us, on the railroad . . . is a RR water station and wood pile, with a cheap and altogether desolate looking frame house; a small low structure of poles, covered with shelter tents and a kind of dugout in the bank, the sides of which are carried up about four or five feet, above the level of the ground, with sods, and the whole is roofed with shingles or boards; this primitive establishment is occupied as a lodging house by the men employed about the station, about twenty in all, when they chance to be here. At present they are all absent on some labor up the road, except the man who attends to pumping the water at the tank (with horse power), a man who attends to sawing the wood, with horse power—one horse in an inclined box treadmill—a small red headed boy, with a very freckled face, short hair and no hat who says that his brother is 19 years old and is a brakeman on the cars, a slatternly woman with unkempt hair who puts her head through a broken pane of glass in a window of the desolate frame building and inquires with some trepidation what is the latest news about the "Injuns."

Being undermanned meant that in some cases the army had to hire Indian and white mercenaries to fill in the gaps in manpower. Frank and Luther North were two seasoned frontiersmen who organized and commanded the Pawnee Battalion that was assigned to guard construction crews.

[A]ll summer long(1867) the Pawnee Battalion continued to do duty along the Union Pacific road for a distance of three hundred miles—from Plum Creek to the Laramie Plains. They had many skirmishes with the hostile Indians and frequently followed them on long rides after stolen horses and mules, which they usually recovered.

Ultimately the North brothers' command grew to four companies of fifty Pawnee men. Each company was commanded by white officers, also civilians, but given army titles and pay. As inveterate and fierce enemies of the Sioux and Cheyenne, the Pawnee were glad to take the pay to do what they wanted to do anyway and only at the sacrifice of submitting to a little discipline. Their respect for the North brothers as frontiersmen and equally fierce and successful fighters was enough to ensure discipline was not a problem.

And so when General Sheridan turned to Major Forsyth and offered him the job of raising and commanding a group of fifty frontiersmen—mercenaries—he had good reasons and precedent for doing it.

LAMB FOR LUNCH

Someone once said that democracy was four wolves and a lamb voting on what to have for lunch. (Ambrose Bierce is usually given the credit.) That may be a little harsh when it comes to the overall political system, but it's not far off when applied to the financing of the Union Pacific and others that came with it. The lamb in this case was the public. But despite the miasma of political corruption surrounding the railroads, it's good to remember that the transcontinental railway *was* built, that vast distances *were* traversed and almost impassable mountain ranges *were* passed, and the West and East *were* connected, as in fact they had to be. It was an achievement worth celebrating. The Union Pacific covered 1,085 miles across the Plains, over rivers and through the mountain passes of the Rockies. The Central Pacific covered 690 miles and passed over the Sierras. The Union Pacific was built mostly by Irish labor. It was guarded by an army officered by professional Civil War veterans and manned by soldiers, many of whom were recent immigrants, along with several cavalry companies of former slaves, a few hundred Indian scouts, and some civilian frontiersmen. The Central Pacific had fewer problems with the Indians and was built mostly by imported Chinese workers. Taken all together, building the transcontinental railroad system was a polyglot effort achieved under difficult and dangerous conditions, both manmade and natural. And while it's impossible to ignore the criminal malfeasance of a few elected officials and a few insider robber barons, their antics should not obscure the work and achievements of the thousands of workers, soldiers, frontiersmen, and friendly tribesmen who made the railroads a reality.

DESTINY

When thinking about the railroads in particular and the settlement of the West in general, it's hard to escape the thought that so much of what happened was inevitable, ineluctable. The western tribes had to relinquish their nomadic ways in the face of unstoppable white migration; there was no choice. That way of life could no longer be feasible. What was the alternative? Leaving the Plains and the western mountains empty for the tribes to hunt in and wander over? Leaving the two sections of the country unconnected and barely able to communicate? Some would say that the federal government's homesteading program and financing of the railroads accelerated and perhaps even caused the western migration, all in the name of a carefully designed policy called manifest destiny. But the government was only recognizing and reacting to a fait accompli. The discovery of gold and silver (and the need for it) was largely responsible for starting the process and no one, including the government or the hostile tribes, was going to stop free people from going to look for El Dorado. And along with the prospectors, or close on their heels, came everything else. Add to the miners the legions of land-hungry and impoverished immigrants and emigrants, and you had a wave that no one could withstand, and few wanted to try. Or even thought it was right to try.

But while so much of Western history seems to have been inevitable, it also seems obvious that it did not have to happen exactly the way it did. The devilment was in the details. The railroads are nicely symbolic of that. The transcontinental railway would most certainly have been built, but the public did not have to be cheated out of millions by their political representatives and by robber baron cronies—a mere handful of crooks. The railroad could have been built honestly, and investors and entrepreneurs could still have become wealthy in return for their vision and their work and the risks they took. They could have had something other than lamb for lunch and still have been well fed.

Similarly, the tribal chiefs and the white officials who signed the treaties might have observed them more scrupulously, instead of using them as stopgaps or fig leaves that allowed continued plundering, by white bureaucrats and ungoverned warriors, alike. A great deal of bloodshed and strife could have been avoided. Granted, the chiefs were correct when they shrugged and said they could not control their young men, but a great many of them, like Satanta or Tall Bull, didn't really want to, and didn't try. The charismatic Cheyenne, Roman Nose, who was not a chief, wanted nothing to do with treaties and was more than content to be a war leader whose reputation attracted other warriors to him. Fighting was the warrior's métier and his raison d'être—literally, his reason for being. For the nomadic horse warrior "violence [was] a way of life, an expression of joy and belief, unlinked to any strategic or tactical necessity." And while it's true that many of the chiefs did not understand all the legalese and terminology of the treaties, many didn't really care and simply signed to get access to the gifts, often including guns and ammunition that came with acceptance, or to acquire rations to sustain them during the lean months of winter. Others signed to forestall attacks from the army and to give themselves time to regroup militarily or at the very least lose themselves in the vastness of the Plains. To characterize them as simpleminded dupes without self-interested agendas is patronizing in the extreme—so, too, to think of them as so many noble, but naive, Hiawathas. They were as capable of cynicism and duplicity as the most seasoned politician. Their preferred tactic in war was decoying the enemy into ambush, i.e., deception. (Even Roman Nose's bravado—"I am going to empty their guns"—was a tactical variation on the decoy theme.) Their object always was victory and obliteration of the enemy. Aside from the occasional woman or child, they took no prisoners. Although George Bent said the Cheyenne did not torture (and that is open to question), other tribes certainly did, and they routinely mutilated the corpses of their enemies, red or white or black. They were a hard, cruel, and resourceful adversary. When they spoke of "their land," most often they were referring to territory they took from other tribes. Their way of life depended on hunting and fighting, with some trading mixed in. It's worth remembering that the Plains tribes had been dealing with wandering Mexican, French, and English traders for more than a century. They understood bargaining and negotiation. The universal sign language of the Plains was primarily a means of negotiation and business. They were horse traders in every sense of the word. They also thought nothing about theft (though generally not from their own people). If a thing appealed to them, they would take it, and if acquiring it meant killing the former owner, well, so much the better, for that's what warriors did. And there was honor in doing so. They did not navigate the Plains by using maps and lived their lives in a borderless and apparently endless territory, so while they might agree to map coordinates that specified reservation boundaries, they did not necessarily believe in those imaginary lines or intend to respect them. It's also worth remembering that many, if not most of the Plains warriors, considered themselves superior to the white men from Washington, those fat men who smelled of cigars and wore unsightly hair on their faces. In fact, they felt superior to white men of any kind. And at the time of the Medicine Lodge conference, the tribes represented there had not been defeated militarily; if they had been, the conferences would have had a very different tone. And despite what many western settlers believed, the Indians were human and had the same capacity for racial hatred as any other group of people. After all, the Cheyenne called themselves Tsistsistas—"people." Even more fundamentally, they had the capacity to hate and fear *the Other*. And if the Indians, with their Asiatic features, dark skins, and strange clothing, were *the Other* to the whites, the Whites were equally *the Other* to the tribesmen. To think otherwise is not only tendentious and paternalistic, it is historically inaccurate.

Finally, there was no unanimity among the chiefs, even chiefs from the same tribes. For every Cheyenne Black Kettle, there was a Tall Bull, a chief of the fierce and recalcitrant Dog Soldiers. And while both signed the Medicine Lodge Treaty, only one perhaps intended to abide by it. Despite what the white negotiators wanted to believe, no one person ultimately spoke for anyone other than himself. And he could—and would—change his mind, if the circumstances changed.

In sum, it's foolish to think that when the chiefs entered into treaty negotiations, they abandoned their way of thinking and became compliant marks for the smooth con men in top hats. "In all my life, I ain't learned but one thing about an Indian. Whatever you know you'd do in his place—he ain't going to do that." That's a line taken from a very good novel *(The Searchers)*, and it encapsulates the hard-earned wisdom of the plainsman, wisdom that the negotiators in frock coats did not have and apparently did not think necessary to acquire. It makes you wonder just who was really smiling to themselves, when the conferences broke up.

For their part, the bureaucrats and agents could have faithfully executed their treaty responsibilities, but many chose instead to plunder both the tribes and the Treasury. There were Indians who were willing to try the reservation idea, and as long as they received the promised annuities; they were at least resigned to a future of settlement in place. After all, the celebrated Red Cloud and Spotted Tail lived up to their promises and retired to their reservations. But even these became either dispirited or infuriated when the promises were broken and the annuities did not arrive, or arrived in the form of bony beef cattle and shoddy blankets. And some of those who were infuriated or simply high-spirited spent the summer months raiding and wandering, but then returned to the agencies to spend the winter in the comparative safety, if not comfort, of the reservation. They were gaming the system, too.

The politicians in Washington could have spent money to recruit, train, and equip an army of sufficient size to do the job it was given, but instead they spent money on an army of bureaucrats and cronies, so that the regular army turned to hired civilians, like Forsyth's fifty scouts, while the settlers took matters into their own hands. Hence, the Third Colorado.

For its part, the regular army could have paid more attention to their recruiting practices, instead of relying on paupers and starvelings just off the boat from Europe, or down at the heel hard men who had wandered west and were just looking for a few square meals before deserting for greener pastures or gold mining camps. And the army could have done a better job of training the men they did get, instead of just outfitting them in heavy woolen uniforms, giving them a rifle, teaching them to march and calling them soldiers. True, the army was undermanned and underfunded, and a few of the professional officers and dedicated non-coms held things together against pretty long odds. But in general the army did a poor job of training and an equally poor job of looking after the men they did have. Desertion rates of more than one third and the large number of deaths from disease are indictments of the system and senior management, not just the poor quality recruiting.

Taken all together, one thing seems clear—the Plains tribes, like the Cheyenne, the army (both regular and volunteer), and the civilians (both West and East)—all had a significant responsibility for the way the west was settled. Few, if any, of the people involved had completely clean hands. And like the passengers on the stagecoaches going west, none of them wore kid gloves. Thinking of that period in the nation's history we'd do well to remember Samuel Johnson—"We are to consider mankind not as we would wish him, but as we find him . . ." The rest of that line reads: "frequently corrupt and always fallible."

When the young Mark Twain was learning the steamboat trade, he apprenticed under an august pilot who peppered him with questions as they navigated the ever-changing Mississippi River. In one instance, the pilot posed a particularly difficult problem, and Twain said, "I was gratified to be able to answer promptly, and I did. I said I didn't know." Similarly, if the details of the inevitable settlement of the west had been different, perhaps more equitable or at least more honest, would the fight at Beecher Island have happened, anyway? The answer to that question comes promptly, too. Maybe. Maybe not. But since all those historical forces were represented at the tiny island in the Arikaree River, does the fight there deserve to be more than a footnote in the history books? Does it become meaningful? Something like a metaphor or an allegory?

II

THE FIGHT AT BEECHER ISLAND

—⁓—

Show me a hero and
I will write you a tragedy.

—F. SCOTT FITZGERALD

4

FROM FORT WALLACE
TO BEECHER ISLAND

In the summer of 1868 Fort Wallace was still in the process of being built. Sandy Forsyth's second-in-command, Lieutenant Fred Beecher, had supervised much of the early construction when he was assigned to the post as acting assistant quartermaster. Beecher worked with the post's first commander, Captain Myles Keogh of the Seventh Cavalry. A favorite of Custer and a stereotypical Irish rogue with an eye for the ladies and a taste for alcohol, Keogh was a soldier of fortune who had served in the Papal Guards before coming to America and fighting in the Civil War. He would die along with Custer at the Little Bighorn, and his horse, Comanche, would be the only living creature left on that hillside.

There would be no walls around Fort Wallace; as usual, it resembled a little village arranged around a square. Most frontier forts were not too concerned about Indian attack. But Fort Wallace should have been, because three hundred Cheyenne attacked in the summer of 1867, and the fort and its seventy or so troopers barely escaped being overrun.

Cheyenne warriors charged through the parade ground, and the fight lasted several hours. Both Captain Albert Barnitz of the Seventh Cavalry and Fred Beecher were part of the force that fought off the attack. It was as the Duke of Wellington said of a slightly larger battle, a "very near run thing." When the Cheyenne withdrew, Barnitz and the others dug rifle pits around the perimeter and waited for another charge. Fortunately for the soldiers, the Cheyenne were satisfied with their work for that day and departed. In the fight, Barnitz's company had six men killed and four wounded. His sergeant, Frederick Wyl-lyams, was killed, stripped, and grotesquely mutilated. A photo taken at the time leaves no doubt about the extent of his injuries, although it's not clear whether his head is still attached.

Barnitz wrote to his wife, Jennie, about the attack he, Beecher, and the others fought off. Jennie must have been made of pretty stern stuff, because Barnitz was not shy about writing to her about the action in detail. And he signed off his long letter with: "By the way, Major Cooper (7th Cav.) shot himself—purposefully—through the head—committed suicide a week or two ago! Reason, 'he had got out of whiskey.'" Cooper was not at Fort Wallace at the time, and Barnitz reports that the few officers who were there and not on patrol or scout were "very good, worthy men and not a drinking set." The part about drinking was not quite true, but otherwise the officers there seemed a reliable bunch. Barnitz also reported that during the Cheyenne attack, the famous Roman Nose was killed. But Barnitz was wrong about that.

Other elements of the Seventh Cavalry were also in the vicinity of Fort Wallace during that summer of 1867. Custer was leading patrols to the north and west. A ten-man patrol led by a Lieutenant Lyman Kidder went looking for Custer with orders to return to the Smoky Hill travel routes, but Kidder was never heard from again. The stripped and mutilated bodies of the entire patrol were later discovered, although the individuals could not be identified. (It was shortly thereafter that Custer left Fort Wallace for his famous and ill-considered ride across Kansas. He said he wanted to get fresh orders and more supplies for

Fort Wallace, but in reality he wanted to see his wife, Libbie. For this inexcusable rashness he was quite properly court-martialed and suspended from duty for a year.)

A picture taken the same day as the Cheyenne attack shows Beecher along with Barnitz and three other officers. Beecher is standing and holding what appears to be a Henry repeating rifle—a sixteen-shot, .44 caliber weapon. Beecher was a good shot. He was also a very good officer. As mentioned, Forsyth described him as: "Energetic, active, reliable, brave and modest, with a love of hunting and a natural taste for plainscraft; he was a splendid specimen of a thoroughbred American, and a most valuable man in any position requiring coolness, courage and tact."

Beecher came from a distinguished family. His aunt, Harriet Beecher Stowe, was of course the "little woman who wrote the book that made this great war," as Lincoln [allegedly] said when he met her. And Fred's uncle, Henry Ward Beecher, was once described as the most famous man in America, because of his popular sermons and even more popular style of delivery. Henry, who baptized Fred, also apparently enjoyed the company of women and was later involved in a well-publicized adultery suit brought by the husband of one of Henry's apparent conquests. It didn't seem to dim his popularity, however, or tarnish his reputation all that much. Wags would say that Henry preached a doctrine of Christian love and that he practiced what he preached. Fred's father was also a minister, but none of the family's calling to the pulpit seems to have rubbed off on Fred, although he was undoubtedly an upright and "thoroughbred American."

Fred went to prep school Phillips Academy, Andover, Massachusetts, an American Eton, and from there to Bowdoin College, the alma mater of the more celebrated Joshua Lawrence Chamberlain, of the Twentieth Maine. Chamberlain was a professor of rhetoric at Bowdoin when Beecher was there. During one vacation from Bowdoin, Fred spent two months hunting and fishing in the Lake Umbagog district. The remote lake sits astride the border between northwestern Maine and

New Hampshire and is still relatively unspoiled country. Fred spent his days fishing for the gorgeously colored brook trout and hunting both waterfowl and big game, like moose and deer, and at the end of the two months he emerged from the woods smiling, refreshed in spirit and heavily bearded, having spent the time much like Hemingway's Nick Adams—in a virtual Eden and far from the rumors of war.

Fred did not seem to have the kind of abolitionist fervor you'd expect from someone from his family. But certainly he disapproved of the peculiar institution, and his service in the Civil War supports that. He volunteered in his final year at Bowdoin, joined the Sixteenth Maine Infantry Regiment, fought and was badly wounded in the leg at Fredericksburg. While recuperating he received his Second Lieutenant's commission. He returned to his unit on crutches in time to fight at Chancellorsville and then at Gettysburg. There, the Sixteenth Maine was heavily involved in the first day's action. As the Union line was being pressed hard by the Confederates and was retreating, the Sixteenth was ordered to hold a position on the Second Division's extreme right "at any cost," so that the rest of the division could get away and fall back on the town. The colonel of the Sixteenth protested that it would mean sacrificing the entire regiment, but he was overruled and ordered to stay. They did and "fought like hell as long as [they] could." In the end only eighty-four of the three hundred men managed to escape. Another report says that only thirty-five men avoided the casualty list. Beecher was not one of them. He was severely wounded again, this time by shell fragments that shattered his right knee.

There are some warriors like Roman Nose who can apparently ride through a battlefield unscathed even though shrapnel and bullets are flying thick as hail. There are others who are just the opposite, like Fred Beecher. His father said of him: "It almost seems like fate—bullets seemed to find him wherever he fought."

The wound in his knee did not heal properly and caused him pain and made him limp for the rest of his life. He was forced to resign from the army, while he recuperated. Part of that recuperation involved a stay at the home of the president of Pennsylvania College (now Gettysburg College), and it seems that one of his nurses was a young woman called Miss Dix. Miss Dix made a big impression on the wounded soldier, and again like a Hemingway hero, he apparently was smitten, although not much is known of the affair except his very occasional references to her in his letters home. He refers to her as "Miss Dix, of blessed memory." It would be entirely too much to expect that the two fell in love, conceived a child while he recuperated from a shattered knee, only to have her die in childbirth—far too much coincidental Hemingway. But something happened, and his letters suggest that he was melancholy about it from that point on, because she disappeared from his life, one way or the other. But she stayed in his memory. (Of course, it is possible that Miss Dix was an elderly spinster who nursed Fred tenderly and reminded him of his mother. But that's not as good a story.)

After the war Beecher worked for a time for the Freedmen's Bureau—an agency organized by the Christian general O. O. Howard and designed to help former slaves make the transition to freedom. Apparently the work was not all that interesting, or maybe he was restless, or missed the army, but for whatever reason he decided to rejoin. It's possible that because of his experience, he was only comfortable in the company of men who had been in the war and had seen what it was like. No one else could possibly understand. In any event, Fred applied for and was granted a second lieutenant's commission in the regular army, and in 1866 he was assigned to the Third Infantry. Initially stationed at Fort Riley, Kansas, he was soon ordered west to Fort Wallace, where he was to supervise the construction of the fort.

If Fred was occasionally melancholy (and his letters home convey that), it's not unusual. Western Kansas was a long way from New England, and Fred was homesick, now and then. But it was more than that. Army life on the Plains was conducive to dark moods. Although Beecher was an outdoorsman and was intellectually curious and was stimulated by the unique nature of the Plains, he was also unsettled by the very differentness of the country. It was a land with no history. The native people who lived there only came to one place now and then and left no marks or monuments, when they moved on. There was no sign anywhere that people ever existed here. Beecher was an easterner. He was used to New England towns built around a village green with a white steepled church at one end and a bandstand in the middle, tree lined streets, houses well maintained, friendly neighbors, or at least, neighbors. The years there had regular seasons with predictable changes in the weather and in the routines of life. There were natural rhythms. Aside from bitter winters and blazing summers, the Plains offered none of that. Not even trees, beyond an occasional cottonwood. The Plains were empty of humanity and seemingly had no past. There was no human context, nothing to make it familiar. There was nothing but grass and sky. Granted, civilization was creeping forward through this vast emptiness, but the tip of that spear was ugly and mechanical and populated by the kind of people society had rejected or foreigners who spoke incomprehensible languages. That noisy future looked no more appealing than the empty past.

So Fred Beecher's curiosity and interest in his new job and his sincere dedication to his profession were balanced by the loneliness. That is of course typical of a young officer sent into a strange land. Many thousands had felt it before and have felt it since, but that does not in any way diminish or invalidate Fred's feelings. But he was there and would make the best of it. He did not dwell on melancholy or let it interfere with his duties. And he did a very good job at whatever came along.

Fred's best friend at Fort Wallace, assistant surgeon Captain Theophilus Turner, also suffered from bouts of melancholy. Turner was from a well-to-do eastern family and had received his medical training from Philadelphia's prestigious Jefferson Medical College. He had also served as a surgeon in the war and afterward had decided to join the regular army, even though it meant service on the frontier, where loneliness and depression were a man's adversaries and where, as

Turner put it, "[T]here was nothing to love." It's tempting to wonder why a man with his education and training would choose such a life, but there is no way of knowing what memories of the war or what other bleak emotions sent him into the frontier. Turner tended the troops at Wallace during the cholera outbreak. Despite his efforts, at least nine men died from it. But apparently Turner had some success with his treatments. As Barnitz wrote to Jennie: "The cholera appears to have lost its epidemic form. One man buried last evening and another this morning, but most of the patients appear to be convalescing." And the commander of the post at the time, Myles Keogh, praised Turner and implied that many more would have died, if not for the doctor's efforts.

During periods of relative peace Turner liked to roam the Plains in search of fossils and one day in the company of chief of scouts, William "Medicine Bill" Comstock, he found the remains of a huge (ultimately forty-foot-long) prehistoric sea creature called a plesiosaur. Turner and some of the troopers spent many days carefully unearthing the find. He sent it piece by piece to the Philadelphia Museum. (It is still on display at Drexel University.)

Turner also struggled with alcoholism. That of course was not uncommon in the frontier army. Even Fred Beecher succumbed to it for a while. But Beecher shook himself out of it (with the good advice of Sandy Forsyth). Turner could not seem to do it; he would die from it at Fort Wallace a few short years later, at the age of twenty-eight. The official cause of death was severe gastritis. Rumors of his drinking were not widespread, though, probably because he was so well liked, even loved, by all those who knew him, including the troops. In modern parlance, he was "enabled." He and Beecher were fast friends, and later when the sorrowing Turner went to look for the battlefield grave of his friend, he was distraught at not being able to find the remains. A sophisticated man, Turner would no doubt have recognized the bitter irony of discovering the skeleton of a prehistoric sea monster but not being able to find the bones of his closest comrade.

In the summer of 1868 while the fort was still being built, General Sheridan recognized Fred Beecher's qualities and assigned him a personal mission to scout and in fact spy on the tribes that were causing so much trouble in the area. Beecher was assisted by four civilian scouts including William Comstock and Sharp Grover. Grover would later go with Beecher and Forsyth on the September patrol. As mentioned, Medicine Bill was the chief scout for Fort Wallace. He had been with Custer and Hancock the previous year during Hancock's ineffective campaign, and Custer admired and respected Comstock:

> No Indian knew the country more thoroughly than did Comstock. He was perfectly familiar with every divide, watercourse and strip of timber for hundreds of miles in either direction. He knew the dress and peculiarities of every Indian tribe, and spoke the languages of many of them. Perfect in horsemanship, fearless in manner, a splendid hunter and a gentleman by instinct, he was an interesting as well as valuable companion.

Comstock was called Medicine Bill because he once saved a Lakota girl who was bitten on the finger by a rattlesnake. The quick-thinking Comstock bit off the finger and so saved the girl. That is the story, anyway. Comstock was darkly handsome man who lived on the Plains and was an Indian trader from the time he was sixteen or so. In 1868 he was still only twenty six, but he was a famous scout and buffalo hunter who once had a contest with Bill Cody to see who could shoot the most buffalo in an afternoon. Cody, who was adept at self-promotion even then, claimed the victory (sixty-nine to forty-six), but Comstock didn't seem to care. Medicine Bill also ran a successful ranch and sold high-quality hay to the army. There were legends about where Comstock came from and stories that he had lived with the Indians and had been born on the Plains, but in fact his father was a successful lawyer in Michigan, and Medicine Bill had come west as a teenager after the family had fallen into financial difficulties.

Ironically, for a man who was said to speak several Indian languages and was also said to know and thoroughly understand the Indian ways, Comstock was the grandnephew of James Fenimore Cooper, the author whose knowledge of Indians started and ended in his colorful imagination. Custer said Cooper was the man to "whose writings, more than to those of any other author, the people speaking the English language are indebted for a false and ill-judged estimate of the Indian character." Mark Twain said about Cooper's literary creations: "In the matter of intellect, the difference between a Cooper Indian and the Indian who stands outside the cigar shop is not spacious." Pouring a little salt into the wound, Twain added that Cooper's "English is a crime against the language." Most likely, not many people read Cooper these days; suspension of disbelief and willingness to slog through his style are necessary prerequisites. Whether Cooper's grandnephew agreed with Custer and Twain or even read Cooper's books is an open question, but it is safe to say that Medicine Bill was not quite the "sprung from the soil" kind of character that he let others believe he was. But this was the West, and it was a time when men could, and did, create their own biographies. Having come west for any number of personal reasons, many of them sorely needed a fresh story and identity. Despite Custer's description of Comstock's gentlemanly instincts, he did have a darker side. He was tried for murder for shooting H. P. Wyatt over a business dispute. Medicine Bill most certainly did the shooting, but the justice of the peace dismissed the case because there was no "felonious intent." He did not explain how it was possible to shoot a man twice in the back without felonious intent, but he did not need to, and the verdict stood. It was the thinnest of fig leaves to cover a man the army needed badly, and, besides, the victim was said to have ridden with Missouri guerillas, William Quantrill and Bloody Bill Anderson, during the war. He would not be missed by many Kansans.

Having finished his summer scouting and intelligence-gathering mission, Fred Beecher returned to Wallace and made his report. Medicine Bill and Sharp Grover, however, ventured into the camp of the

Cheyenne Turkey Leg to continue their assessment of the Indians' mood. There are different versions of what happened next. According to George Bent, a Cheyenne war party ambushed the scouts as the two men left the village, after an apparently friendly conference. The Cheyenne killed Comstock and wounded Grover, who managed to fight them off using Comstock's body as protection, and then to get away in the dark. That was Grover's story, too. Later stories, most notably told by trooper Reuben Waller of Company H of the Tenth Cavalry, have it that Grover killed Comstock in order to get possession of Comstock's valuable ranch and that Grover was wounded in a shootout with Comstock, not the Cheyenne. The following year Grover was shot to death in a bar in Pond Creek, so there's no way of knowing the truth. Grover's body was returned to Fort Wallace and buried in the cemetery there.

In any event, however Grover acquired his wound, he recovered sufficiently to sign on later that summer as chief scout for Sandy Forsyth's patrol—a patrol that would lead them to a rendezvous with Roman Nose at a place that would come to be called Beecher Island.

FORSYTH GETS UNDERWAY

On August 29, 1868, Major Sandy Forsyth received the following orders from General Sheridan: "I would suggest that you move across the headwaters of Solomon [River] to Beaver Creek, thence down that creek to Fort Wallace. On arrival there report to me by telegraph at this place."

Actually, Beaver Creek flows northeasterly, and so Forsyth would have followed it upstream, not down, as he traveled west and south. But he undoubtedly understood what Sheridan meant, and so with a glad heart, he left Fort Hays and led his men on a march across the Plains to Fort Wallace, the westernmost army post in Kansas, thirteen miles west of the Kansas Pacific's current terminus.

Crossing the Sabine River and south fork of the Solomon we struck Beaver Creek, where Short Nose Creek empties into it. Here the Indians had evidently held a great sun-dance, where probably they decided to go to war with the whites. Moving thence up Beaver Creek, beyond timber line, I struck the trail directly for Fort Wallace, reaching there the night of September 5th, not having seen an Indian during the march.

Since the sun dance is one of the most important Cheyenne rituals and was often performed as part of a larger ceremony known as the Medicine Lodge, it's not likely that Forsyth found the remains of one. The Medicine Lodge and accompanying sun dance are attended by large gatherings of the people. Ceremonies last for several days, and involve various intricate rituals, sometimes including "renewal" of the medicine arrows. The ceremony and rituals are of such importance that the Cheyenne would not have risked holding it anywhere close to white installations, for fear of profane interruption and violence. The sun dance self-torture involved inserting skewers into the chest muscles and then struggling to tear them out by straining against ropes that attached the skewers to a lodge pole or heavy object, like a buffalo skull. It was performed by an individual as part of his personal vow, so it is possible although unlikely, that Forsyth saw some indications that the ritual had been performed: "Unless the man making the vow specified a definite occasion when he would perform the sacrifice, he was at liberty to choose his own time. He might declare that he would swing at the pole in the Medicine Lodge or that he would perform the same sacrifice alone in the hills." It is certain, however, that the Cheyenne had not gathered in that camp to decide to make war on the whites. They had already decided that long ago. Most likely, the camp Forsyth came across was that of a war party bent on attacking the Smoky Hill travel routes or settlements. Once again, Forsyth was writing his memories of the operation twenty five years after the fact, and his account has a number of other mistakes in it, most of them understandable, some unavoidable. By that time he had no reason to exaggerate or falsify the record. But he did get some things wrong.

The exhilaration of independent command would have worn off after the first day or so, leaving Forsyth with the more practical responsibilities of command in a hostile place. The Plains are sometimes as flat as a pool table, which is good news for a farmer who makes his living with a plow and a mule, but is not so good for a soldier in a hostile country. It would be possible for fifty well-armed men to fight off many more times that number of attackers, if the men had a good defensive position. But on the flat Plains there are no good defensive positions—or at least none readily available or visible. Therefore, being caught in the open by a large force of well mounted enemy was pretty much a death sentence. Even worse, there were occasional arroyos or miniature canyons in the apparently featureless flatland. A rider might not see them until he was almost at their edge, but they could easily conceal a large group of mounted warriors who could come bursting forth while the soldiers were thinking they were all alone in the universe and not particularly enjoying the sensation. Other parts of the Plains are not flat and call for the inevitable comparison to huge rolling waves at sea, although no sailor would relish that kind of sea. The rolling hills are several hundred feet high in spots. Behind these waves there were innumerable places for an enemy to wait, unseen, and then to swoop over the top of the small hills and fall upon the soldiers flank. And so Forsyth would have posted men to ride on each side of the column as well as a man "on point" far ahead. These were lonely assignments for those men. Then, too, there was occasional broken ground on the Plains, strange eruptions of rocky patches and small escarpments and stony hollows—ground that a geologist could explain but that seems to be there for no reason an amateur could understand. Sometimes there was a small rivulet passing through the bottoms of these breaks, and over centuries it's possible that the little streams, flooded by seasonal rains, carved the broken ground. On the other hand perhaps it was the result of some ancient upheaval that might explain the strange looking deposits of stone and mounds of what looks like petrified ash or slag. Forsyth was not a graduate of West Point and so did not have had the benefit of the Academy's quite excellent courses in natural sciences. He would wonder at the variety of the Plains topography but, more important, worry about the exposure of his command to sudden attack from well-hidden enemies coming at him from any direction. Trees of course were scarce. In fact, lumber for the Fort Wallace had to be imported from Colorado. But now and then there would be a grove of cottonwoods or willows lining a creek or dry bed. But even these were rare. And above it all was the endless sky and the harsh sun of summer.

Forsyth doesn't say much about his march across the Plains to Fort Wallace, aside from describing the pleasures of having an independent command. But it's worth repeating the notes of Captain Barnitz of the Seventh Cavalry who was also in and around Fort Wallace at the time:

> Have had a hard and tiresome march today—over the hot plains—the torrid plains—prairie fires surging everywhere in the distance and clouds of dust rising along the column for it has only rained twice [in the last few months] and the heat has been fearful at times, and the grass looks as though it has been dried in an oven and the streams are all dry—even the Smoky is dry—not a drop of water to be found except by digging in the dry sand of the channel, and it (the water which we obtain thus) isn't very delicious—tastes as though it had been filtered through several mud holes (which is the fact).

The sun beating on the Plains in late August was more than enough to dry out the grass, but prairie fires caused by summer lightning added to the miseries of horses on the march, for they depended to a large extent on grass for fuel. The Cheyenne knew this as well and commonly set fire to the combustible dry grass to make life harder for the troopers' animals. As for water, Forsyth's scouts carried trenching tools with them. They would come in handy for more than just digging in a dry creek bed for water.

When Forsyth and his men arrived at Fort Wallace they found:

> [T]wo barracks 120 feet by 30 each, with cook and mess house in the rear, two store houses for the Quartermaster and Commissary, 130 by 30 each, a large stable for horses and mules, a bake house, guard house, three commodious houses for officers, together with the hospital which measured 70 feet by 35. [. . .] The buildings were faced with stone taken from a neighboring quarry and worked up by a detail of men. A mill was built and a saw for sawing the stone set, by means of which blocks were cut.

It doesn't sound too bad, although photos of the period show some officers standing outside a rude shed that served as commandant's quarters. Barnitz reported that the officers lived in tents, perhaps the three houses were still being built or were being reserved for more senior men.

Forsyth and his men arrived on the evening of September 5. They were met with a message telling of an attack against some teamsters near Sheridan, Kansas, which was thirteen miles east of the fort and the place that the Kansas Pacific had halted construction. The teamsters fought off the attack, but the Cheyenne killed and scalped two who had been lagging behind and also ran off some of the stock. There was another message from the governor of Kansas asking for help in protecting settlers in Bison Basin, which was farther south and east of the fort. Forsyth decided that the wagon train attack was of more immediate concern, since the war party would have left a fresh trail that might lead him to significant contact. And so, leaving two of his men sick in the hospital under the care of Dr. Turner, Forsyth, Beecher, and the rest of the scouts set off for scene of the attack.

At the scene Forsyth, Beecher, and Sharp Grover examined the trail. Forsyth freely admitted that the other two men were his superior in plainscraft and reading signs. Beecher may have been an easterner by birth and education, but he was an experienced outdoorsman, too, and had quickly adapted to the challenges of the Plains. He had a lively intelligence and enjoyed studying and learning the ways of this totally different environment, which was a far cry from the lakes and pine and birch forests of Maine and New Hampshire. What's more he did not waste the opportunities of learning from men like Bill Comstock. Having spent the summer on the Plains as Sheridan's spy, Beecher pretty well knew what he was doing. Beecher and Grover determined that somewhere between twenty-five and thirty-five Cheyenne had made the attack, and the trail led off to the northwest, toward the Republican River. They felt sure that the war party was now returning to a larger camp, and so Forsyth decided that if, or rather, when they found the main body, he and his men would attack, or in picturesque army parlance "give them battle." He asked Beecher and Grover's opinions about that. Beecher said nothing, a sign that perhaps he remembered the old army saying that the most dangerous man in the world is a new second lieutenant with a map and a compass. The "new lieutenant" in this case was a major, but the basic concept seemed to apply—inexperience combined with ambition could be more dangerous to the men under his command than to the enemy. Sharp Grover's opinion was that they would probably not be able to overtake the war party before they were able to reunite with the main body, and when they did, it would pose a significantly a bigger challenge. He probably expressed himself more colorfully than that, but that was the gist.

Forsyth considered the counsel of his two more experienced men and dismissed their reservations:

I therefore cut short the discussion by saying that I had deter-mined to find and attack the Indians, no matter what the odds might be against us. If we could not defeat them, we would show them that the government did not propose that they should escape unpunished for want of energy in their pursuit.

Forsyth's memoir is naturally couched in nineteenth-century style, but the fact was, he was looking for a fight and he meant to get it. Forsyth decided that, at the very least, he needed to make some kind of demonstration, one that would impress the tribesmen with the government's resolve and tenacity. One small battle would not lead to the Cheyenne's reform, but without severe and continued reprisals for their attacks, the Indians would have no incentive to give up and accept the reservation system. That was the army's position at the time, and it's hard to argue with it. If there were no repercussions from raids, why stop? It's what the Cheyenne and their allies did, what they lived for, their métier. Forsyth would therefore understand his proposed attack would be part of a continuing strategy of pressure and punishment. Furthermore, Forsyth reasoned, the odds were good that most of his command would not suffer the fate of Fetterman's command. "I thought, with fifty one men, even if we could not defeat them, they could not annihilate us." If Beecher and Grover expressed doubts, they did so mildly or in such a manner that allowed Forsyth to make the decision he wanted to make. In fairness to Forsyth, he was following Sheridan's orders. "[I]t was expected that the command would fight the Indians, and I meant it should do so." Of course, the commander in the field has wide discretion about where, when, and how to fight. Forsyth might be criticized for deciding to attack without knowing the extent of the problem. That is mostly historical hindsight, however, and it's always well to remember that troops going in harm's way cannot know what may happen next. Officers are forced to make decisions amid perplexing uncertainty, decisions that historians, professional and amateur, can second-guess with impunity. And of course Forsyth would tell himself that he could always change his mind, if the situation warranted. All things considered, he did exactly what Sheridan expected of him.

Ironically, Forsyth's deliberations about whether to "give battle" became irrelevant. The Cheyenne had already made up their minds about that.

That evening Forsyth and his men camped alongside the trail of the war party, and in the morning they resumed the chase. Beecher and Grover rode in front of the column and studied the signs. Not surprisingly, at least not to Beecher and Grover, the trail began to disintegrate as individual horsemen split off from the group and went in a different direction. It was as though the trail were breaking into a delta, like a river. That could indicate the war party knew Forsyth and his men were following them. But not necessarily. It was a common Cheyenne precaution after a raid. After a while, there was no trail at all, because the last of the Cheyenne horsemen, maybe two or three at most, had ridden purposefully over rocky ground where their horses left no tracks. The war party had scattered and disappeared. They would rejoin at some designated spot up ahead or perhaps at the camp of the main body. But for now, Forsyth and his scouts were without any clues. Nonetheless, they continued northwesterly toward the Arikaree branch of the Republican River, which was just across the Kansas line into northeastern Colorado.

George Bent said:

Mean time this war party [the one Forsyth was following] had reached their village which was made up of Dog Soldiers under Tall Bull, White Horse and Bull Bear and a number of Sioux lodges under Bad Yellow Eyes and Two Strikes; a few young Arapahos were also there with friends in the Cheyenne village. [. . .] I doubt if there were more than two hundred Cheyenne.

Bent does not say whether the two hundred Cheyenne were all warriors, but subsequent events indicate that they were. What's more, there were some friends arriving in the vicinity: "A Sioux war party returning from a raid on the South Platte River . . ." What's more, they had "discovered Forsyth's men. They watched the scouts and late in the day brought the news to their village. Messengers were sent over to the Dog Soldiers camp with the news." Forsyth and his men did not know they had been spotted, though the experienced men among them no doubt were aware of the possibility. The report from the Sioux war party merely confirmed what Cheyenne already knew, because not only had their war party returned but also two Cheyenne who had been hunting buffalo had spotted the scouts about twelve miles away on the Republican River. Bent says with the addition of the Sioux "there were between three hundred and three hundred fifty fighting men in the village."

Since war parties commonly scattered as a precaution against pursuit, Forsyth could not be sure he was heading in the right direction. He assumed there was a substantial village somewhere up ahead, but there were no indications where it might be. He continued his march up the Republican River. Then he got lucky. Along the banks of the river, one of his men discovered what Forsyth called a "wickie-up"—a temporary shelter made of willow branches and grasses on the banks of the river. Two Cheyenne had apparently spent the night there— perhaps the two buffalo hunters. A small trail from there led for several miles along the river and then broadened into a larger trail, with tracks of more horses. At the fork of the river where the Arikaree enters the Republican, the trail grew even larger and showed signs of many horses and travois poles that had carved ruts in the ground. There were also discarded items of equipment and clothing. Camp litter. It was obviously the trail of a village on the move. War parties did not drag travois with them. At this point, several of Forsyth's men (he does not name them) asked if they could have a few words with him:

> [S]ome of the men of the command ventured to approach me with a protest. They said that if we followed the Indians to their villages, we would be met with overwhelming numbers and stood no show [i.e., "chance"] whatever for our lives.

Forsyth listened calmly and then said that in his judgment, they were in greater danger if they decided to withdraw; he thought it would be safer to "advance and attack." Forsyth reasoned that it would be more dangerous to be caught and surprised on the open Plains by a large force of attackers than it would be to maintain the initiative and choose the time, if not the place, to attack. Forsyth may have also been familiar with Sun Tzu's dictum: "Attack is the secret of defense." Perhaps wondering at Forsyth's conclusion, the men returned to their positions without further objections. Forsyth congratulated himself on the fact that half or more of his men had been soldiers at one time and so were used to accepting orders, even though they might not like or agree with them. That is "the difference between an army and a mob," he said.

It's useful at this point to remember that Forsyth was a very experienced soldier and fought in many desperate Civil War battles, especially in Sheridan's Shenandoah campaign. He was no innocent rookie in the ways of combat or in the management of men. He was not autocratic or blustery, not a martinet or a fool; and he was well liked and respected for his personality and his professionalism. He was willing to listen to the counsel of his subordinates, but he was fully aware that he was in command and that final decisions would be his alone and, moreover, that he would be held accountable for them. Nor did he underestimate the fighting qualities of his adversary—quite the contrary. He also shared with them the *gaudium certaminis*—"joy of battle." As Michael Sheridan, the general's brother, said of Forsyth: "[He] was ready at any time to risk his life, even though it was not actually necessary, and seemed to take joy in entering a fight." That may suggest a level of impetuosity that would trouble the more cautious soldier or civilian, but it was the kind of attitude that won respect among the professionals, including Sheridan, Beecher, and, later, Custer. Forsyth's only inexperience, therefore, lay in the particular matter of fighting Indians, and he was well aware of that. But he had a solid record in combat and had earned the right to have confidence in his own military judgment. Like most soldiers who have been in tight spots and emerged from them more or less in one piece, he undoubtedly had a sense that this situation, too, could turn out all right. And with a bit of luck it might turn into a success of the kind he had been sent to deliver. He had his orders, and he had his ambitions, and he had his record. Against those was the unknown, which may or may not be something to worry about. Therefore, he decided to proceed, even though this new trail indicated they were facing a much larger challenge than he first thought. Despite the size of the trail and the village at its end, he felt "the necessity of fighting them and decided to do so, even though I doubted my force to be strong enough to do more than partially cripple them for the time being."

There was another consideration that argued for continuing. The regular army, and indeed the volunteers, rangers, and civilian posses, all knew that the biggest problem in fighting the Plains tribes was finding them. To be able to locate and attack a hostile village was the desideratum of all commanders. For one reason, the Indians almost never had sentries posted. It was not hard to surprise them, if you were careful about the approach. And for another, one of the greatest fears was that a village, when alarmed, would scatter, just as war parties scattered on the trail. Individual warriors would think first of their families and since there was no unified military command structure, and since they were not expecting an attack, it would be every man for himself and his family. Even those who chose to stay and fight would operate as individuals. Custer's biggest worry at the Little Bighorn was that he'd been discovered and the Indians would get away. That worry led in part to his precipitous attack. In retrospect, that seems darkly laughable, but it was common army wisdom and borne out by experience. Indians generally only fought when they wanted to and only on their own terms. They preferred surprise and ambush and were rarely in the mood for a set-piece battle. When conditions were not favorable in their eyes, they made themselves scarce. The year before, during his unsuccessful campaign, Hancock was enraged when the huge Cheyenne village was suddenly empty. The people had gone in the night, and Hancock burned their teepees in frustration. Therefore, to discover the trail of a large village that could be attacked was a rare and golden opportunity. Any regular officer, even one more experienced with Indians, would see it the same way. And there was something else—since finding the hostiles was so difficult, and since it was conventional army wisdom that when their village was attacked, they were more likely to run than to fight, Forsyth surely gave a fleeting thought to what would be said about him back in headquarters, if he turned off a hot trail and retreated without even sighting a Cheyenne. He had wanted an independent command; Sheridan had faith in him and given him what he wanted. Even if deep down he wanted to turn around, he couldn't. And all indications are that he didn't want to. Quite the contrary.

But there was a problem. When the scouts went into camp alongside the Arikaree, it was the night of September 16, and "we were nearly out of supplies, save salt and coffee." The seven days of rations and any extras packed on the four mules were almost gone. As it was, the scouts would be on short commons, even if they turned around right then and went back. And they were a hundred miles from Fort Wallace. Hunting would avail them little or nothing—"No game had been seen for two days." The very large Indian village Forsyth was following had probably frightened away any buffalo or antelope that might otherwise have been near the water. At night, a few wolves or coyotes lurked around just beyond the firelight, but no one fancied them for dinner, even if they came close enough to be shot—which they didn't. The horses and mules had run out of grain and were now dependent on grazing. And much of the late summer grass was dried and burned by the sun. Forsyth would need to find a spot where the grass was at least acceptable. In short, Forsyth and his men had reached the extreme edge of their possible range. In fact, considering the distance back to Wallace, they were really beyond it. Forsyth knew he was pushing his luck by continuing, and subsequent events would prove just how wrong he was to do it. But his blood was up, and the last thing he wanted was to return to Wallace after ten days of wandering over the dry prairie, with his horses played out and his men worn out and nothing to show for it. That had been the experience of too many cavalry patrols, and Forsyth was not about to have his first independent command result in another useless trek though the barren Plains. He was on a hot trail, and he was going to follow it. So, having decided to press on and provoke a battle, Forsyth had no time to waste. If there was going to be any action, it had better come soon—"If it were done when tis done, 'twere well it were done quickly."

Ironically, the Cheyenne and Sioux felt the same urgency as Forsyth, but for different reasons. They were afraid the scouts would get away or become alarmed, somehow, and hurriedly find a defensive position. In that case, they would dig in and wait, and they would be difficult to dislodge. Even though the Indians would outnumber Forsyth seven to one, attacking fifty frontiersmen who were firing from defensive positions would be a formidable and dangerous proposition. The Sioux had learned that bitter lesson at the Wagon Box and Hayfield fights. And the Sioux and the Cheyenne were obviously close friends who shared intelligence. They all knew what had happened in those earlier fights. Moreover, the Indians could not know that the scouts had run out of food and grain. If they had known, they might have decided to wait until the scouts inevitably started home and then attack them in the open. But like all warriors, the Cheyenne had to assess the situation with incomplete information, and so they felt they must act sooner, rather than later. And their blood was up, too. The plan therefore would be to wait until Forsyth's scouts made their evening camp, wait and watch until "the morning star," and then attack with the entire body of warriors, while the scouts were still waking up. The scouts would be overwhelmed by several hundred mounted warriors riding down on them from all sides. It was a good plan. Accordingly, Bent said, "Criers rode through the village announcing that no small parties would be permitted to go out and attack the troops; all must wait and go in a body, Sioux and

Cheyenne; anyone attempting to steal out would be severely punished." It may be remembered that one of the roles of the Cheyenne warrior societies was to act as policemen in situations like this. It may also be remembered that individual warriors often paid no attention.

THE ATTACK

On the afternoon of September 16, Forsyth and his men went into camp alongside the Arikaree River, in a "well grassed valley about two miles in length." The river at that season was nearly dry, with only a thin line of current and a few pools of standing water in the otherwise sandy riverbed, which "wound in and out of wild plum thickets, alder bushes and swamp willows." At other seasons when the spring and summer rains came, the Arikaree, like all western rivers, would overflow its banks and wash away the willows and sandbar islands or create new ones by depositing sand and debris from further upstream. But now there was nothing much to it, and the willows and alders had survived or others had grown, so that there was waist high cover. All around the little valley were the rolling hills, "from forty to fifty feet in height."

> Dismounting about the middle of the valley, we encamped on the bank of the stream opposite the center of a small island, which had been formed in the sand in the middle of the bed of the stream [. . .] the little island in the center of its bed was fully seventy yards from the bank on either side. [. . .] Long sage grass grew on its [the island's] head, and a thicket of alders and willows shot up four or five feet in height above the center, which just at its foot stood a young cottonwood tree of about twenty feet in height.

Forsyth posted sentries around his bankside camp. He gave orders to hobble the horses and also to make sure that the picket pins were firmly planted and that the rope tying the horse to the pin was securely knotted. If they were attacked, each man was to grab his rifle and stand by his horse to prevent stampede. As mentioned, they were a hundred miles from Fort Wallace in hostile territory, and losing their horses would most likely mean the end of them all. Forsyth also knew that trying to run off the enemy's horses was a favorite Cheyenne tactic as well as a fruitful way of capturing new wealth and earning prestige. That was likely to be the Indians' opening gambit.

After their meager dinner, the men rolled into their blankets, but Forsyth didn't sleep much. He wandered the perimeter and checked on the sentries. He was apprehensive, feeling, with good reason, that their enemies were close.

As Forsyth surveyed the ground, he must have realized then that if an attack came with the morning star, as he thought it could, the island across the sandy riverbed might make a better defensive position than his current campsite. The island was raised above the streambed by a couple of feet, but that elevation was better than nothing. Forsyth might not be well versed in Sioux and Cheyenne tactics, but he could read the ground and the cover as well as the next man, and he understood cavalry action. He could see that if attacked, his men stood a better chance if they were dug in on the island than if they remained where they were. The foliage on the island would provide good cover, especially once the scouts dug rifle pits. True, the foliage was a mixed blessing— useful on the island, but troublesome on the riverbanks. The tall grass and willow bushes were thick along both banks of the river. Beyond the banks the bushes gradually disappeared and gave way to the usual brown grass of the late summer Plains and then to the bare hills that surrounded the little valley. But from the island, the streambed would give him a decent field of fire. As he wrote, there were at least seventy yards of open streambed on either side of the island and more than that at either end, upstream and down. Beyond the bankside bushes and even on the slopes of the surrounding hills, the Indians would be visible, as they assembled to attack. They would quickly come into range of the scouts' Spencer carbines, which could hit with power at five hundred yards, although Forsyth would have his men wait until the range became more practicable. Even so, a shot fired at extreme range but aimed into a crowd of warriors might do some damage, and the scouts had plenty of ammunition. (While hunting with Bill Comstock, Fred Beecher killed an antelope with a Spencer carbine at five hundred yards, which proves not only that Beecher was a very good shot but also that the Spencer was serious at that range.)

Mounted Indians would have to start their charge from the brown hills that surrounded the little river valley and then cross the gradually flattening land on the way to the river. Finally they would have to burst through the willows along the river bank and into the seventy yards of open riverbed. For the last few seconds they would be clear and very close targets. The same would be true if they came charging down the streambed from either direction. The scouts could put up a tremendous volume of fire. Properly handled, the Spencers could deliver upward of fourteen well-aimed shots per minute. A few of the men, including Beecher, had Henry repeaters, which fired an equal or greater volume once they were fully loaded with sixteen rounds, although their effective range was shorter and the bullet somewhat smaller. All things considered, the little island gave the scouts just that slight bit of extra protection and a marginally better field of fire than their campsite beside the river. Discipline, firepower, good cover, and entrenchment could balance off the Cheyenne and Sioux advantage in numbers.

There was also the possibility that the Indians would dismount and fight on foot. That way they could hide in the willows and alders opposite the island and fire on the scouts from short range. Even at seventy yards, an arrow would be more than sufficient, and a rifle shot would be virtually point blank. Dug in on the island, his men would be hard to see, but so would dismounted attackers crawling through the bushes opposite. And as George Bent writes, contrary to their popular image, the Sioux liked to fight on foot. And although the Cheyenne preferred the exhilaration of a mounted charge, they were not fools and would dismount to fight, if the situation called for it. Most likely, Sharp Grover would have said something about that to Forsyth.

Still, despite the willows on both riverbanks, the island seemed like a better defensive position. If the dawn brought the anticipated attack, Forsyth knew what he would do, but he still spent a fitful and watchful night.

In the Indian camp "the warriors had made ready their war rigs and put on their sacred face paint." And that same night they started out for the last reported position of Forsyth's camp. The plan was to surround the camp in the dark, wait until dawn and then attack in full force. They would have the advantage of surprise and overwhelming numbers, and the fight would be over in minutes, just as it was at the Fetterman battle. But when they reached the reported campsite, they discovered that Forsyth's men had moved, and in the dark there were no clear signs of where they went. The warriors decided to pause for the night and resume the search in the morning. Everyone was cautioned again to be patient and stay in camp, for fear of accidentally alerting the white men.

"But in spite of the strict orders, Starving Elk and Little Hawk, Cheyennes, with six Sioux, all young men, mischievously agreed to slip out and find the whites." The temptations were too strong for the boys. The eight mischief makers eluded any watching policemen and stole out of camp. They searched through the night, trying to spot the light from the campfires of the scouts. But they had no luck until, that is, just before dawn. Then they saw the glow of firelight. The burning campfires should have told them that the whites were not still rolled in their blankets. "Even at this early hour Forsyth's men were moving about camp and getting ready to start."

Although the scouts were up and about, the eight warriors figured they still had the element of surprise working for them. They decided to attack. They were after the horses, anyway, and not trying to overwhelm or even fight the white men. If one or more of them could count coup, so much the better. But to be first in action against the white men and to come away with the soldiers' horses would be a feat worth bragging about, not only for its daring, but also for its tactical usefulness. It would put the scouts afoot and make them easy game for the rest of the warriors. The boys would become famous in the villages! And so they charged, yelling their war cries and most likely blowing eagle-wing-bone whistles to ward off enemy bullets.

Forsyth was talking to a sentry when he first saw some movement along the hills nearby and then spotted three riders coming at break-neck pace toward the horses. Then five others immediately followed. Forsyth and the sentry fired at them, and Forsyth shouted for the men to gather up their arms and their horses, for it was clear the Indians were trying to stampede the animals. They were "beating Indian drums and rattling dry hides" to spook the animals. The "beating of Indian drums" sounds a little unlikely, but no doubt the eight warriors were making plenty of noise and probably waving blankets, which was their more usual way of stampeding enemy horses. But Forsyth surely thought these eight were only the first of many more to come. And they were.

The eight swooped down the hill and into the camp's picket lines. "Starving Elk's little party startled them by making a rush toward the horses and mules. The white men opened fire on the raiders, but some of the stock was stampeded and swept off by Starving Elk and his friends." The warriors got away with two horses and two mules. The other animals, although badly frightened, were firmly picketed and the men, as ordered, quickly rushed to settle them. Some of the scouts managed to get off some shots at the raiders as they disappeared into the gloom. But as quickly as it started, it was over. Forsyth says he or the sentry emptied one of the Indian saddles, but that probably didn't happen. Bent says that none of the raiders was hurt. Forsyth might have seen one of the boys duck down beneath his horse's head in a warrior's typical style when under fire. The eight attackers were unharmed and rode off into the still dark morning with their four prizes. But the scouts were now thoroughly on the alert. As Bent wrote: "[T]hese wild young men spoiled everything."

The gloom of early morning was quickly giving way to dawn, and as the men hurriedly gathered their equipment and prepared to mount up, the horizon and the near foreground suddenly appeared to be alive. "Grover who stood by my side, placed his hand on my shoulder and said 'Oh heavens, general, look at the Indians." Grover might have used more forceful language, but Forsyth was writing for the late Victorian audience at this point. On the other hand, Grover might have felt that under the circumstances, blasphemy was a bad idea. Regardless, the morning was suddenly filled with hundreds of hostile tribesmen. Obviously, the eight mischief-makers had not gotten too far ahead of the main body, for the bulk of the war party had shown up just after first light, attracted to the scene by the shots from the scouts. The hills and the floor of the little valley were covered with horsemen who seemed to materialize "out of the very earth," and they all began to unleash "wild cries of exultation." Well they might cheer. They had the scouts just where they wanted them. The noise was deafening and not a little unsettling. So too the sight of painted warriors who looked like nothing if not creatures from another nightmarish world. They were all around, although there did seem to be an opening to the east. That sounds very much like an invitation to Forsyth's men to retreat in that direction, where they would be surprised by an ambush on the far side of the hill. If it was a ruse, Forsyth did not fall for it, and in fact in his memoir he mentions that he recognized it as a potential trap. Besides, he had already decided what to do:

> The command was ordered to lead their horses to the little island just in front of us, to form a circle facing outward, securely tie their horses to the bushes just outside of the circle so formed, throw themselves on the ground and entrench themselves as rapidly as possible, two men working together, protecting each other in turn as they threw up the earth to cover themselves.

To Forsyth and his men it seemed as if the ground everywhere was sprouting the Indians. And that is not surprising, because there were at least 350 Cheyenne and Sioux on horseback or standing on the sides of the little hills. (Other accounts given to George Bird Grinnell by Cheyenne who were there say the number was six hundred.) What's more, women and children from the huge village had followed the warriors and now began to appear on the highest ridges to the north of the scouts' island. They too were raising an unholy din. Having spectators there to watch a fight was unusual, but it was known to happen when the warriors believed they had an overwhelming advantage over an enemy who was trapped, or seemed to be, and when the village was therefore in no danger. George Custer encountered the same thing in his campaign against these same tribes in the Yellowstone valley in 1872. It's not hard to imagine the scouts' reaction to seeing and hearing the audience, for it plainly indicated the presumed hopelessness of their situation and no doubt reminded many of the rumors of atrocities committed by Indian women in the aftermath of a battle. Whether those rumors were true or not didn't matter. They were widely believed.

But there was at least time enough for Forsyth to get his men on the island. That suggests that Forsyth might have explained his thinking to his men the evening before, because they quickly crossed to the island and began digging in. But once they got to the island the Indians did not waste any more time demonstrating and began their attack. "Many of the mounted warriors sprang from their horses and, running forward, they lined both banks of the river, and from the reeds and tall grass poured a steady and galling fire upon us." Several of the scouts panicked and shouted that they must make a run for it, but in classic fashion Forsyth stood in their midst with his pistol in his hand and said he would shoot any man who tried to run. Beecher added, "You addled headed fools, have you no sense?" Once again, he may not have said it quite that way. On the other hand, he was the son and nephew of preachers, so it's possible. The mini-panic was over quickly, as most of the men recognized that fighting from a good defensive opposition was far better than trying out outrun hundreds of Cheyenne on the open Plains. No doubt the Cheyenne recognized the same tactical situation. It would have been far better for them, if the scouts had panicked and tried to run. Also it seems reasonable to think that the Indians' initial demonstrations on the surrounding hillsides were designed to frighten the scouts into bolting. If so, it might have worked, if not for Forsyth's and Beecher's steadiness.

One of the scouts was nineteen-year-old Jack Stilwell. Forsyth sent him and two others to the northeastern end of the island. Instead of digging in, they found a hollowed out section of the river bank that offered good protection and a clear field of fire. Because of the foliage around their blind and because of the clouds of gun smoke, these three men were never discovered by the Indians:

> This party did a great deal of damage to the Indians [. . .] Weasel Bear [. . .] in a mad rush on the island, rode close to Stilwell's party hiding in a hole on the bank. He was shot in the back just above the hips and fell from his horse in the grass not far from Stilwell's party. As the scouts were keeping up a heavy fire at this time and the smoke hung low, it was not noticed how Weasel Bear had been shot. Some time later White Thunder [. . .] went down to carry off Weasel Bear and he, too, was shot by these scouts.

The rest of the scouts were simultaneously trying to fight off attackers and dig trenches. The scouts were firing from behind and around their horses who were stamping and rearing from fright and from wounds. They were systematically being killed and dropped in place. Scouts were also firing from behind the dead horses' bodies and from behind packs and cases. Some used teamwork as one fired while the other dug. Most of their shovels must have gone off with the stampeded mules, for the reports of the action have the scouts cutting through the sod with their butcher knives and digging in the sand with tin plates and anything else that came to hand. They dug a body length pit about eighteen inches deep and threw up sod and sand in front and behind, because there were Indians firing at them from high grass on both sides of the river. It should be remembered that although there were at least 350 warriors there, each was following his own ideas about how best to fight, now that the battle was underway. In many ways that made it even more difficult for the scouts, because there were no massed formations and no way to know from which direction they might attack in force. They were fighting hundreds of individuals who played by no known military rule book. On the other hand, the scouts benefitted from the Indian's inability or unwillingness to coordinate their charges. Had hundreds of warriors come at the island en masse, the scouts would have been overwhelmed and annihilated, forthwith.

Forsyth was walking among his men as they dug their rifle pits and shot at the enemy. It was the kind of thing that an officer under fire was supposed to do, and a veteran of the Civil War would understand that. It was not just for show and not just to reassure his men with his coolness. He was also stopping by each trench, assessing the men's positions and their shooting. He was ordering them to keep calm and to aim properly, because in the excitement some were firing too rapidly with their repeaters. (This natural tendency was one reason many army theorists argued for single-shot rifles.) Forsyth could feel fairly confident about his supply of ammunition, but even so, there was none to waste. He walked among the men, saying, "Don't shoot unless you can see something to hit. Don't throw away your ammunition, for our lives may depend on how we husband it." Here again, his memoir language was probably cleaned up for the Victorian reader, but Forsyth was doing his job properly. Farther down the island, which was no more than a hundred yards long, Forsyth saw Beecher, "whose every shot was as carefully and coolly aimed as though he was shooting at a target."

At one of the trenches Forsyth came across Sig Schlesinger, the boyish immigrant from Hungary, who had signed on because he needed a job and was accepted for no particular reason; he was not prepossessing in any way and had no particular experience of the Plains. But when the fighting started he pulled his weight. Afterward, Forsyth referred to him as "that brave and active young Israelite." Nor was Forsyth surprised by Schlesinger's performance, for he said, "My experience with men of his race during the civil war, with a single exception, had strongly impressed me in their favor as being brave men and good soldiers." Schlesinger later said:

> My plan of observation was to work the barrel of my carbine in saw fashion, through the sand from the edges on top of my hole downward, obtaining by these means a sort of loophole through which I could see quite a distance; also taking a general observation by suddenly jumping up and as quickly dropping back into my hole, which enabled me to take a shot, or as many as the size of the target warranted, without undue exposure and yet be in touch with the general situation. In such instances I have seen Indians crawl behind a knoll and saw several times two horsemen drag a body away between them. Indian boys came from behind a knoll shooting arrows at us. I saw bodies of Indians both on foot and horseback coming toward us. These I considered good targets.

For his action Sig was later enshrined in army lore by a poem printed in an army publication: "When the foe charged on the breastworks, with madness of despair, And the bravest souls were tested, The little Jew was there. When the weary dozed on duty, Or the wounded needed care, When another shot was called for, The little Jew was there." Was this an example of casual anti-Semitism? If so, there seems to be no malice in it. Sig was the "little Jew" in the same way Germans were Dutch and Irish were Micks and Swedes were Squareheads and the Slavs were Hunkies. And the troops of the Tenth and Ninth Cavalries? They were the "brunettes." On the battlefield, those things didn't matter. Combat was a great reagent of prejudice—that and humor.

Having completed his inspection of the trenches Forsyth sensibly took cover himself, but as soon as he laid down he was hit in the right leg by a bullet that ranged "upward" in his thigh but then stayed lodged in the flesh. The pain was intense and Dr. John Mooers who was "doing splendid service with his rifle, as he was a capital shot," told Forsyth to join him in his trench. As a couple of the men were helping Mooers enlarge the trench, Forsyth was still lying on the ground and was hit again in the other leg. The bullet shattered the bone "midway between knee and ankle." And from that point on Forsyth was pretty much reduced to "something of a spectator." But he remained in command, and even though the pain from his wounds was intense, he stayed fully conscious.

The fight settled down to an hour or so of desultory but regular firing on both sides. The Indians were shooting at men and the horses, obviously now more interested in killing all the scouts than salvaging their valuable animals. Finally, the last horse was killed, and the scouts heard someone yell "There goes the last damned horse, anyhow" in a perfect American accent. Forsyth figured this must have been one of the Bent brothers, and since George does not claim to have been there, it might well have been his younger brother, Charlie, who was every bit as wild a Cheyenne warrior. Perhaps more.

Looking up to see what was going on, Forsyth was hit again—this time a bullet blew off his hat and grazed the top of his head, knocking him back into his trench, "almost senseless." It was later found that he had a fractured skull and several pieces of bone had to be removed. But just then it appeared to be just a glancing blow, but one that caused a severe headache. Around the same time Dr. Mooers was firing at a pair of warriors who were dashing around the perimeter on horseback. Forsyth reports that Mooers shot one of them through the head and then said, "That rascally redskin will not trouble us again." Maybe he

really said that. It doesn't matter. But a moment later Forsyth heard
the distinctive sound of a bullet hitting bone. Mooers uttered "I'm
hit," and pitched forward on to the sand. Forsyth turned him over to
see where he was wounded. The bullet had struck Mooers squarely
in the forehead, and he never said another word, although he would
linger for three more days before dying.

Another of the scouts, named Frank Herrington, was also hit in the
forehead, this time by an arrow. His mates tried to remove the arrow
but couldn't and had to cut it off. The arrowhead stayed lodged in the
bone. Moments later a bullet came from the side and hit the man a
glancing blow on the forehead. The shot dislodged the arrowhead, and
both bullet and arrowhead dropped into the sand. The half-stunned
scout recovered, wrapped a bandage around his head, and kept firing.

The first charge of mounted warriors from the main body came
shortly thereafter. "In a tumult of shouting and shooting, singing war
songs and death songs, the Indians charged up the streambed, many
of the Sioux with streaming war bonnets of eagle feathers, the Dog
Soldiers wearing their peculiar bonnets of crow feathers without a tail."
Coming up the streambed meant that the Indians were attacking the
end of the island, but even though only a handful of the scouts were
placed there, they loosed a volume of fire that surprised the attackers
by its intensity. The other scouts faced to the side and began fire, too.
"The rifle fire of those new repeaters was continuous and unlike anything the Indians had ever before experienced," said George Bent.
While the Sioux, especially, had vivid memories of the attacks at the
Wagon Box and Hayfield Fights, the troops there were using single shot
rifles, and although the new trapdoor mechanism made the Springfield
easier and faster to reload, the volume of fire was nothing like what the
scouts were able to put up with their repeaters. Charging down
the streambed meant that the attackers were offering relatively easy
shots to the scouts because they were coming straight at them. There
was little relative motion, until that is the attackers reached the island,
but instead of riding over the dug in scouts, the Indians swooped

down both sides of the island—all except one, their leader. He made a mad dash over the island and through the scouts' circle of trenches.

> Wolf Belly, or Bad Heart, half Cheyenne, half Sioux, whose med-icine was so strong that bullets could not harm him, headed that charge, armed only with lance and shield. He wore a breechcloth and a panther skin thrown over his shoulder. Unlike the others he never faltered under the terrific rifle fire from the island and rode through the scouts and up the river bank, then turned and, to show his strong heart, charged back again through the entrenched whites.

Wolf Belly's medicine that day was indeed good, because he was not hit despite his wild ride through the scouts' entrenchments. The other attackers thundered by and continued up the stream. Despite the rate of fire from the scouts, there were few Indian casualties, except among the ponies, many of whom were hit and killed. The riders, when thrown off their mounts, were able to run or crawl into the tall grass along the banks. During this action, Bent reports that only one Indian was killed, and he was shot while circling the island "on the prairie" and beyond the streambed.

Wolf Belly led, if that's the word, only about sixty warriors. Most likely he simply said something like "Now I am going!" and a few dozen warriors decided to go, too.

It's worth noting Bent's phrase "to show his strong heart." Bent, who was half-Cheyenne by blood and more than that by tempera-ment, intentionally or unintentionally put his finger on the essence of the Cheyenne warrior culture. If the object of Wolf Belly's ride was simply to kill as many scouts as he could, he went about it the wrong way, surely. Armed only with a lance, he might have thought he could skewer one or two scouts once he was on the island, but he didn't even seem to try that. He had no gun, no bow, not even a war club. He could have gotten hold of a pistol, which is the normal cavalry weapon in a close fight like this one. But he carried only a lance and shield which was more symbolic than practical. And while a heavy buffalo-hide shield might deflect a fifty caliber bullet that came at an angle, it would not stop a bullet fired directly at it from close range. Nor would a warrior, for that matter. But a warrior's shield was as much a talisman as anything. But what an opportunity for display and for gathering accolades! Hundreds of his comrades were there, all focused on the island, watching the action. Women and children from the village were watching from the hillsides. There could not have been a better stage. The first time through was so exhilarating that he turned around and rode through again.

Forsyth was full of admiration for the warrior's exploit, the warrior who, he assumed, was Roman Nose. He described him in almost Cooperesque purple:

> [H]e was the very beau ideal of an Indian chief. [. . .] He was a man over six feet and three inches in height, beautifully formed and save for a crimson silk sash around his waist and his moccasins on his feet, perfectly naked. His face was hideously painted in alternate lines of red and black and his head covered by a magnificent war bonnet from which just above his temples and curving slightly forward, stood two short two short black buffalo horns, while its ample length of eagle feathers and heron plumes trailed wildly in the wind behind him, and as he came swiftly on at the head of his charging warriors, in all his barbaric strength and grandeur, he proudly rode that day the most perfect type of savage warrior it has been my lot to see.

Of course, it would have been impossible to know the height of the warrior was who was galloping through the island amid clouds of gun smoke and dust and in the excitement of the action. But Forsyth was writing for an audience that was used to scenes like this and expected them. His description of Roman Nose as an impressive physical specimen is probably lifted from an earlier description that was written after an earlier conference with the Cheyenne. But that is quibbling. Forsyth deserves credit for acknowledging the gallantry and style of a deadly enemy—a fellow beau sabreur complete with "crimson sash" and panache, both literal and figurative. But the man he saw charging through his lines was not Roman Nose. That Cheyenne warrior had not joined the fight yet and was still encamped, a dozen or so miles from the battlefield.

The mounted charge by the Cheyenne was beaten off by the high volume of fire, but it was not without result. When it was over Forsyth, who had fought the action almost flat on his back and only supported himself by his elbow so that he could fire his pistol, was shocked to see Fred Beecher stand up shakily, then lean on his rifle and stagger, fall, and drag himself toward Forsyth.

"I have my death wound, general. I am shot in the side, and dying." Here again, this seems a little literary, but there was nothing made up about Forsyth's reaction: "Oh, no, Beecher—no!"

"Yes. Good night." Then he lost consciousness. A few moments later Forsyth heard Beecher whisper, "My poor mother." And it's not at all hard to believe that those were his actual last words. The stunned Forsyth was deeply saddened to lose "one of the best and bravest officers in the United States army." And Custer, who was not easily impressed and not one to praise his fellow officers universally, wrote: "He was one of the most reliable and efficient officers doing duty on the Plains. Modest, energetic and ambitious in his profession, had he lived he would have undoubtedly had a brilliant future."

To repeat what Beecher's father said afterward, "It almost seems like fate—bullets seemed to find him wherever he fought." Oddly, many of Beecher's Cheyenne adversaries of the day believed much the same thing, and they avoided the use of metal implements as much as possible, thinking that by using them they acquired some sort of mystical magnetism that attracted Fate in the form of enemy bullets.

ROMAN NOSE AT HIS TENT

During the first few hours of the fight, Roman Nose was in his tent, several miles from the action. Like Achilles, he was thinking things over. But unlike Achilles he was not sulking about the loss of a woman, although a woman had been partially responsible for his current problem.

George Bent knew Roman Nose "very well and found him to be a man of fine character, quiet and self-contained." Bent says that when Roman Nose was a young man, he had camped on an island in a Montana lake and had fasted for four days. There he dreamed of serpent with a single horn in the middle of its forehead—a kind of fantastic and perhaps sinister unicorn. Later Roman Nose told White Bull about his dream. White Bull was "one of the most famous of the old time Northern Cheyenne medicine men," White Bull used that vision to make Roman Nose a war bonnet that would protect him in battle.

> Instead of having two buffalo horns attached to the head band, one on each side, it had but one rising over the center of the forehead; it had a very long tail that nearly touched the ground even when Roman Nose was mounted. This tail was made of a strip of young buffalo bull hide and had eagle feathers all along its length, first four red feathers, then four black ones, then four red feathers again and so on, forty feathers in all. In making this famous war bonnet White Bull did not use anything that had come from the whites, no cloth, thread or metal.

Years later, in conversations with George Bird Grinnell, White Bull said the bonnet also displayed the skins of a bat, a kingfisher, an eagle, and a barn swallow. The bonnet would convey the different attributes and powers of those creatures. "In battle the enemy may shoot at the person on horseback but what he is shooting at is not really there, in the flesh, as he appears to be. The real person is up above." He was "up above" like the bat, or swooping like the swallow, but not anywhere a bullet could find him. In short, the war bonnet would make Roman Nose invulnerable.

When White Bull had finished making the war bonnet, he presented it to Roman Nose along with some specific instructions. To violate any would weaken or even cancel its protective powers and would require a series of lengthy and elaborate purification ceremonies to restore the bonnet's power. First, he must never shake hands with anyone—"If you do, you will certainly be killed." In battle he was to imitate the cries of the kingfisher, which is a kind of cross between a police whistle and a screech. What's more, his horse had to be painted with certain prescribed patterns and colors. He was also told to wear a special war paint: three horizontal bars that would cover his entire face—yellow on the forehead, red over the nose and cheeks and black across the chin and jaw. And finally "he was never to eat food that had been taken from a dish with a metal instrument."

It was a lot to think about, but in the eight years Roman Nose had worn the bonnet in battles, he had followed the rules and had never been touched by a bullet, despite his daring and almost maniacal courage in charges against the soldiers and in fights against civilians. "Roman Nose had entire faith in this war bonnet, and it was believed that it had always protected him in battle. He had worn it in many fights, especially in the year 1865, when on several occasions he rode back and forth within twenty five or thirty yards of lines of white troops, all of whom shot at him without effect." And it seems more than reasonable to assume his courage was legitimate—something more than simple faith in an elaborate talisman. For in spite of his belief that he was invulnerable, when the bullets were flying and his horses were shot from under him and he saw his comrades going down, Roman Nose would have been less than human if he didn't have a doubt or two. He certainly knew of other warriors who claimed to be invulnerable, but turned out not to be. If there was a seed of doubt, it may have been planted by an arrow wound suffered in a fight against the Pawnee. But protection against bullets was the bonnet's special quality, and Roman Nose had never been hit.

Now, however, in camp with the Sioux and after a feast, he learned that he had unknowingly eaten bread that a Sioux woman had lifted from the pan with an iron fork. He usually gave instructions to the women about his special requirements for food preparation, but this time he had forgotten to do it. Cheyenne women in his village would have known without being told, but in the village he was visiting, the Sioux women had no way of knowing. It's not hard to imagine his sense of shock when he learned what happened. The timing could not have been worse. There'd be no opportunity to conduct the purification ceremonies that would restore the bonnet's power, because the Cheyenne leaders at the battlefield had sent emissaries to him, saying they needed him. His reputation and his prowess would be an inspiration to the others. Not only that, they said, there was a great opportunity to achieve a famous victory over these surrounded white men. There would be historic honor in it. All the people were watching. Surely, they said, Roman Nose could not resist this chance for further glory.

So Roman Nose came, knowing he was going to his death. There seemed little doubt about that. After all, he had always followed the prescriptions for the past eight years, and he had been protected. Now having violated a taboo, he had cancelled his power. It was just a careless mistake, but even heroes must pay for their mistakes. The taint of metal would draw bullets to him.

When Roman Nose arrived at the battlefield, there was a lull in the fighting. It was late in the afternoon of the first day. "There was a great deal of excitement among the Indians at the news that the great Roman Nose had come up. An old man rode up to the group of chiefs and reproached Roman Nose for not getting into the fight." Others urged him to lead the next charge. He agreed. He prepared to go, painting his face and preparing his war bonnet, and then saying: "I have done something I was told not to do. [. . .] I know I shall be killed today."

He mounted his white horse and started for the island. Other mounted warriors joined him, but not so many as in the morning's charge. Some of the others probably reasoned that Roman Nose may or may not be invulnerable, but they certainly were not. They had seen what the scouts' volume of fire could do to a charge of horsemen. Those who had tried before were lucky to get away, and they were not eager to try their luck again. Fighting on foot from the bankside bushes seemed a smarter option. But Roman Nose went, and a few others followed him.

The Cheyenne warriors swooped down the hillside toward the island. Issuing the shrill cry of the kingfisher, Roman Nose came thrashing through the high grass along the riverbank. He must have seemed like a figure conjured by an evil and sinister genie with his weird bonnet and face paint—the stuff of nightmares. The scouts had seen plenty of Indians in their day, but usually the warriors were not wearing war paint and war regalia. Many, if not most of those whites who had seen such phantasmagoria had not lived to talk about it. The sight of Roman Nose in full display must have been unsettling, at the very least, and of course to unsettle the enemy is the point of wearing it—that and to acquire its ritual protective power. Roman Nose was galloping toward the northeastern corner of the island where Jack Stilwell and his comrades were hiding. Once again the Cheyenne charge was met with a high volume of fire from the scouts, although Stilwell and his mates crouched down and held their fire. Faced with the heavy fusillade, most of Roman Nose's party peeled off and rode away. But Roman Nose kept coming. Apparently he intended to ride over the island and through the scouts. If he was going to die, he was going to do it in desperate style.

Like all the other Cheyenne that day, he did not see Stilwell in his blind. Roman Nose came thundering past the blind, splashing through the thin line of current. Stilwell and his mates waited until he passed and then fired. Roman Nose was hit in the back "just above the hips." Some reports say he fell into the riverbed near the far bank, and after a while was able to crawl into the tall grass on the bank, where some warriors were able to reach him and carry him off. George Bent says he did not fall, but rode back to the Cheyenne lines and collapsed there. That sounds more likely, because if he fell in the dry riverbed and tried to crawl away, Stilwell and the others most assuredly would have kept shooting him. At that range, they would not have missed a wounded, crawling man, and they would not have hesitated to finish him. In any event, Roman Nose made it back to his lines. Then he was taken to the village, most likely carried there on a travois by women who came to retrieve the dead and wounded. He lingered through the night, in considerable pain. There was nothing that any medicine man could do for him. By morning he was dead, just as he knew he would be.

"Roman Nose was buried on a scaffold." Some of the women helped his wife "bring up the lodge poles and raise this scaffold for his burial. . . . As the most famous of the Northern Cheyenne Roman Nose was regarded as the hero of this fight" Roman Nose had two wives, one named Island and the other Woman With White Child. It's not clear which wife arranged for the scaffold. Of course, all the women in the village mourned the loss of their hero. In the old days they would have slashed themselves with flints or cut off a little finger, but Bent says the northern Cheyenne women had stopped this form of mourning in 1865. He does not say why.

On the island Forsyth and his men could hear the "wails of passionate grief and agony [rise and fall] in the air in a prolonged and mournful cadence of rage and despair." To the white ears most native chanting and song sounded mournful and strange, but in this case Forsyth was probably correct in thinking he was hearing an outpouring of grief.

Roman Nose's comrades were naturally saddened, too. Some undoubtedly shook their heads at the bad luck of the metal fork, although the incident only reaffirmed to all of them the necessity of strict adherence to rituals and careful observance of taboos. Yes, it was bad luck and very sad. On the other hand, Roman Nose had died while he was still a vigorous young man who had won vast acclaim from the people. In that sense, it was a good death. As the father of the warrior killed in a fight with the whites said, "[I]t is well. It is better to be killed in battle than to die a natural death. We must all die. Do not let the killing of these young men make you feel badly."

Just before dark the scouts could see rustling in the tall grass on the riverbank. The Cheyenne were trying to retrieve their own wounded and dead. The scouts fired at the movement, but the Cheyenne were able to retrieve a couple of their wounded. Using ropes they tied one end to the wounded men's feet and dragged them backward.

It had been a bitter day in some ways for the Cheyenne. They had lost their greatest warrior and a half dozen others killed, and there were many more wounded. And they had not achieved the great victory they had expected. The eight mischievous boys had spoiled the surprise, but there is no record of their being punished. It was the kind of thing young men did, and it was understandable. But it was certainly too bad. But tomorrow was another day. And surely the outnumbered and surrounded scouts would run out of ammunition or supplies sooner or later. It was simply a matter of keeping up the pressure until the white men exhausted their supplies and both their will and ability to fight. Then the Cheyenne could ride over them, counting coup and killing them all. Or perhaps the whites would try to sneak away in the darkness, in which case the Cheyenne could find their trail in the morning and annihilate them on the open Plains. Either way, there was still the promise of success and plunder and glory.

On the island Forsyth assessed his situation. Beecher and three others were dead. Mooers was still alive, somehow, but beyond hope and soon would die. There were seventeen wounded, including Forsyth. Of those, six or seven were wounded badly enough to make them useless in future attacks, Forsyth among them. The other wounded, though, could still fight. On the plus side of the ledger, Forsyth had plenty of ammunition and a strong defensive position, which the scouts set about improving by digging connecting trenches and building up their breastworks. They also had water. One of the men had dug a small well. There was also a slight rivulet in the streambed, although someone would have to expose himself to fill the canteens. That would have to be done in the dark. There wasn't much firewood available on the island, and finding some on the riverbanks would also have to wait until dark. There was food, of a kind. Forsyth ordered some of the men to cut steaks off the horses and bury the meat in the sand to delay spoilage. He ate a few mouthfuls of raw horseflesh to keep up his strength. Later, when they ran out of salt and the horseflesh became increasingly rotten, the men would sprinkle it with gunpowder to disguise the taste. At least for the time being they were in decent shape, but they would need help to survive. That was clear to all of them.

Forsyth gathered the men around his rifle pit and asked for volunteers to go for help. As mentioned, they were a hundred miles or more from Fort Wallace, but that was the place where the nearest help could come from. What's more the scouts needed medical supplies. The few things they brought had been packed on mules, but were lost in the move to the island. The scouts were using torn clothes and bandannas as makeshift bandages. Their surgeon, Dr. Mooers, was mortally wounded and unconscious. They needed a doctor, medical supplies, and an ambulance for the wounded. Soon they would need food, because it was abundantly clear that they were almost out. And even traveling at their best pace, the scouts who went would take at least three days, probably four to get to Wallace. Thirty miles a day on foot through hostile Cheyenne and Sioux, many of whom would be on the lookout for just such a mission, would take at least that long. The scouts would have to travel at night and hide during the day. What's more the Plains were rolling in some places, flat in others, and there were no real landmarks to travel by. The scouts could not possibly travel in a straight line, and that would add to the distance and the difficulty. Assuming they did make it to Wallace, it would take another three or four days for a rescue party, complete with an ambulance and supply wagon, to get organized and make the return trip. At the very least Forsyth and his men would have to wait a minimum of seven days before they could even start to look for help to arrive.

When Forsyth asked for volunteers, a number of men raised their hands, and not because it meant safe passage out of there. The odds were against anyone who tried to get to Wallace. Forsyth selected Pierre Trudeau and young Jack Stilwell. He gave Stilwell his map (he does not mention a compass). Stilwell and Trudeau filled their canteens and pocketed some slices of horsemeat. Then they took off their boots, and hung them around their necks, wrapped some strips of leather on their feet to simulate moccasins, wrapped themselves in blankets and left very quietly. They walked backwards in the sandy ground to imitate the footprints of the enemy in case the tracks were discovered. Heading southeast, the two men disappeared into the night. There were no shouts from the Indians and no shots were fired. It was possible they got away, but there was no way to be sure. Time would tell, but as far as the scouts were concerned, time would be rather slow about providing the answer. If Stilwell and Trudeau got through, all might still be well. If they didn't, well, everyone knew what that would mean.

After improving their trenches, the scouts settled down for the night. They anticipated another fight in the morning. Then it started to rain.

THE SECOND DAY

The rain shower that night was welcome. The sun that day had been blisteringly hot, and the men in their trenches had been hard-pressed to get any water from the seepage in the small well they dug. They were only able to fill their canteens after it was dark. At least the refreshing rain cooled their sunburnt skin and soaked their clothes which had become stiff with dried sweat and in some cases, blood. But the night soon turned cold. Although the days were very hot under the beating sun, the late September nights were chilly on the Plains. The dry air gave no resistance to the rising heat of the day. There was no wood to speak of for fires, either for cooking or warmth. And although Forsyth believed the Indians never fought in the night, he and the men were wary about a campfire that might attract a marksman hidden on the far bank.

In the morning "a large party" of Cheyenne horsemen appeared. They were a couple of hundred yards from the island. Forsyth told the men to hold their fire. The warriors didn't seem interested quite yet in attacking and seemed instead to be reconnoitering. About twenty of them dismounted and came forward in a kind of skirmish line, as if unsure whether the scouts were still there or had escaped in the night. The approaching warriors were still beyond the riverbank bushes and would make decent targets in the open, as would the men who were still mounted and waiting. But Forsyth wanted them to get closer before firing. "At this juncture, one of the men, probably by accident, discharged his piece."

This time it was a scout whose mischief spoiled the surprise, and Forsyth was annoyed. It had been a good chance to do some real damage, but it had been lost. As for the gun going off accidentally, that seems possible, but unlikely. The mounted men dived for the ground as did the skirmishers. Forsyth ordered the scouts to open fire, and although he believed they killed one of the skirmishers, they did no other damage. From that point on for the rest of the day, there were no mounted charges. The warriors resumed their careful approaches on foot and took up positions in the weeds of the riverbank on both sides of the island. They fired when they saw a target, as did the scouts. But the scouts built-up breastworks and deeper trenches protected them from any significant harm. One of the scouts was grazed by a bullet, but that was the extent of the damage. Similarly, the cover on the riverbanks protected the warriors. The warriors had also dug rifle pits and were quite as well protected as the scouts. The fight was settling down into a stalemate of sniping. "It was now apparent that they meant to starve us out, for they made no further attempts to attack in the open." From Forsyth's position it might have been better if the

Indians had tried to attack. At least then there would be a battle. The scouts with their firepower and trenches might have been able to inflict severe casualties and, although they would have suffered, too, they might have been able to discourage the warriors and make them decide to give it up until some other time. Taking the chances of a decisive battle is usually preferable to enduring a siege. But a siege appeared to be what the scouts were facing.

The prospect was all the more discouraging because the wounded men were suffering badly, Forsyth included. He said the first wound he suffered, the one in the flesh of his thigh, was excruciating. There was little if any medicine. The men were pinned down in their trenches and any movement to come to the aid of one of the wounded might bring an arrow or bullet from the tall grasses opposite. The rain had been welcome in the night, but the morning brought the wretched sun again. It beat down on the scouts and added to their miseries. The sun also beat on the carcasses of the horses and accelerated the process of decay. Already the scouts could smell the beginnings of rotting horseflesh. Flies buzzed and swarmed around the wounds of the men and the carcasses of the horses, especially where the men had cut steaks. And added to their troubles the Cheyenne and Sioux women on the hills to the north continued their "dismal wailing and beating of drums." Then there was the matter of their own dead. They would need to be buried soon. But that work would have to wait as long as the Indian snipers were active on both banks. But surely the sight of the lifeless Beecher and the others was more than a little dispiriting. No doubt they were covered with blankets but the sight was only a little less depressing. Also depressing were the incoherent mumblings of the unconscious Dr. Mooers.

All things considered, however, Forsyth felt that the scouts might just be able to survive. The Indians might get bored with the siege game; it was not something they traditionally did. It did not sit well with their warrior ethic. And they had apparently given up the idea of a frontal attack, at least for the time being. And so it became a matter of simply enduring, until help arrived. But that was the rub. Would help arrive before the Cheyenne and Sioux got bored with waiting and decided on an all out attack? Would help arrive before the scouts ran out of food? Or more to the point, would help arrive before the only food, the horseflesh, had rotted to the point of being inedible? And even more fundamentally, would help ever arrive, period? Forsyth no doubt wondered what the Indians were thinking. What would he do in their situation? But whatever answer he came up with would be the wrong one, for he was new on the Plains and had not yet learned the lesson of the plainsman: "In all my life, I ain't learned but one thing about an Indian. Whatever you know you'd do in his place—he ain't going to do that." Maybe Forsyth was smart enough to know what he didn't know. But it really didn't matter. For the time being, there was nothing to do but wait and watch.

That night Forsyth again called for more volunteers to go for help. There was of course no way to know whether Stilwell and Trudeau got through. Sending another pair of messengers only made sense. "Two more of my company were sent out at eleven o'clock at night to try to make their way to Fort Wallace, but they found the Indians guarding every outlet, and returned to the command about three the next morning." That was disheartening, not least because it raised doubts in all of their minds about whether the first two messengers had made it. Granted there had been no shots when Stilwell and Trudeau the night before, but there were lots of ways the warriors could kill a man silently. Once again the scouts settled down for a night of restlessness and watching.

THE THIRD DAY

The next morning was cloudy and promised some rain, or, if not that, at least relief from the fearsome sun. The men were stoic, knowing that they had days of waiting before them. The wounded were still suffering but at least they were not being attacked. There were occasional shots from the usual locations, but no one was hit. Nor did the scouts do any damage to their enemies that they could see.

Around noon Sharp Grover came over to Forsyth's trench and told him that the Cheyenne women who had been the source of the dismal keening were leaving their places on the hilltops to the north. That seemed a hopeful sign, since the women had been such "interested spectators" from the first. Now if they were leaving it might mean that there would be nothing more to see. No more attacks.

Soon afterward the scouts saw a delegation of Cheyenne coming toward them under a white flag of truce. Forsyth was in no mood for palaver and ordered several men to stand and shout and gesture to tell them not to come nearer. Forsyth was sure they were trying to assess the condition of the scouts before deciding on their next moves. The Cheyenne emissaries ignored the warning gestures and kept coming. Then Grover yelled at them "in their own language" to stay away, but they paid no attention and kept coming. Finally, Forsyth ordered the men to fire a "half dozen shots" in their direction. That decided them, and they retreated, but a number of their entrenched warriors fired a return volley which convinced Forsyth that they were not sincere about a parlay and were using it as a ruse.

Still later in the day as the men endured the afternoon heat, they noticed a fat Cheyenne who was calling to them from the Indian lines. The Cheyenne assumed he was out of range, well over a thousand yards, and he was taunting the scouts. "He was perfectly naked and his gestures were exceedingly exasperating." Forsyth doesn't specify, but it's not hard to imagine what was going on. At the risk of generalization, the Plains Indians had a robust and bawdy sense of humor. That should not be surprising. Their domestic culture—the communal living, one room homes with utterly no personal privacy, men with several wives, no sanitation, domestic animals in abundance—it was not the sort of life that would develop Victorian delicacy about functions or pleasures of the flesh. Many commentators who had visited the tribes in their villages remarked on their lively sense of fun and playfulness among themselves, which contrasted completely with the stereotype of the dour and stoic red man or, for that matter, the dignified philosopher of the Plains and woodlands. In any event, the antics of this lone Cheyenne caused Forsyth to call over three of the men who happened to have the Springfield trapdoor rifles in addition to the Spencers they had been issued. The Springfields had a better range, several hundred yards more than the Spencers. (In fact, they could be lethal at a thousand yards and could carry a good twelve hundred.) He had the three men raise their sights to the maximum and fire at the scampering Cheyenne. "At the crack of the three rifles he sprang into the air with a yell of seemingly both surprise and anguish, and rolled over stone dead, while the Indians in his vicinity scattered in every direction." It probably didn't happen quite that way. The target, whose name was Killed by a Bull, would not have heard the noise of the shot at that range, not before he was hit by the bullet or bullets. And the Cheyenne say that, far from making obscene comic antics, he was helping carry some wounded to the rear. But the story illustrates that two sides in a battle generally see things differently. In this case both versions could be true to some degree. In any case, Forsyth says it "was a matter of intense satisfaction to all of us." Further, it must have given the Cheyenne something more to think about. Despite his name, Killed by a Bull was in fact killed by a very, very long-range shot.

Speaking of rifles, Forsyth wrote in the memoirs that the Indians were well supplied with modern weapons. "[I]n the matter of arms and ammunition they were our equals in every respect. The Springfield breech loaders that they captured at Fort Phil Kearny formed part of their equipment as well as Henry, Remington and Spencer rifles." In mentioning Fort Phil Kearny, Forsyth is referring to the Fetterman fight. He is saying the Cheyenne and Sioux collected the Springfield breechloaders from Fetterman's troops and after annihilating them. But the new Springfields were delivered to the troops at Phil Kearny after the Fetterman disaster and showed up for the first time at the

Wagon Box and Hay Field fights the following summer of 1867. Forsyth also says after the fight at Beecher Island he and his men picked up a number of brass cartridge cases which indicate that the Indians had plenty of new rifles, Springfield trap doors included. Where they got them remains a question. But it is certainly possible the Cheyenne and Sioux received the newest model Springfields as well as Spencers and Henrys from Indian traders. George Custer notes in the confrontation with Hancock the year before the Cheyenne were armed with the latest weapons. "[E]ach [warrior] was supplied with either a breech loading rifle or a revolver, sometimes with both, the latter obtained through the wise foresight and strong sense of fair play which prevails in the Indian Department." This was a very sore subject with the army for obvious reasons, and they had every right to complain about traders who provided rifles to the Indians either under terms of a treaty or simply to make a profit from the sale.

George Bent says most of the Cheyenne rifles were old, muzzle loaders, and that most of the warriors "were armed with lances and bows." So there are, as usual, at least two versions. In this case, however, the evidence in the form of shell casings seems to support Forsyth's version, especially since the men killed were all hit by bullets. And the desultory but regular sniping for three days running was all rifle fire. A few scouts were also hit by arrows in the initial hours of the fight, but aside from that, rifles on both sides did the bulk of the damage. Forsyth doesn't mention the pistols his men had, although he did manage a few shots with his Colt revolver, after he'd been wounded and was lying flat on his back during the first charge.

In the afternoon, Forsyth decided that he had better try to send out more messengers. He wrote a dispatch to send to the commanding officer at Fort Wallace, but unfortunately headed his note "On Delaware Creek, Republican River, August 19, 1868." Forsyth and his scouts were not really sure where they were. If the messengers were not able to return with the relief force, that mistake could cost both the besieged and relief forces precious time.

To Colonel Bankhead, or Commanding Officer, Fort Wallace:

I sent you two messengers on the night of the 17th instant, informing you of my critical condition. I tried to send two more last night, but they did not succeed in passing the Indians pickets and returned. If the others have not arrived, then hasten at once to my assistance. I have eight badly wounded and ten slightly wounded men to take in, and every animal I had was killed, save seven which the Indians stampeded. Lieutenant Beecher is dead, and Acting Assistant Surgeon Mooers probably cannot live the night out. He was hit in the head Thursday and has spoken but one rational word since. I am wounded in two places—in the right thigh, and my left leg broken below the knee. The Cheyenne alone numbered 450 or more. Mr. Grover says they never fought so before. They were splendidly armed with Spencer and Henry rifles. We killed at least thirty five of them, and wounded many more, besides killing and wounding a quantity of their stock. They carried off most of their killed during the night, but three of their men fell into our hands. I am on a little island and still have plenty of ammunition left. We are living on mule and horse meat, and are entirely out of rations. If it were not for so many wounded, I would come in and take the chance of whipping them if attacked. They are evidently sick of their bargain. [. . .] You had better start with not less than seventy five men and bring all the wagons and ambulances you can spare. Bring a six pound howitzer with you. I can hold out here for six days longer if absolutely necessary, but please lose no time.

The request for a howitzer is interesting and makes good sense. Indians intensely disliked being shot at with the "gun that shoots twice," meaning a cannon firing exploding shells. As mentioned earlier, the mountain howitzer could be disassembled and packed on a mule, and it had proved decisive in two previous battles between native tribes and outnumbered troops. If Forsyth had brought one along, the battle would have taken a very different form. There would certainly have been no crowds of spectators on the ridges.

There is no further mention of the three "who fell into our hands." Certainly they were not taken prisoner. Perhaps they were Cheyenne shot and dropped on the island or in the streambed during the first attack.

Forsyth selected Jack Donovan and Allison Pliley as messengers—"two of my best men." They left at midnight. Once again, there was no firing from the Indian lines. Forsyth and the others began to hope that the Indians had decided to abandon their siege.

THE FOURTH DAY

At dawn the Cheyenne fired a heavy series of volleys against the island, but the scouts were huddled in their trenches and were not hurt. As the morning advanced and the sun rose the heat became intense and accelerated the already well advanced decomposition of the horses. The stench was becoming intolerable. Worse yet, there was the growing odor arising from some of the wounded. There was the distinct possibility of gangrene. Putrefaction of dead horses was one thing, gangrene in living flesh was something else again. Several of the men were out of their heads from fever and were mumbling or raving. Dr. Mooers was still breathing but was well past the point of no return.

The Indians continued their occasional fire throughout the day, if only to remind the scouts that they were still around. The scouts returned fire now and then whenever a warrior provided a target however brief. But no Cheyenne were hit that day, either.

The pain in Forsyth's thigh wound was intense. The bullet shifted slightly against his flesh whenever he made even the slightest move. He could see the bullet lying below the surface of the skin. It was dangerously close to the artery. He was worried that the bullet might scrape the wall of the artery and open it, which would mean the end of him. He asked several of the men to cut it out for him, but when they examined the wound and saw how close the bullet was to the artery, they declined. They did not want to take the responsibility. Forsyth then sent for his saddle bags and got out his straight razor. He asked two of the men to "press the adjacent flesh back and draw it tight." Then he did the surgery himself. "I managed to cut it out myself without disturbing the artery, greatly to my almost immediate relief."

As the afternoon wore on and the stench of the dead horses intensified, there was less and less firing from the Cheyenne. Forsyth began to wonder if maybe they had decided to call it a day. After all, the women and children had left the hillsides the day before. It would make sense that the warriors would have waited a day or so to let the village get underway. Then, it would be time for them to go, too. Forsyth needed to look around for himself. He could not stand by himself, so he had several of the men lift him up in a blanket. As soon as he was upright about twenty hidden Cheyenne opened fire, and the men holding Forsyth quite naturally hit the ground. They dropped Forsyth and his broken leg shattered further. A piece of newly broken bone thrust though his skin. Not surprisingly Forsyth screamed and swore and then collapsed back into his trench. The Cheyenne, evidently, had not left, after all. It looked very much as if they intended to let the scouts starve or at least become so weak as to be defenseless.

The day wore on. There were a few shots in both directions, but no one was hit. The stench grew even worse, and hunger was staring the scouts in the face. In fact, it had already gripped them. They tried boiling the rotted meat to make a kind of soup, but they had to be careful and keep the heads down while building and tended the fire. They had been able to collect some firewood in the night, and boiling the rotten meat might help them get it down. But they couldn't do it. A few of the men found some wild plums and stewed them as well and gave the tea they made to the wounded, Forsyth included. The scouts who were unhurt did their best to look after the wounded, but without medical supplies all they could do was give them water and keep them cool during the day and warm at night. Toward the end of the day, Forsyth examined his leg and was distressed to see maggots beginning to infest the wound.

By nightfall the wolves were watching from the hillside. They were of course drawn by the odor of the dead horses. A few of the scouts tried to shoot one. Even boiled wolf or coyote would be welcome at this stage. But they had no luck. A couple of scouts carefully stole out of camp in the darkness hoping to find some game—a jackrabbit or a sage hen. Anything. But there was nothing.

They settled down to another night of fitful watching and waiting. It was the last day of summer.

THE JOURNEY OF THE SCOUTS

Although he was only nineteen Jack Stilwell was in charge of the two-man mission. He selected Pierre Trudeau to go with him. Years later Stilwell described Trudeau to the celebrated artist, Frederick Remington:

> [He was] an old French Rocky Mountain trapper. [. . .] He was about fifty-five years old, but had led a rough life with the American Fur Company and was much more aged than his years warranted. Also he had consumed what whiskey he could lay his hands on, and that had not improved things. He dressed in greasy buckskin and wore long hair, goatee and mustache and would have made a proper looking member of Napoleon's Old Guard. He had a very limited English vocabulary but made up in profanity when he lacked words.

Trudeau went by the nickname "Avalanche," because he once had his leg broken by a kick from a mule. The break was pretty severe, and he had to be carted off in a medical wagon. "That was the onliest time I ever rode in an avalanche," he said.

Stillwell hadn't chosen Trudeau for comic relief but because he spoke Cheyenne and Sioux and could possibly answer any challenges they might encounter in the dark. They were going to respond to any Cheyenne challenges in Sioux, and vice versa. When they left that first night, they avoided the little valleys where the Cheyenne would expect a messenger to sneak through and instead walked over the open hillsides wrapped in blankets as though they were warriors on the prowl. They were not challenged and headed southeast.

When the sun came up they hid in a hollowed out place in a hillside and waited out the day. They could hear firing coming from the island. That night they continued south and in the morning they were unsettled by coming upon a large village on the banks of the South Branch of the Republican. They hid in a swamp and again waited for nightfall and watched riders coming and going from the village. The next night they made good time and in the day, according to legend they hid in a dried out carcass of a buffalo bull. (Buffalo Bill told the scouts' story in his autobiography and embellished it a bit by adding a rattlesnake that joined the scouts in the carcass.) Underway again at night the two men made good time. Figuring by then that they had passed the villages and camps, they carried on during the day. Avalanche Trudeau made the mistake of drinking water from a buffalo wallow and became sick. Mark Twain might have said it was because Trudeau wasn't used to water.

Four and a half days after leaving Forsyth they arrived, foot sore, hungry, and thirsty at Fort Wallace. It's not clear exactly how they navigated. Perhaps Forsyth had given Stilwell a compass, or perhaps they traveled by the stars. The landmarks were few, and in the night they would be even harder to see and recognize. But they must have come in a fairly straight line because they covered more than one hundred miles on foot, and over terrain that was rolling hills for much the journey, and they did it in just over four days. And while the grass-covered Plains look soft and easy from a distance, in reality the footing can be loose and gravelly in spots. It would not be comfortable walking. And whether they actually shared a dried-out buffalo carcass with a rattlesnake, they certainly walked by more than a few. The Plains had no shortage of them. At night they would have been serenaded by the howls of wolves and coyotes, and the last thing they would want was to have to fire a shot to chase away a hungry wolf or, worse, a pack. In any event, they made it. They reported to the commander at Fort Wallace, Captain (Brevet Colonel) H. C. Bankhead. Bankhead organized a relief party consisting of "wagons, ambulances, ammunition and provisions [. . .] and a strong party of men." The party left Wallace at four the next morning. Beecher's best friend, Dr. Theophilus Turner, was part of the force. He was in a sorrowing mood no doubt because he would have learned of the death of his friend. To their enduring credit, Stilwell and Trudeau joined the relief column as guides, although one report says their feet were in such poor condition and "suppurating" that they had to ride in the ambulance. If so, that was presumably Avalanche Trudeau's second experience.

Not surprisingly there are several versions about what happened with the other two messengers—Jack Donovan and Allison Pliley. Both men were highly regarded by their comrades, and Forsyth described them as two of his best men. Donovan, twenty-three, was born in New Brunswick, Canada, but moved to Wisconsin as a boy. He was invariably lighthearted and free-spirited. "Jack was as good and brave a boy as we had on the island," said another of the scouts. Pliley was equally popular. Only twenty-four, he had extensive experience on the Kansas Plains, having fought as part of the Fifteenth Kansas Volunteer cavalry during the war. Most of his wartime service involved battles with Confederate bushwhackers and guerillas and with the Indians who were raiding the settlements. After the war he studied law for a time but found it too tame and joined the Eighteenth Kansas Volunteers as a scout and later found himself at the Medicine Lodge peace conference as an observer. He was greatly admired by his comrades for his intelligence and modesty but also because he was someone who "delighted in a desperate situation and was a natural leader." Well, if he in fact "delighted in a desperate situation," he must have relished his new assignment.

The two men started out on the third night. Unfortunately the horsemeat they had for rations was now three days old, and the blazing sun had done its damage. The meat was almost past the point of being edible, and the men still had four days of traveling ahead of them. But there was no other food to give them. Donovan and Pliley put on moccasins so that their tracks would not be suspicious. One report says the moccasins were taken off two dead warriors. It's possible that these were two of the three dead that Forsyth mentioned earlier. As Pliley said later about the moccasins, "In crawling away from the island [the moccasins] got wet and the cactus thorns which were very plentiful went through them into our feet like pins in a cushion." These were small ground hugging cactus plants, hardly visible even in the daytime, let alone at night. The men soon picked up enough spines to make the rest of their trip south a miserable pain filled journey on increasingly swollen and infected feet.

Instead of heading southeast, Donavan and Pliley started almost due south. They set their course for Cheyenne Wells, Colorado, where the Smoky Hill stage line road ran east and west. They figured they could catch the eastbound stage at Cheyenne Wells and so get to Wallace faster than by going straight southeast to the Fort. That first night they stopped for an hour or so to bathe their sore feet in the South Fork of the Republican. Then they continued southward. On the fourth night they reached the road and a ranch that lay alongside it. They were given food and fresh water. Their feet "were swollen to twice their normal size," and Pliley was sick and "prostrated from eating vile horsemeat and drinking [bad] water," but he and Donavan caught the stage coach for Fort Wallace. Pliley was too sick to go very far and got off at the Goose Creek station, which was about twelve miles west of Wallace. Donavan kept going and reached the Fort only to find out the Stillwell and Trudeau had gotten there hours before and had started on the return trip with Captain Bankhead's relief force.

Here the story gets a little cloudy, but the most likely version of events has Donovan resting briefly and then riding out again to catch up to Bankhead's relief column. Meanwhile, Bankhead had sent four couriers west to find Captain Carpenter and the two companies of the Tenth Cavalry, Company H and Company I. Carpenter was just beginning a long scout against the marauding Indians and he and his troops were camped about on the Colorado line, which is forty or so miles from Wallace. The four couriers had a message from Bankhead ordering Carpenter to head north to the forks of the Republican to relieve Forsyth's besieged men. Fortunately, Carpenter had prepared for a long scout against the Cheyenne who had been attacking along the Smoky Hill, and so his force was reasonably well equipped to rescue Forsyth's scouts. The command consisted of about seventy troops, sixteen civilian scouts, thirteen supply wagons and an ambulance. One of the guides was J. J. Peate, a civilian who had been attached to Forsyth's column but who had been left behind because of some mis-understanding of orders. The two companies headed north, although they were unfamiliar with the country and were unsure exactly where Forsyth might be besieged. If Bankhead had sent either Stillwell or Trudeau along with the messengers, Carpenter's men might have had a better idea of where to go. But they knew they would have to go north to the area of the forks of the Republican, and so they wasted no time getting underway.

Two days later they reached area of the South Fork of the Repub-lican and began to see signs of the Cheyenne camp. They also started to encounter scaffolds of the dead. Peate says they examined these bodies and found they had all been killed by gunfire. They were getting close. One of the scaffolds "was in a tepee, and the body was wrapped in a fine buffalo robe. The corpse was not disturbed but Carpenter did carry away a drum that he later gave to the Pennsylvania Historical society."

The suggestion that the scaffolds and the dead were not disturbed strains credulity. And George Bent reports that the soldiers tore down the scaffolds, which sounds more likely. After all, if the troops exam-ined the bodies and discovered that they all died from gunshots, and if the scaffolds such as Roman Nose's were made of the lodge poles, as reported by George Bent, are we really to believe that a soldier climbed up eight feet or so, examined the body, and then slid down again without disturbing the corpse? Or is it more likely that the troops pulled the scaffolds down, checked the body, took a few souvenirs and then moved on? The troops would have had no delicate feelings for the dead Indians. And the Cheyenne who left the bodies there would not be surprised by the action. After all, they knew the animals and birds would soon be feasting on the corpses, anyway. It hardly mattered whether the creatures who tore them down walked on two legs or four. "The body of a man who died in battle . . . was left lying on the prairie, sometimes covered with a blanket, oftener not covered. Men thought it well that wolves, coyotes, eagles, buzzards and other animals should eat their flesh and scatter their bodies far and wide over the prairie." The body of a warrior, as the Psalmist said, "shall be a portion for foxes."

Not knowing where he was going and with guides who were unfamiliar with that country north of the Smoky Hill, Carpenter had to explore every possible dry creek or small stream that wandered through the hills. They heard no firing from the north, and they had no way of knowing exactly where Forsyth and his scouts were. But on the morning of the twenty-fifth, Carpenter's outfit saw riders coming up from the southeast. They turned out to be the intrepid Jack Donovan who had caught up with Bankhead and had volunteered to go ahead with four other civilian scouts to tell Forsyth that help was coming. Donovan told Carpenter that he and his troops were about twenty miles south of Forsyth's position. With Donovan leading the way, Carpenter and his companies of the Tenth Cavalry hurried to cover the last twenty miles.

THE LONG WAIT

The Cheyenne seemed to be gone by the last day of summer. But Forsyth could not be sure. In any event, there was little enough he and his men could do but wait, even if they seemed to be all alone in an empty universe. The sufferings of the wounded, Forsyth included, were intense. Forsyth's wound was infested with maggots and the smell of increasing gangrene among the other wounded was added to the noxious smell of decaying horseflesh. Some of the wounded were delirious and all of them were feverish. Flies were swarming and the sun was beating down on them with what seemed like venomous intent. The men tried boiling the horsemeat and then adding gunpowder to the concoction to disguise the revolting smell and nauseous taste, but even though they were famished, they could not get or keep the stuff down. When it seemed that it was reasonably safe to leave the rifle pits, some of the unwounded went hunting. One of the scouts managed to shoot a small coyote, and the men shared what little flesh the animal had. Coyotes generally spend their lives on short commons, so there wasn't much to it. Later the men boiled the head several times to make a soup and capture the last measure of nutrition, such as it was. Some of the men found a few wild plums. But that was all the bounty the Plains would deliver. At night the wolves lined the hillcrests and howled dismally, but although they were probably in range they did not leave the darkness to offer a shot.

The unwounded men tended their suffering comrades as well as they could, but there was really very little they could do. There were no medical supplies and what first aid the men knew was only the rough sort of knowledge picked up through hard experience. There was nothing they could do about gangrene except recognize the signs and reassure the sufferer that he would be all right and that help was on the way.

On the evening of the sixth day, Forsyth reached a decision. He called the men around his rifle pit and explained the situation as he saw it. The Indians were gone, probably. They might have left a few patrols to watch the scouts and then to summon the main body back, if the scouts attempted to leave. But Forsyth felt that it was more likely that they had simply grown tired of the siege, and further that they had had enough of the scouts' firepower. He estimated that they had killed at least thirty five and had wounded many more. In that case, he said, it would probably be safe for those scouts who were still well enough to travel to head for Fort Wallace immediately. There was no way to know if the two sets of messengers had gotten through. If they had, help was surely on the way. But if they hadn't, those men who were still relatively healthy could make it to the fort and bring word. Even on foot twenty plus men would make a formidable unit that the Indians would probably not want to tangle with, especially after their losses of the last few days. So he believed, although in reality the Cheyenne would have overwhelmed the wretched scouts and killed every one of them with relative ease. But whether he knew that or not, Forsyth was putting the best face on the situation, and he felt, as any good commander would, that it was only fair to release the men who stood some chance to live. The wounded would wait here for the relief, whenever it came. And if it did not come in time, well, they were soldiers and "knew how to meet our fate."

The men rejected the offer. Forsyth's first sergeant, McCall, the Civil War brevet general who had fallen on hard times and who was himself slightly wounded, spoke for the others. According to Forsyth, McCall said, "We've fought together and by Heaven if need be we'll die together." While this sounds again a bit like Victorian melodrama and probably is not very close to the language McCall and the others used, the basic sentiment is no doubt accurate, because the men did refuse to leave. They could have, but they didn't. The scouts had been through a harrowing experience of combat and now some were suffering from wounds and they all were on the verge of—if not star-vation, quite yet—then very real and painfully debilitating hunger. The experience had certainly bonded them. Small unit comradery must have been at work to some extent. The men who were comparatively well would not leave their wounded and dead, even though Forsyth gave them the chance, and even though their odds of survival here on the island looked pretty thin.

The next two days were worse. There was no relief from the heat and sun, no relief from the pain of wounds, and no relief from the agony of hunger. The men were about at the end of their endurance.

On the morning of the ninth day, the men, who were now a gang of haggard scarecrows, were alarmed to see riders on the crest of hill to the south. That was a bad sign, because if help was to come from the Fort, it would not be coming from due south. Perhaps the Cheyenne had returned for the coup de grace, not that any of the scouts believed there would be any grace about it.

It was Jack Donovan and J. J. Peate. They were only a mile or so ahead of Carpenter's troops. Donovan and Peate gave a whoop and came galloping down the hillside, waving their hats so that the sentries wouldn't fire at them, and soon they were on the island and amid the scouts who were now delirious not only with fever and hunger but with rapture at the surprise of being rescued. Then Carpenter's troops arrived along with the ambulance and wagons.

In his memoir *History of a Slave Written by Himself at Age 86*, trooper Reuben Waller, of Company H, Tenth Cavalry, wrote:

> Colonel Carpenter and myself as his hostler rode into the rifle pits and what a sight we saw—30 wounded and dead men right in the middle of 50 dead horses that had lain in the hot sun for ten days. [. . .] The men were in a dying condition when Carpenter and myself dismounted and began to rescue them.

The story also goes that when Carpenter approached Forsyth's rifle pit, where he had been immobilized almost for the whole period of the siege, Forsyth "affected" to be casually reading *Oliver Twist* and looked up to Carpenter and said, "Welcome to Beecher Island." It was a beau geste, and done in fine style, and no doubt Carpenter understood and appreciated it for the ironic gesture it was. Probably neither man saw the literary parallel in the story of an orphan who is rescued by a kindly deus ex machina. But maybe they did, afterward. Forsyth also says that when he saw Carpenter it was "all I could do to keep from breaking down, as I was sore and feverish and tired and hungry, and I had been under a heavy strain from the opening of the fight until his arrival."

Reuben Waller said:

> By this time all the soldiers were all in the pits and we began to feed the men from our haversacks. If the doctor had not arrived

in time we would have killed them by feeding them to death. The men were eating all we gave them, and it was plenty. Sure, we never gave a thought that it would hurt them. [. . .] We were not aiming to hurt the boys. It was all done through eagerness and excitement. God bless the Beecher Island men. They were a noble set of men.

If Waller also smiled at the irony of black troops coming to the rescue of white soldiers and scouts, he didn't mention it. It's quite possible that the Tenth had become used to the service and the problems of frontier service and fights with the Plains tribes, so that this event, while dramatic, was still just another chapter in an unfolding story, one in which they were just doing a job. Waller also says that the men of Company H buried the men who had died there.

We buried the five men who were killed. Lieutenant Beecher, Doctor Mooers, Louis Farley and others with military honors. We used the funeral flag of Company H to bury the dead, which flag I now have in my possession.

It's a little hard to believe that the scouts waited the full nine days before burying their comrades, especially once it seemed that the Cheyenne and Sioux had left and it seemed safe to move around on the island. But by the time of his writing, Reuben Waller was an old veteran of eighty-six. So it's possible he forgot a few things. In any event, it is certain that the five men were buried on the island that Forsyth had already begun calling "Beecher."

Carpenter then set up a camp a quarter of a mile away from the overpowering stench of the island and moved the wounded into tents where Dr. Jenkins Fitzgerald treated the wounded, and the soldiers from the Tenth passed out food to the others. The doctor reckoned that Forsyth could not have lasted another day without treatment, and one of the wounded scouts died after his leg had been amputated.

The gangrene had apparently gone too far or the man was too weak from loss of blood and hunger to be able to withstand the shock of amputation. That made six dead from the fight.

Twenty-six hours later Captain Bankhead and his column arrived at the camp, so that there were now plenty of wagons and at least two ambulances to carry the scouts back to Fort Wallace. Dr. Turner was with Bankhead and went to see the place where his friend was buried. Turner doesn't say why they decided not to take the bodies back at that time, but Captain Bankhead wrote that "it was found impracticable to remove Lieutenant Beecher's remains when the command returned." It's likely that the bodies were so decomposed that it would have been severely unpleasant for all the men. Turner probably felt it was better to let the work of decomposition finish, so that he could later retrieve what remained and would last. Maybe he was too upset. Maybe it was a combination of those things. In any event, he did return there in December to collect the bodies, but by then all traces of the five men were gone, except for a few rags in the graves that told Turner they had the right spot. Someone or something had dug up the bodies and scattered the remains. And so in a macabre symmetry, the soldier and the scouts, like their Cheyenne adversaries, became "a portion for foxes," either four-legged, or two.

WHAT, IF ANYTHING, DID IT ALL MEAN?

Was it a victory or a defeat? If so, for whom? That depends on which people you ask. Generally speaking, it is considered a victory if one side retains the field and the other side retreats. But if you asked Forsyth's bedraggled and suffering command if they had won the battle, they would have to think long and hard about it. About the best they could say is that most of them survived it. And the Cheyenne's casual withdrawal looked nothing like a retreat and more like an audience leaving the theater at the end of a play.

Another way people keep score is with casualties. And there is no agreement among the army and scouts about Indian casualties at Beecher Island. That is not surprising. The assessment of Cheyenne and Sioux casualties in this and almost all fights with the army are generally inaccurate—almost always inflated on the army's side. Big numbers made good reading in the after action reports. In fairness, unless bodies were recovered, and that was often difficult to do, there was no way to tell how many warriors were killed in any of these fights. Warriors made every effort to rescue wounded comrades, and, when possible, to carry off the bodies of the killed. Nor did they always conveniently erect scaffolds to be found and examined afterward. Also, in the heat of a fight, it is hard for anyone to see things accurately—especially in action on the dry Plains where the dust of rampaging horses coupled with black powder gun smoke made it impossible to see more than a few yards during any kind of serious engagement. And, given the state of Native medical knowledge and treatment, there would be a high percentage of mortality among those who were wounded, especially by large caliber bullets that devastated tissue and bone and increased the chances of infection. (The large number of amputations in the Civil War was due as much to the severity of wounds as to the state of medical knowledge, and the weapons used were many of the same weapons used on the frontier.) Fortunately, we have George Bent's account of this and other engagements. Bent says that there were nine Indians killed in the fight, and he names them. Since he knew many of the Cheyenne warriors who were there, including Roman Nose, the most famous of all, and since the Cheyenne had no incentive to minimize the extent of their injuries (they had no politicians or newspapers to answer to), their accounts of casualties are generally thought to be more accurate than the accounts of the troops or civilians. Add to this the Cheyenne warrior was generally much more experienced in combat and could be more dispassionate in assessing the situation afterwards. He was a better observer than the understandably excited and excitable settlers or troops. (Like all generalizations, though, this comes with a portion salt. After all, the Cheyenne warrior thrived on the acclaim of his people and could be as tempted as any other man to exaggerate his exploits.) Bent also says that there were about 350 to 400 Cheyenne, some Sioux, and a handful of Arapaho in the fight. Other Cheyenne later told Grinnell that there were six hundred Indians. Both figures could be correct, since the warriors could have come and gone as they liked during the first few days of the battle. And certainly the warriors did not form ranks to be counted before going into battle, nor did they stay together afterward, so any number is necessarily an estimate. Whatever the number, there is no denying that the scouts were vastly outnumbered, and all the Indian sources agree that the only thing that saved the scouts was their quick move to the island and their equally quick entrenchment. Forsyth's professional eye for terrain saved them—that and their superior weapons. And of course, the eight "mischievous" young men helped by ruining the surprise. Even so, there were only nine tribesmen killed and an unknown number of wounded who may or may not have survived.

On the other side of the story, Reuben Waller said:

Let me say here that I had many fights with the Indians for ten years after the Beecher fight, and I never saw anything to equal it. I say it was the greatest fight that ever was fought by any soldiers of the regular army at any time not excepting the Custer fight or the massacre at Fort Phil Kearney, and I say further that in all the fights with the Indians—I mean the regular army—we never killed as many Indians. I saw Lone Wolf, who was in the Beecher fight, and he told me they lost 400 killed and fatally wounded in the Beecher fight.

It seems clear that Lone Wolf was pulling Reuben Waller's leg, or else something was lost in translation. And Waller wasn't there for the fighting, so he could only report what others told him.

Sandy Forsyth's account of the battle falls somewhere between these two extremes. "During the fight I counted thirty-two dead Indians: these I reported officially. My men claimed to have counted far more, but these were all that I saw lying dead, and I have made it a rule never to report a dead Indian I have not seen myself." Unfortunately, this cannot be true, because Forsyth was wounded badly in both legs in the first few hours of the battle, and from then on he could not even raise himself up without help. Add to that a head wound and fractured skull. Even after the rescue he was at death's door, and he was utterly incapable of wandering over the battlefield counting bodies, even if they were there. In his memoirs, George Custer says that after the battle Forsyth led "the life of an invalid for nearly two years" and only then recovered sufficiently to return to duty to await "the next war to give him renewed excitement."

Regardless of the inflation of the body counts, the story of the scouts' fight and rescue went down well with the public. And why not? It was a good enough story without any embellishment. And the army was happy to have some good public relations for a change. The settlers could cast the event as a kind of Thermopylae (successful this time) or Horatio at the Bridge—the Cheyenne hordes had been stopped and dispersed. The eastern press might even find something good to say about the army. But was it a victory? In the army's eyes, maybe. But an objective observer would call it a draw.

Over time the events at Beecher Island have become a mere foot-note of history. That is partially a function of the battle's modest military impact and partially the result of modern society's historical amnesia or, frankly, indifference. Among those who do think about the fight, there is general agreement that it wasn't all that important, stra-tegically. The Cheyenne didn't think it was particularly significant—not in military terms. Or, rather, they felt it was no more significant than any other fight that they had, and their history was one of constant warfare—with enemy tribes, white settlers, and the army. George Bent said: "The whites gave this fight much importance, but the Indians take it as an ordinary incident." Historian Robert Utley agrees: "It had been an action of little consequence." However, Utley goes on to say: "But [it was] one that would long be remembered and glorified in the annals of the Indian fighting army." What's more, despite their credible dismissal of the fight as just another incident, militarily, the Cheyenne long remembered it, too. Why?

For the Cheyenne it may not have been an important battle, but it was an important *story*—primarily because of Roman Nose, his exploits and his death. Without a written language, stories were the means by which bards and elders communicated the lessons of their culture and protected and perpetuated it. Interestingly, the bards were extremely careful to narrate the stories the same way every time; they had an innate understanding of the importance of structure and precise language. They did not want the meaning of a story altered or diluted by improvisation. It that sense, storytelling was no different from other important ceremonies and rituals that also had to be scrupulously observed and performed. Deviate at your peril. What's more, the Cheyenne celebrated their heroes, whether they were mythological culture heroes who harnessed or overcame supernatural powers, or real men who fought bravely against the People's human enemies. It's commonplace to say that the Cheyenne were fighting to defend their way of life. But, in fact, fighting *was* their way of life. It was not a means to an end; it *was* the end. It made life matter. So naturally their heroes were warriors. And Roman Nose was one of the most celebrated of all. He was famous before he arrived at Beecher Island and even more famous afterward. "All the Cheyennes held him in great esteem and talk of him a great deal to this day." And heroes were essential to the Cheyenne because "heroes also imply the idea of the sovereign individual, even if they ultimately succumb to the force of circumstance." "The sovereign individual"—surely that is the presiding idea of Cheyenne culture and an idea they were careful to preserve and celebrate in their stories.

History might read the story of Roman Nose in another way: that Roman Nose's life and death are symbolic of the fate of the Cheyenne and all of the warlike nomads of the Plains. He was facing what he knew was certain death, but he attacked anyway, perhaps with a heavy heart and knowledge that what he was about to do would end in failure. That reading of the story implies that the Cheyenne knew they were doomed, but were refusing to submit. That also fits well with the broader interpretation of the western tribes as victims of a rapacious white race that was marching in the name of manifest destiny.

That interpretation may be tempting, but it is too simple. To cast the Cheyenne as victims and anoint Roman Nose their doomed symbol ignores their complexity and their participation, in fact, their complicity in the Western violence. Roman Nose is a symbol of his people, but not as a victim. A hero is never a victim. A hero may be defeated in war, but only because he is outnumbered or outgunned or outgeneraled or unlucky. To portray the Cheyenne as mere victims ignores the reality and authenticity of their warrior culture, and *that* is what Roman Nose more accurately represents.

It's also possible to read the story of Roman Nose as a kind of Greek tragedy. "The essentials of . . . [classical] tragedy are that the various aspects of the hero's character should combine with events to lead to a disastrous issue. [. . .] The disastrous issue must in retrospect appear to have been inevitable." It is often said that tragedy also results from a flaw in the hero's character, but according to Aristotle, the hero's downfall is actually the result of a mistake, not some glaring character fault. The hero is not evil or foolish; he is in most respects admirable. The hero's catastrophic demise is not entirely his fault and *that* makes it much more pitiable. In fact, tragic. And it arouses fear in the audience—"If it could happen to him, what could happen to me? If one so high could fall so far, what chance do the rest of us have?" Hence Aristotle's notion that tragedy arouses both fear and pity. All Roman Nose did was unknowingly eat contaminated bread. He made a mistake, he realized it, and he knew what would happen, but he went to battle, anyway. There was nobility in the act and inevitability in the fall. The plot would have played well in classical Athens.

There were heroes among the scouts, too—Jack Stilwell and the other three who made the epic and hazardous journey for help, and Sandy Forsyth, who cut a bullet out of his own leg. But the main hero of their story is Fred Beecher. While he may not fit the mold of the classical Greek tragic hero, he is perhaps, archetypal in another sense. Gentlemanly and good-natured, popular with his troops and colleagues, he represents countless young men who went off to do their duty and were killed, leaving behind sorrowing parents and friends and, perhaps, a sweetheart. He left the settled campuses and villages of New England to meet his end in the desolate, featureless prairie. What sort of urge brought him to the Plains and finally to that island? Was it classic American restlessness? A sense of duty? Lost love? Lost illusions? Or something else entirely? He seemed to sense that he was doomed, hence the strain of melancholy—a recognizable theme in stories about young men. Hemingway heroes again come to mind. But there are many others. Fred Beecher happened to be real, but he has plenty of fictional counterparts, many such "legends of the fall." As F. Scott Fitzgerald said: "Show me a hero and I will write you a tragedy."

It's also possible to look at the Beecher Island story as an allegory. After all, all the important participants in the conflict for the West were represented there—the red, the white, the black. And among the whites there were all levels of society—immigrants and outsiders like Sig Schlesinger, men from the establishment like Fred Beecher and Dr. Mooers, self-made professionals like Forsyth, classic Western frontiersmen like Sharp Grover, brave young adventurers like Jack Stilwell, drifters like William McCall, even dissipated, seriocomic figures like Avalanche Trudeau. The men were representatives of the advancing culture of the whites. And confronting these men were the famous horsemen of the Plains—the Cheyenne, the Sioux, and the Arapaho, people from a radically different culture. They were there to assert their own identities, to destroy their detested enemies and perhaps halt or at least delay the mass migration these white men represented and prefigured. These people from very different worlds fought in a single place, on and around a temporary stage that was no more than one hundred yards long. And that stage was set amid the vast emptiness of the Plains—emptiness that meant and symbolized different things to the participants on both sides. And when the fighting was over and the red men had retired, who of all people should come to the rescue of the beleaguered and exhausted white men, but black troops who only a few years ago had been slaves? The *West* in a one-act allegory, with a dash of irony? A kind of morality play? You could see it that way. Is it also an over-simplification? Of course. Allegories generally are.

Beecher Island—a footnote of history, Cheyenne legend, classical tragedy, allegory of the West? Maybe it's all those things. But at the very least it's a tale of heroic action in the ageless and endless struggles between different peoples. And for that alone it deserves to be remembered. It feeds what Jacques Barzun calls our "primitive appetite for stories."

EPILOGUE

The Cheyenne left the battlefield on the last day of summer, the time they called "when the cherries were ripe." It's possible to read some significance into that. Perhaps in the context of the story, the change of seasons can seem meaningful—the end of something. That is not anything the Cheyenne would have thought about, but the story allows room for such things. The Cheyenne did know of course that autumn was coming and, after that, the bitter winter. Perhaps they left just because it was time to get on with other things. After all, to everything there is a season.

It had been a good summer for the Cheyenne. The raiding had been productive and important for the young men. There had been successful fights and others that were less so. Honor had been won, trophies had been taken, enemies killed, horses stolen, plunder gathered, warriors killed. That last part was sad, of course, but everyone must die. Better that way than some other. People come and go. Summer ends. It was all in the way of things, the inevitable way of things.

Years after the fight, there was a great flood, and the Arikaree overflowed its banks and swept away the lone cottonwood and all the willows that had protected both Cheyenne and white men. It washed away the sandy island. When the flood receded, the Arikaree was no longer divided. Today at the site of the fight you can jump over the stream without much trouble. Today, also, there are some settled places on the Plains. But even though wheat has taken the place of native grass in some places, there are only a few scattered hamlets along the Colorado-Kansas border, and the prairie still seems mostly empty. Fort Wallace is gone. All that is left is the cemetery, and even the remains of the soldiers have been removed and reburied in army cemeteries elsewhere. Only a few civilians lie there now, including Sharp Grover, gunned down in a sod saloon only a few months after surviving the ordeal. Reuben Waller said it was in retaliation for killing Medicine Bill Comstock. Other people said it was for some other reason. It hardly matters. Standing beside his grave today you can turn and look 360 degrees across the mostly flat country. Through all points of the compass there is an ocean of grass stretching as far as you can see. Other than that, there is nothing. Just the lone prairie.

BIBLIOGRAPHY

Beecher Island Battle Memorial Association. *The Battle of Beecher Island Annual.* Wray, CO: Beecher Island Battle Memorial Association, 2007.

Brady, Cyrus Townsend. *Indian Fights and Fighters.* Lincoln: University of Nebraska Press, 1971.

Brown, Dee. *The Fetterman Massacre.* Lincoln: University of Nebraska Press, 1962.

Bunting, Josiah, III. *Ulysses S. Grant.* New York: Times Books, 2004.

Calhoun, James. *With Custer in '74: James Calhoun's Diary of the Black Hills Expedition.* Provo, UT: Brigham Young University Press, 1979.

Coddington, Edwin B. *The Gettysburg Campaign: A Study in Command.* New York: Scribner's, 1968.

Cremony, John C. *Life Among the Apaches.* Lincoln: University of Nebraska Press, 1983.

Criqui, Orvel A. *Fifty Fearless Men: The Forsyth Scouts and Beecher Island.* Marceline, MO: Walsworth, 1993.

Custer, George A. *My Life on the Plains, or, Personal Experiences with Indians.* Norman: University of Oklahoma Press, 1962.

Eisenhower, John S.D. *So Far From God.* Norman: University of Oklahoma Press, 2000.

Forsyth, George A. *Thrilling Days in Army Life.* Big Byte Books, 2015.

Fuller, J.F.C. *Grant and Lee.* Bloomington: Indiana University Press, 1982.

Glasrud, Bruce A., and Michael N. Searles. *Buffalo Soldiers in the West: A Black Soldiers Anthology.* College Station: Texas A&M Press, 2007.

Grinnell, George Bird. *By Cheyenne Campfires.* Lincoln: University of Nebraska Press, 1971.

———. *The Cheyenne Indians: Their History and Ways of Life,* volumes 1 and 2. Lincoln: University of Nebraska Press, 1972.

———. *Two Great Scouts and Their Pawnee Battalion: The Experiences of Frank J. North and Luther H. North.* Lincoln: University of Nebraska Press, 1973.

———. *The Fighting Cheyennes*. Norman: University of Oklahoma Press, 1956.

Guelzo, Allen C. *Fateful Lightning: A New History of the Civil War and Reconstruction*. Oxford: Oxford University Press, 2012.

———. *Gettysburg: The Last Invasion*. New York: Alfred A. Knopf, 2013.

Gueniffey, Patrice. *Napoleon and DeGaulle, Heroes and History*. Cambridge: Harvard University Press, 2020.

Hassrick, Royal B. *The Sioux: Life and Customs of a Warrior Society*. Norman: University of Oklahoma Press, 1964.

Hormats, Robert D. *The Price of Liberty: Paying for America's Wars*. New York: Times Books, 2007.

Hyde, George E. *Life of George Bent: Written from His Letters*. Edited by Savoie Lottiville. Norman: University of Oklahoma, 1968.

Josephy, Alvin M., Jr. *The Indian Heritage of America*. New York: Alfred A. Knopf, 1968.

Junger, Sebastian. *War*. New York: Hachette, 2011.

Kaplan, Robert D. "Introduction." In *Taras Bulba*, by Nikolai Gogol; translated by Peter Constantine. New York: Modern Library, 2003.

Keegan, John. *Warpaths: Travels of a Military Historian in North America*. London: Hodder & Stoughton, 1995.

Kitto, H.D.F. *Greek Tragedy*. New York: Doubleday Anchor, 1950.

Leckie, William H. *The Buffalo Soldiers: A Narrative of the Negro Cavalry in the West*. Norman: University of Oklahoma Press, 2003.

LeMay, Alan. "*The Searchers.*" In *The Western: Four Classic Novels of the 1940s & 50s*, edited by Ron Hansen. New York: Library of America, 2020.

Liddell Hart, Basil Henry. *Sherman: Soldier, Realist, American*. New York: Da Capo, 1993.

Lubetkin, M. John. *Jay Cooke's Gamble: The Northern Pacific Railroad, the Sioux, and the Panic of 1873*. Norman: University of Oklahoma Press, 2006.

McPherson, James M. *Battle Cry of Freedom*. New York: Oxford University Press, 1988.

Monnett, John H. *The Battle of Beecher Island and the Indian War of 1867–1868*. Niwot: University Press of Colorado, 1992.

Moody, Ralph. *Stagecoach West*, Lincoln: University of Nebraska Press, 1998.

Mort, Terry. *Thieves' Road: The Black Hills Betrayal and Custer's Path to Little Bighorn*, Amherst, MA: Prometheus, 2015.

———. *The Wrath of Cochise: The Bascom Affair and the Origins of the Apache Wars*. New York: Pegasus, 2013.

Nelson, Scott Reynolds. *A Nation of Deadbeats: An Uncommon History of America's Financial Disasters*. New York: Alfred A. Knopf, 2012.

Ormsby, Waterman L. *The Butterfield Overland Mail: Only Through Passenger on the First Westbound Stage*. San Marino, CA: Huntington Library, 1942.

Parkman, Francis. *The Oregon Trail*. New York: Library of America, 1991.

Schubert, Frank N. *Voices of the Buffalo Soldier: Records, Reports, and Recollections of Military Life*. Albuquerque: University of New Mexico Press, 2003.

Sears, Stephen W. *Gettysburg*. New York: Houghton Mifflin, 2004.

Sherman, William T. *Sherman: Memoirs of General W. T. Sherman*. New York: Library of America, 1990.

Stanley, Henry M. *My Early Travels and Adventures in America and Asia: Volume 1*. London: Gerald Duckworth, 2001.

Twain, Mark. *Life on the Mississippi*. New York: Signet, 2001.

———. *Roughing It*, New York: Oxford, 1996.

———. *The Gilded Age*, New York: Harper & Brothers, 1915.

Utley, Robert M. *Frontier Regulars: The United States Army and the Indian, 1866–1891*. Lincoln: University of Nebraska, 1973.

———. *The Indian Frontier of the American West, 1846–1890*. Albuquerque: University of New Mexico Press, 1984.

———, ed. *Life in Custer's Cavalry: Diaries and Letters of Albert and Jennie Barnitz, 1867–1868*. Lincoln: University of Nebraska, 1977.

———. *Frontiersmen in Blue: The United States Army and the Indian, 1848–1865*. Lincoln: University of Nebraska, 1967.

———. *Cavalier in Buckskin*. Norman: University of Oklahoma Press, 1988.

Wagoner, Jay J. *Early Arizona*. Tucson: University of Arizona Press, 1975.

ENDNOTES

INTRODUCTION

p. ix — better imagined than described: Forsyth, *Thrilling Days*, 2.

p. x — They don't know anything about fighting Indians: Mort, *Thieves' Road*, 55.

p. xii — either in the field, or by torture at the stake: Forsyth, *Thrilling Days*, 3.

p. xiv — than of an order of nobility: Guelzo, *Gettysburg*, 10.

p. xv — dedicated soldier [and] a skilled scout: Criqui, *Fifty Fearless Men*, 12.

p. xv — position requiring coolness, courage and tact: *Fifty Fearless Men*, 28.

p. xv — he always wanted to see a real, live wild Indian: *Fifty Fearless Men*, 30.

p. xvi — an opportunity for advancement or distinction: Forsyth, *Thrilling Days*, 9.

p. xvi — Oh, hell, Beecher, sign him up: Criqui, *Fifty Fearless Men*, 185.

p. xvii — trapping along the northwestern border: *Fifty Fearless Men*, 33.

p. xvii — a cool head made him a valuable man: *Fifty Fearless Men*, 33.

p. xvii — butcher-knife, tin plate and tin cup: Forsyth, *Thrilling Days*, 5.

p. xvii — cooked rations in his haversack: *Fifty Fearless Men*, 5.

p. xix — enemy's country ever holds for a soldier was before us: *Fifty Fearless Men*, 10.

p. xix — "the time when the cherries are ripe": Grinnell, *Cheyenne Indians*, vol. 1, 72.

PART I: THE ANTAGONISTS
1: THE CHEYENNE

THE PEOPLE

p. 3 — which means, roughly, "foreign speakers": Grinnell, *Cheyenne Indians*, vol. 1, 2.

p. 5 — shortened the name to Sioux: Josephy, *Indian Heritage*, 116.

THE SACRED DOG

p. 8 — Trans-Mississippi West had horses: Utley, *Indian Frontier*, 13.

p. 10 — they want the lands of the Indians: *Indian Frontier*, 61.

NOMADISM VERSUS SETTLEMENT: AN IRRECONCILABLE DIFFERENCE

p. 14 — *who seek to limit or redirect it:* Keegan, *Warpaths*, 296; italics added.

p. 16 — race of brave men fighting against destiny: Sherman, *Sherman*, 926.

p. 16   when we settle down we grow pale and die: Stanley, *My Early Travels*, 265.

p. 17   "uncomplicated by sentiment": Utley, *Frontier Regulars*, 9.

THE MARK OF THE WARRIOR

p. 17   unlinked to any strategic or tactical necessity: Kaplan, "Introduction," xiv.

p. 17   all seemed so desirable: Grinnell, *Fighting Cheyennes*, 12.

p. 18   and threatened the punishment he feared: Grinnell, *Cheyenne Indians*, vol. 1, 103–04.

p. 18   condemnation and contempt were to be dreaded: *Cheyenne Indians*, 103.

pp. 18–19   no weapon that would do harm at a distance: Grinnell, *Cheyenne Indians*, vol. 2, 30.

p. 19   the boy who did it to the greatest credit: *Cheyenne Indians*, 29–30.

p. 20   *and took orders from no one*: Mort, *Thieves' Road*, 78; italics added.

p. 22   somewhere around 3,500 people: Grinnell, *Cheyenne Indians*, vol. 1, 21.

p. 23   justice, honesty, veracity, regard for each other's claims: Mort, *Wrath of Cochise*, 104.

VILLAGE POLITICS

p. 25   fell into disfavor: Hyde, *Life of George Bent*, 294.

p. 26   shall hold the chief and his tribe responsible: Stanley, *My Early Travels*, 55.

"WE FEW, WE HAPPY FEW."

pp. 27–28   of mutual aid, will attack resolutely: Guelzo, *Gettysburg*, 309.

p. 31   rider might get off and pick up the object: Grinnell, *Cheyenne Indians*, vol. 2, 70.

p. 31   taunted with it wherever she went: Grinnell, *Cheyenne Indians*, vol. 1, 156.

THE EDUCATION OF A WARRIOR

p. 33   and that was that: Grinnell, *Cheyenne Indians*, vol. 1, 294.

p. 34   even killed them on the wing: *Cheyenne Indians*, 114.

p. 34   wrapping them with sinew: *Cheyenne Indians*, 174.

pp. 34–35   a revolving pistol of that time: *Cheyenne Indians*, 177.

BARDS

p. 36   wisdom and perhaps, strangely, the spider: Grinnell, *Cheyenne Indians*, vol. 2, 88.

p. 38   courage to conquer their enemies: *Cheyenne Indians*, 102.

pp. 38–39   the head chief of the buffalo: Grinnell, *Cheyenne Campfires*, 263.

p. 39   and all animals for the coming year: *Cheyenne Campfires*, 53.

MEDICINE

p. 40   **animals typified or which took their shape:** Grinnell, *Cheyenne Campfires*, 87.

p. 42   **natural and supernatural remedies:** *Cheyenne Campfires*, 127.

p. 43   **the damage would almost always be life threatening:** Guelzo, *Gettysburg*, 364.

ROMAN NOSE

p. 44   **"Now I am going to empty their guns":** Hyde, *Life of George Bent*, 239.

p. 44   **feathers set all along its length:** *Life of George Bent*, 307.

p. 45   **"sacred medicine paint":** *Life of George Bent*, 307.

p. 45   **black across the mouth and chin:** *Life of George Bent*, 307.

p. 45   **he would not be hit by a bullet:** Grinnell, *Cheyenne Indians*, vol. 2, 108–09.

p. 46   **killing of these young men make you feel badly:** Grinnell, *Fighting Cheyennes*, 296.

p. 46   **the warriors set up a yell and charged:** Hyde, *Life of George Bent*, 240.

BEAU SABREURS AND CAVALIERS

p. 47   **without stint or measure:** Custer, *My Life*, 22.

p. 49   **the brilliancy of his deeds than anything else:** Utley, *Cavalier in Buckskin*, 34.

2: THE ARMY

p. 51   **as often as you can and keep moving on:** Fuller, *Grant and Lee*, 78.

p. 53   **deaths came from combat, the others came from disease:** Eisenhower, *So Far from God*, 369.

p. 53   **died from disease as from combat injuries:** McPherson, *Battle Cry*, 485.

p. 53   **fatal wound in the abdomen:** Guelzo, *Gettysburg*, 364.

p. 55   **three thousand Klansmen:** Mort, *Thieves' Road*, 147.

CONGRESS AND THE POSTWAR ARMY

p. 57   **shell fragments and other large projectiles:** Guelzo, *Gettysburg*, 278.

pp. 57–58   **to give the infantry a chance:** *Gettysburg*, 41.

pp. 58–59   **lost 932 of its 2,216 horses to sickness:** *Gettysburg*, 40–41.

p. 60   **thirty infantry divisions versus ten of cavalry:** *Gettysburg*, 41.

p. 60   **they can't stand that:** *Gettysburg*, 279.

p. 62   **covered themselves in glory:** Utley, *Indian Frontier*, 92.

p. 64   **handful of cartridges a year:** Utley, *Frontier Regulars*, 24.

p. 64   **much less an Indian:** Utley, *Life in Custer's Cavalry*, 97.

p. 64   **reach the camp the same day at all:** Utley, *Frontier Regulars*, 49.

p. 66   **officers and enlisted men:** *Frontier Regulars*, 12.

p. 66   **one thousand Indian scouts:** *Frontier Regulars*, 11.

THE RANK AND FILE

p. 68   **bummers, loafers, and foreign paupers:** Utley, *Frontier Regulars*, 22.

p. 69   **as their native-born comrades:** McPherson, *Battle Cry*, 606.

p. 70   **two-thirds of them had deserted:** Mort, *Wrath of Cochise*, 59.

p. 70   **poured the charge of powder on top of it:** Utley, *Frontier Regulars*, 41.

p. 71   **an Indian within easy range proved:** Custer, *My Life*, 202.

p. 71   **anywhere from 25 to 40 percent:** Utley, *Frontier Regulars*, 23.

p. 71   **as 30 percent of its men from desertion:** *Frontier Regulars*, 23.

BUFFALO SOLDIERS

p. 71   **of almost 180,000 in uniform:** Leckie, *Buffalo Soldiers*, 5.

p. 71   **as high as 750,000:** *New York Times*, April 2, 2012.

p. 72   **Lee's suffered 20 percent:** McPherson, *Battle Cry*, 472n.

p. 73   **the respect of all the army:** Guelzo, *Fateful Lightning*, 381.

p. 73   **exclusively from the volunteer services:** Leckie, *Buffalo Soldiers*, 6–7.

p. 74   **the Popedom of Rome:** Utley, *Cavalier in Buckskin*, 39.

p. 74   **"bitter and unmeasured.":** Guelzo, *Gettysburg*, 125.

p. 74   **has nice notions about religion:** *Gettysburg*, 125.

pp. 74–75   **at worst the victims of social shunning:** *Gettysburg*, 125.

p. 76   **a corporal in the Philadelphia Brigade:** *Gettysburg*, 289.

p. 77   **Tenth Regiment of Cavalry, United States Army:** Leckie, *Buffalo Soldiers*, 15.

p. 77   **unqualified endorsement to lead the Ninth Cavalry:** *Buffalo Soldiers*, 7.

p. 78   **officers, clerks and mechanics:** *Buffalo Soldiers*, 13.

p. 78   **whose duty shall include the instruction:** 1866 army appropriations bill.

p. 78   **for the cavalry soldiers:** Schubert, *Voices*, 24–25.

p. 78   **with Satanta and his Kiowa:** *Voices*, 17.

p. 79   **are as brave as the occasion calls for:** Utley, *Frontier Regulars*, 56.

p. 79   **their conduct in the army:** *Frontier Regulars*, 27.

LIFE ON A FRONTIER ARMY POST

p. 83   **he will eat almost anything:** Mort, *Wrath of Cochise*, 152.

p. 83   **step back to keep from it:** Utley, *Life in Custer's Cavalry*, 57.

p. 84   **six thousand teamsters and worked 45,000 oxen:** Mort, *Wrath of Cochise*, 157.

pp. 84–85   **inside the War Department?:** *Wrath of Cochise*, 153.

p. 85   **as safe as possible:** Utley, *Frontier Regulars*, 94.

p. 87   **inhumanity of the man masters:** Mort, *Wrath of Cochise*, 214.

p. 87   **prairie dog villages might be called *forts*:** Utley, *Frontier Regulars*, 82.

p. 88   **row before being shot and killed:** Leckie, *Buffalo Soldiers*, 22.

p. 89   **expired in delirium tremens:** Moody, *Stagecoach West*, 218.

p. 90   **the road to Fort Yuma:** Wagoner, *Early Arizona*, 395, 400.

p. 90   **we are all right:** Mort, *Wrath of Cochise*, 165.

p. 90   swallowed a kerosene lamp: *Wrath of Cochise*, 166.

p. 91   hauled in an ambulance: Utley, *Life in Custer's Cavalry*, 293.

p. 91   hold a commission in the army: *Life in Custer's Cavalry*, 269.

p. 91   of all right thinking men: *Life in Custer's Cavalry*, 52.

p. 91   deprivation and poverty: Mort, *Wrath of Cochise*, 214.

p. 92   human nature is capable: *Wrath of Cochise*, 215–16.

p. 92   post hospital each year: Utley, *Frontier Regulars*, 86.

p. 92   not remarkably fond of Indians: Utley, *Life in Custer's Cavalry*, 86.

p. 92   an enemy bullet: Utley, *Frontier Regulars*, 87.

p. 93   was ordered out to eat them: *Frontier Regulars*, 87.

p. 94   untrained men in little danger: Junger, *War*, 123.

p. 94   locked in a sweatbox: Utley, *Frontier Regulars*, 84.

p. 94   foreign and domestic, were a hard set: *Frontier Regulars*.

pp. 94–95   for such they are as a general thing: Utley, *Life in Custer's Cavalry*, 136.

p. 95   their means of purchasing of late: *Life in Custer's Cavalry*, 128.

p. 95   ordered the deserter shot: Mort, *Thieves' Road*, 144.

p. 96   wood chopping and haymaking: Utley, *Frontier Regulars*, 83.

p. 97   isolation of duty on the Plains: Quoted in Utley, *Frontier Regulars*, 82.

3: THE CIVILIANS

"THE MINERS, FORTY NINERS . . ."

p. 99   where the gold was to be found: Mort, *Thieves' Road*, 284.

p. 100   thought the whites were crazy: Hyde, *Life of George Bent*, 106–07.

p. 102   might be needing diversion: Twain, *Roughing It*, 89.

p. 103   his secretary of the treasury, Salmon Chase: Hormats, *Price of Liberty*, 67.

pp. 103–04   dubious quality or simply counterfeit: *Price of Liberty*, 75.

p. 104   certain convertibility into gold or silver: Mort, *Thieves' Road*, 31.

p. 104   previously invested in these instruments: Citation TK.

BLACK HILLS

pp. 105–06   was in a hunter's paradise: Parkman, *Oregon Trail*, 230.

p. 107   hunting about here after gold: Mort, *Thieves' Road*, 12.

CIVILIANS: EAST AND WEST—NEVER THE TWAIN . . .

p. 111   great measure responsible for the war: Twain, *Life on the Mississippi*, 46.

p. 112   Nearer by, they never get anybody's: Twain, *Roughing It*, 149.

p. 112   womanly grace and beauty: Harte, *Railway Reading*, 87.

pp. 112–13   wild beast of the desert: Custer, *My Life*, 13.

p. 114   the most savage savage: Cremony, *Life Among the Apaches*, 128.

p. 115   deprives him of his identity: Custer, *My Life*, 20–21.

p. 115   a book of unceasing interest: *My Life*, 19.

p. 115   vices thrown in without stint or measure: *My Life*, 23.

p. 118   but decidedly my superior: Mort, *Wrath of Cochise*, 64.

VOLUNTEERS VERSUS REGULARS

p. 118   gets cuffs from both sides: Mort, *Wrath of Cochise*, 65.

p. 118   the army was the Indian's best friend: Custer, *My Life*, 16.

p. 119   strangely indifferent to what is going on: Stanley, *My Early Travels*, 185.

p. 119   food and merchandise from the East.": Utley, *Frontier Regulars*, 290.

p. 120   Others place the numbers higher: Utley, *Life of George Bent*, 159n.

p. 120   was in sympathy with the Indians: Utley, *Frontier Regulars*, 294.

p. 120   civilization cannot sanction it: Stanley, *My Early Travels*, 154.

p. 120   as impolitic as it is barbarous: *My Early Travels*, 59.

p. 121   spare none but the women and children: Utley, *Life in Custer's Cavalry*, 93.

p. 121   his face was streaming with blood: Hyde, *Life of George Bent*, 219.

p. 122   cutting off Denver from the East: Utley, *Indian Frontier*, 93–94.

p. 122   Chivington's "great victory" at Sand Creek: Hyde, *Life of George Bent*, 180.

p. 123   were ripe for plucking: *Life of George Bent*, 287.

p. 123   sugar the ponies could carry: *Life of George Bent*, 172.

FETTERMAN

p. 125   "Most cordial feelings prevail" among the Indians: Utley, *Frontier Regulars*, 99.

p. 125   borrowed from the fort's band: *Frontier Regulars*, 195.

p. 126   even to the soles of the feet: Brown, *Fetterman Massacre*, 188.

p. 127   survivors knew that perfectly well: Grinnell, *Cheyenne Indians*, vol. 2, 22.

p. 128   never be taken alive by the Indians: Custer, *My Life*, 122.

p. 128   well treated and adopted into the tribe: Hyde, *Life of George Bent*, 296.

pp. 128–29 only made a flesh wound in her breast: Grinnell, *Two Great Scouts*, 197.

p. 129   floating down the Platte: Stanley, *My Early Travels*, 149.

p. 130   an area of about 10,000 square miles: Utley, *Life in Custer's Cavalry*, 90.

p. 131   eating rations and drawing pay: Custer, *My Life*, 25.

p. 131   desired a war with the Indians: *My Life*, 26.

p. 131   extermination, men, women and children: Quoted in Utley, *Frontier Regulars*, 111.

p. 132   Black Kettle's reputation: Hyde, *Life of George Bent*, 164.

PEACE COMMISSION

p. 136   sheep and hogs to stock his farm: Stanley, *My Early Travels*, 263.

p. 137   we will now offer you the way: *My Early Travels*, 271.

p. 137   putting us on a reservation: *My Early Travels*, 269.

p. 138   territory outside the reservations: Utley, *Life in Custer's Cavalry*, 116.

p. 138   terms of present and previous treaties: *Life in Custer's Cavalry*, 115.

p. 140   affect the sanguinary savage: Stanley, *My Early Travels*, 129.
p. 140   military posts and frontier settlements: *My Early Travels*, 37–38.
p. 140   might trespass without Indian consent: Utley, *Frontier Regulars*, 135.
p. 141   were still in sight along the trail south: Brown, *Fetterman Massacre*, 225.

RESOURCES
pp. 142–43 beating of old tin kettles: Mort, *Thieves' Road*, 13.
p. 143   heathen barbarianism into oblivion: Calhoun: *With Custer*, 40.
p. 145   fighting warriors at the Wagon Box fight: Brown, *Fetterman Massacre*, 223.

THE INDIAN BUREAU
p. 147   ranged in search of prey: Utley, *Indian Frontier*, 36.
p. 149   a blunter instrument to solve the problem: Quoted in Utley, *Indian Frontier*, 36.
p. 151   is something of a mystery: Stanley, *My Early Travels*, 248.
p. 152   chief and his tribe responsible: *My Early Travels*, 55.
p. 152   make them sue for peace: Brown, *Fetterman Massacre*, 217.

CORRUPTION
p. 154   to forward to his superintendent: Custer, *My Life*, 166–67.
p. 157   his promised treaty annuities: Mort, *Thieves' Road*, 114–15.
p. 158   desirable office in the gift of the government: Custer, *My Life*, 176.
p. 158   to their common foe: *My Life*, 33.
p. 159   the cause of most Indian unrest and hostility: Mort, *Thieves' Road*, 116.
p. 160   the big bowl dangling from his belt behind him: Hyde, *Life of George Bent*, 172.

THE SMOKY HILL
p. 161   flocked westward along the Smoky Hill: Moody, *Stagecoach West*, 156.
p. 161   somewhat safer route in the north: *Stagecoach West*, 281.
p. 162   could "charm a bird out of a tree": *Stagecoach West*, 280.
p. 162   constructed bridges and relay stations: *Stagecoach West*, 282.
p. 163   several mud holes (which is a fact): Utley, *Life in Custer's Cavalry*, 95.
pp. 164–65 surroundings had been different: Twain, *Roughing It*, 57.
p. 167   I shall not undertake it again: Moody, *Stagecoach West*, 244.

THE MAIL
p. 171   perpetrated on the country by the slave holders: Mort, *Wrath of Cochise*, 187.
p. 171   "white pants or kid gloves": Ormsby, *Butterfield Overland Mail*, 52, 94.
p. 172   and this happened but seldom: Hyde, *Life of George Bent*, 295.

p. 173   **established through their country:** Utley, *Frontier Regulars*, 95.

pp. 173–74 **the present and previous treaties:** Utley, *Life in Custer's Cavalry*, 115.

IRON HORSE

p. 176   **they resembled disks of flame:** Lubetkin, *Jay Cooke's Gamble*, 20.

FINANCING A RAILROAD

p. 179   **filling with wood and brush:** *Jay Cooke's Gamble*, 64.

p. 180   **contributors small and large:** Bunting, *Ulysses S. Grant*, 123.

p. 182   **the neighborhood of $30 million:** Mort, *Thieves' Road*, 104.

p. 183   **look after their own property:** Bunting, *Ulysses S. Grant*, 135.

p. 183   **similar Crédit Mobilier bribes:** Mort, *Thieves' Road*, 105.

p. 183   **so they are not ashamed of it:** Twain, *Gilded Age*, 262.

p. 184   **protection to the construction workers:** Utley, *Indian Frontier*, 109.

p. 184   **as safe as possible:** Utley, *Frontier Regulars*, 94.

p. 186   **south toward the Republican [River]:** Hyde, *Life of George Bent*, 276.

p. 187   **latest news about the "Injuns":** Utley, *Life in Custer's Cavalry*, 153–54.

p. 188   **which they usually recovered:** Grinnell, *Two Great Scouts*, 145.

DESTINY

p. 190   **strategic or tactical necessity:** Kaplan, "Introduction," p. xiv.

p. 192   **he ain't going to do that:** LeMay, *Searchers*, 356.

PART 2 THE FIGHT AT BEECHER ISLAND
4: FROM FORT WALLACE TO BEECHER ISLAND

p. 198   **worthy men and not a drinking set:** Utley, *Life in Custer's Cavalry*, p. 68.

p. 199   **position requiring coolness, courage and tact:** Criqui, *Fifty Fearless Men*, 28.

p. 200   **three hundred men managed to escape:** Guelzo, *Gettysburg*, 192.

p. 200   **thirty-five men avoided the casualty list:** Sears, *Gettysburg*, 221.

p. 200   **to find him wherever he fought:** Criqui, *Fifty Fearless Men*, 28.

p. 201   **"Miss Dix, of blessed memory":** *Fifty Fearless Men*, 21.

p. 204   **as well as valuable companion:** Custer, *My Life*, 65.

p. 205   **ill-judged estimate of the Indian character:** *My Life*, 13.

p. 205   **the cigar shop is not spacious:** Mark Twain, *The Complete Humorous Sketches and Tales of Mark Twain* (Garden City, NY: Doubleday) 832.

p. 205   **a crime against the language:** Twain, *The Complete Humorous Sketches and Tales of Mark Twain*, 832.

p. 206   **get away in the dark:** Hyde, *Life of George Bent*, 285.

FORSYTH GETS UNDERWAY

p. 206   **telegraph at this place:** Forsyth, *Thrilling Days*, 10.

p. 207   **an Indian during the march:** *Thrilling Days*, 11.

p. 207   **the same sacrifice alone in the hills:** Grinnell, *Cheyenne Indians*, vol. 2, 213.

p. 209   several mud holes (which is the fact): Utley, *Life in Custer's Cavalry*, 95.

p. 210   by means of which blocks were cut: Criqui, *Fifty Fearless Men*, 17.

pp. 211–12   for want of energy in their pursuit: Forsyth. *Thrilling Days*, 13.

p. 212   they could not annihilate us: *Thrilling Days*, 13.

p. 212   I meant it should do so: *Thrilling Days*, 13.

p. 213   two hundred Cheyenne: Hyde, *Life of George Bent*, 298.

p. 214   Dog Soldiers camp with the news: *Life of George Bent*, 298.

p. 214   fighting men in the village: *Life of George Bent*, 298.

p. 214   whatever for our lives: Forsyth, *Thrilling Days*, 14.

p. 215   "advance and attack": *Thrilling Days*, 14.

p. 215   difference between an army and a mob: *Thrilling Days*, 14.

p. 215   joy in entering a fight: Criqui, *Fifty Fearless Men*, 10.

p. 216   cripple them for the time being: Forsyth, *Thrilling Days*, 14.

p. 217   nearly out of supplies, save salt and coffee: *Thrilling Days*, 14.

p. 217   "No game had been seen for two days": *Thrilling Days*, 14.

pp. 218–19   would be severely punished: Hyde, *Life of George Bent*, 298.

THE ATTACK

p. 219   well grassed valley about two miles in length": Forsyth, *Thrilling Days*, 15.

p. 219   alder bushes and swamp willows: *Thrilling Days*, 15.

p. 219   of about twenty feet in height: *Thrilling Days*, 15–16.

p. 222   put on their sacred face paint: Hyde, *Life of George Bent*, 298.

p. 222   slip out and find the whites: *Life of George Bent*, 299.

p. 222   getting ready to start: *Life of George Bent*, 29.

p. 223   Starving Elk and his friends: *Life of George Bent*, 299.

p. 224   wild young men spoiled everything: *Life of George Bent*, 299.

p. 224   look at the Indians: Forsyth, *Thrilling Days*, 18.

p. 224   "wild cries of exultation": *Thrilling Days*, 18.

p. 224   earth to cover themselves: *Thrilling Days*, 18.

p. 225   the number was six hundred: Grinnell, *Fighting Cheyennes*, 291.

p. 225   a steady and galling fire upon us: Forsyth, *Thrilling Days*, 19.

p. 225   have you no sense: *Thrilling Days*, 19.

p. 226   shot by these scouts: Hyde, *Life of George Bent*, 302.

p. 227   depend on how we husband it: Forsyth, *Thrilling Days*, 20.

p. 228   brave men and good soldiers: *Thrilling Days*, 22.

p. 228   I considered good targets: *Battle of Beecher Island*, 66.

p. 228   The little Jew was there: Brady, *Indian Fights*, 110.

p. 229   join him in his trench: Forsyth, *Thrilling Days*, 21.

p. 229   back into his trench, "almost senseless": *Thrilling Days*, 25.

p. 229   rascally redskin will not trouble us again: *Thrilling Days*, 25.

p. 230   crow feathers without a tail: Hyde, *Life of George Bent*, 300.

p. 230   the Indians had ever before experienced: *Life of George Bent*, 301.

p. 231   again through the entrenched whites: *Life of George Bent*, 301.
p. 232   it has been my lot to see: Forsyth, *Thrilling Days*, 27.
p. 233   undoubtedly had a brilliant future: Custer, *My Life*, 135.
p. 233   bullets seemed to find him wherever he fought: Criqui, *Fifty Fearless Men*, 28.

ROMAN NOSE AT HIS TENT

p. 234   quiet and self-contained: Hyde, *Life of George Bent*, 307.
p. 234   Northern Cheyenne medicine men: *Life of George Bent*, 307.
p. 234   no cloth, thread or metal: *Life of George Bent*, 307.
p. 235   a bullet could find him: Grinnell, *Cheyenne Indians*, vol. 2, 120.
p. 235   you will certainly be killed: *Cheyenne Indians*, 122.
p. 235   dish with a metal instrument: *Cheyenne Indians*, 120.
p. 235   shot at him without effect: *Cheyenne Indians*, 121.
pp. 235–36 fight against the Pawnee: Hyde, *Life of George Bent*, 308.
p. 236   for not getting into the fight: *Life of George Bent*, 303.
p. 236   I know I shall be killed today: Grinnell, *Fighting Cheyennes*, 286.
p. 237   "just above the hips": *Fighting Cheyennes*, 287.
p. 238   as the hero of this fight: *Fighting Cheyennes*, 291–92.
p. 238   "Woman With White Child": Hyde, *Life of George Bent*, 308.
p. 238   cadence of rage and despair: Forsyth, *Thrilling Days*, 32–33.
p. 239   make you feel badly: Grinnell, *Fighting Cheyennes*, 296.

THE SECOND DAY

p. 242   discharged his piece: Forsyth, *Thrilling Days*, 36.
p. 242   attempts to attack in the open: *Thrilling Days*, 36.
p. 243   wailing and beating of drums: *Thrilling Days*, 36.
p. 244   about three the next morning: *Thrilling Days*, 36.

THE THIRD DAY

p. 245   gestures were exceedingly exasperating: Forsyth, *Thrilling Days*, 36.
p. 246   scattered in every direction: *Thrilling Days*, 36.
p. 247   which prevails in the Indian Department: Custer, *My Life*, 33.
p. 247   armed with lances and bows: Hyde, *Life of George Bent*, 300.
p. 248   please lose no time: Forsyth, *Thrilling Days*, 37–38.

THE FOURTH DAY

p. 250   to my almost immediate relief: Forsyth, *Thrilling Days*, 39.

THE JOURNEY OF THE SCOUTS

p. 251   when he lacked words: Criqui, *Fifty Fearless Men*, 226.
p. 251   in an avalanche: *Fifty Fearless Men*, 227.
p. 253   and a strong party of men: *Fifty Fearless Men*, 230.
p. 253   ride in the ambulance: *Fifty Fearless Men*, 230.
p. 253   as we had on the island: *Fifty Fearless Men*, 95.

p. 253   was a natural leader: *Fifty Fearless Men*, 175.

p. 254   pins in a cushion: *Fifty Fearless Men*, 96.

p. 254   horsemeat and drinking [bad] water: *Fifty Fearless Men*, 180.

p. 255   supply wagons and an ambulance: Beecher Island Battle Memorial Association, 78.

p. 255   Pennsylvania Historical society: Leckie, *Buffalo Soldiers*, 35.

p. 256   bodies far and wide over the prairie: Grinnell, *Cheyenne Indians*, vol. 2, 163.

THE LONG WAIT

p. 258   "knew how to meet our fate": Forsyth, *Thrilling Days*, 41.

p. 258   Heaven if need be we'll die together: *Thrilling Days*, 41.

p. 259   to rescue them: Schubert, *Voices*, 25.

p. 259   the fight until his arrival: Forsyth, *Thrilling Days*, 42.

p. 260   They were a noble set of men: Schubert, *Voices*, 26.

p. 260   which flag I now have in my possession: *Voices*, 26.

p. 261   remains when the command returned: Criqui, *Fifty Fearless Men*, 26.

WHAT, IF ANYTHING, DID IT ALL MEAN?

p. 263   there were six hundred Indians: Grinnell, *Fighting Cheyennes*, 291.

p. 263   wounded in the Beecher fight: Schubert, *Voices*, 27.

p. 264   I have not seen myself: Forsyth, *Thrilling Days*, 42.

p. 264   to give him renewed excitement: Custer, *My Life*, 143.

pp. 264–65 Indians take it as an ordinary incident: Hyde, *Life of George Bent*, 305.

p. 265   in the annals of the Indian fighting army: Utley, *Frontier Regulars*, 148.

p. 265   a great deal to this day: Hyde, *Life of George Bent*, 307.

p. 265   succumb to the force of circumstance: Gueniffey, *Napoleon and De Gaulle*, 272.

p. 266   appear to have been inevitable: Kitto, *Greek Tragedy*, 112.

ACKNOWLEDGMENTS

A thousand thanks to Deb Goodrich and the staff at the estimable Fort Wallace Museum, Wallace, Kansas. Their cheerful help and extensive knowledge were immensely important in the planning and writing of this book. Melissa Rau created the figure of Roman Nose and Ken Weidner recreated the dress, accoutrements, and the war bonnet.

INDEX

〜〜〜